Taylor's Guide to Heirloom Vegetables

Benjamin Watson

HOUGHTON MIFFLIN COMPANY

Boston • New York 1996

For information about permission to reproduce selections from this book, write to Permissions, Houghton Mifflin Company, 215 Park Avenue South, New York, New York 10003.

For information about this and other Houghton Mifflin trade and reference books and multimedia products, visit The Bookstore at Houghton Mifflin on the World Wide Web at http://www.hmco.com/trade/.

Taylor's Guide is a registered trademark of Houghton Mifflin Company.

Library of Congress Cataloging-in-Publication Data
Taylor's guide to heirloom vegetables / [edited by] Ben Watson.
        p. cm
    Includes bibliographical references (p.   ) and index.
    ISBN 0-395-70818-4
    1. Vegetables — Heirloom varieties. 2. Vegetable gardening.
I. Watson, Benjamin.
SB324.73.T38 1996   95-33230
635 — dc20   CIP

Printed in Hong Kong

DNP 10 9 8 7 6 5 4 3 2 1

Cover photograph © by Rosalind Creasy

Contents

Consultants   vii

In Praise of Heirlooms   1
Seed-Saving Basics   7
Organic Control of Pests and Diseases   14

The Plant Gallery
A Word About Color   21
Photographs of Plant Varieties   22

Encyclopedia of Plants
A Note on the Varieties   125
Plant Descriptions A–Z   126

Hardiness Zone Map   302
Notes   304
Mail-Order Seed Sources   307
Seed Trusts and Historic Seed Programs   314
Further Reading   318
Bibliography   322
Photo Credits   324
Index   325

Consultants

The following persons assisted the author during the research and writing phases of this book, reviewing preliminary lists of heirloom varieties and passing along their comments, critiques, and suggestions.

Suzanne Ashworth is the curator of eggplant and other crops for Seed Savers Exchange. She is also the author of *Seed to Seed,* a handbook on seed saving.

David Cavagnaro is a freelance photographer and former Garden Manager at Seed Savers Exchange in Decorah, Iowa.

Rosalind Creasy is a well-known garden writer whose books include *Cooking from the Garden* and *The Complete Book of Edible Landscaping.*

Janika Eckert is Research Assistant at Johnny's Selected Seeds in Albion, Maine.

Ron Engeland runs Filaree Farm in Okanogan, Washington, a mail-order supplier of garlic to organic gardeners and small farmers. He is also the author of the book *Growing Great Garlic.*

Lawrence Hollander is the director of CRESS (Conservation and Regional Exchange by Seed Savers), a project of the Eastern Native Seed Conservancy, Inc., based in Great Barrington, Massachusetts.

Rob Johnston, Jr., is the founder and chairman of Johnny's Selected Seeds in Albion, Maine.

Wendy Krupnick is Horticulture Advisor for Shepherd's Garden Seeds in Felton, California.

Shepherd Ogden is the cofounder of The Cook's Garden seed company in Londonderry, Vermont, and a garden writer whose works include *Step by Step Organic Vegetable Gardening* and *The Cook's Garden.*

Michael Orzolek is Professor of Vegetable Crops in the Department of Horticulture, College of Agricultural Sciences, Penn State University.

In Praise of Heirlooms

Have you ever leafed through an old, pre-1940 seed catalog, perhaps while browsing through a good used bookstore? There's a certain disarming innocence in the descriptions of vegetable and flower varieties, and the beautiful color plates seem more like works of art than mere "product shots." For something designed to have only a year's worth of useful life, these old catalogs have stood the test of time and offer us a glimpse back to a society and a world-view that, while familiar, is strangely disconnected from our modern-day experience.

Glancing through the catalog's pages, one comes across some well-known names of vegetables, plants that are still widely grown and highly regarded by gardeners today. 'Golden Bantam' sweet corn. 'Black Beauty' eggplant. 'Chantenay' carrots. But what about all the other, less familiar, names such as 'Norfolk' spinach or 'Boston Marrow' squash? It's hard to find these old favorites in today's splashy color seed catalogs. What ever became of them?

The answer is that some varieties have survived, while many others have been lost forever, dropped by seed companies over the years and replaced in the main with newer, hybrid vegetables. The argument made by people in the seed trade was, and still is, that hybrids perform better than the old standard varieties, ensuring higher, more consistent yields over a wider range of growing conditions. In large part this claim is true. But in recent years a grassroots movement — forged by home gardeners, preservationists, and small regional seed companies — has begun to bring back the fine old vegetables that our parents and grandparents once enjoyed so that our generation, and those that follow, can rediscover through these heirloom varieties the rich plant heritage we all share.

What Is an Heirloom Vegetable?

Defining an heirloom vegetable precisely is a tricky thing; like beauty and truth it is not a fixed quantity but exists at least partially in the eye of the beholder. Unfortunately the word "heirloom" itself confuses the issue, conjuring up images of antimacassars, demijohns, and Grandpa's bay rum cologne — all quaint anachronisms that may have some nostalgic appeal but offer little of practical value in our modern, high-tech society. Of course, a seed is not a museum piece but, like ourselves, a living thing. A particular variety may have been grown since prehistoric times, but an individual seed of that variety is only as ancient as its last harvest date, and it remains alive only as long as humans continue growing it out and saving new generations of seeds.

Bearing this in mind, this book defines an heirloom variety using three basic criteria:

1. The variety must be able to reproduce itself from seed. Almost all heirlooms are *standard* or *open-pollinated* (OP) varieties. This means that they will grow "true to type" from seed, as opposed to F1 hybrid plants, whose seeds generally prove sterile or revert to one of the hybrid's parent forms. (The term *F1 hybrid* refers to the "first filial generation"; these plants are typically the product of crossing two separate, genetically uniform parent strains. Offspring of self- or cross-pollinated F1 hybrids are known as F2 plants, and so on.)

A few modern hybrids have been successfully "stabilized" through careful selection over many generations, so that they now reproduce themselves true to type. One example is the popular 'Sweet 100' cherry tomato, which originated as a hybrid but has been stabilized as an OP strain by various gardeners and plant breeders. These OP plants are no longer really "hybrids" in the strictest sense of the word, but most are also too recently introduced to qualify as heirloom varieties (see rule 2).

One major exception to this "true to type" rule are those plants, many of them perennials, that gardeners most commonly propagate from roots or cuttings rather than from seed. In this book the group is represented by artichokes (globe and Jerusalem), asparagus, garlic, potatoes (regular and sweet), and rhubarb. The seeds of these plants, when available, tend toward genetic variability, so they don't necessarily produce seedlings that resemble the parent plant.

2. The variety must have been introduced more than 50 years ago. Fifty years is, admittedly, an arbitrary cutoff date, and different people use different dates. The 50-year cutoff is a little like the convention of calling a 100-year-old highboy an "antique," while one that is only 99 years old doesn't yet qualify.

With the increased interest in heirloom vegetables, many fine old-fashioned varieties have been reintroduced recently by various seed companies. These "new" varieties still qualify as heirlooms because, even though they were previously unavailable to most gardeners through the seed trade, they have been preserved over the years by families or by ethnic, religious, or tribal groups, who handed down the seeds from generation to generation.

A few people use an even stricter definition, considering heirlooms to be only those varieties developed and preserved outside the commercial seed trade. To my mind, this distinction ignores the very real and useful contributions made over the years by professional plant breeders and explorers, who have greatly expanded our store of useful plants. Thus, the varieties profiled in the encyclopedia section of this book represent a mixture of plants developed or selected by individuals, ethnic or cultural groups, indigenous peoples, and seed companies.

3. The variety must have a history of its own. Perhaps the variety was brought to America by immigrants, or saved and improved over the years by a single family or religious group (like the Amish or the Hutterites). Perhaps it figured importantly as a staple or ceremonial crop for indigenous peoples. Or perhaps it has simply become well suited to the climate and growing conditions of a particular region.

Sometimes an heirloom variety has a well-established history and a clear date of introduction. More often, though, old varieties have a probable or "folk" history and can only be dated by the first mention of their existence by a garden writer or in a commercial seed list. Part of the fun of growing heirlooms is uncovering their stories. However, since not all varieties have a definite history, and because this guide is intended to introduce readers to a broad range of heirloom vegetables, the historical facts and dates found in the encyclopedia section are necessarily limited. As heirlooms increase in popularity, more information will no doubt surface on plants about which we now know very little.

Why Grow Heirlooms?

Just a few years ago, it was difficult to find a seed catalog that devoted space to heirloom varieties of vegetables. Today it is almost as hard to find a catalog or gardening magazine that doesn't mention at least a few old-fashioned favorites. Heirloom vegetables have definitely reappeared in a big way, but their growing popularity (no pun intended) constitutes more than just a passing fad in the gardening world. Fans of heirlooms range from environmentalists and scientists concerned with maintaining the genetic diversity of our food crops to backyard gardeners, who have rediscovered a fascinating world of unusual tastes and shapes and colors. From 'Belgian White' carrots to 'Cherokee Purple' tomatoes, 'Black Mexican' sweet corn to 'Moon & Stars' watermelon, the sheer number and wide range of heirloom varieties now available makes perusing midwinter seed catalogs more exciting (and educational) than ever before.

There are many qualities that make modern hybrid vegetables important to large-scale commercial growers: maximum yield, uniformity in size and shape, the ability to ripen fruit all at once for mechanical harvesting, a tolerance for chemical fertilizers and pesticides, tough skins that withstand long-distance shipping and handling, and an extended "fresh" shelf life. These same qualities, however, are entirely irrelevant to most home gardeners and small local growers, who prize above all else taste, freshness, and an extended harvest.

It all comes down to this: if you are only transporting a tomato from the backyard to the kitchen table, you don't need a thick-skinned, tasteless fruit like the ones you find in the supermarket. Granted, *any* variety of tomato tastes better when grown and harvested vine-ripe at home, but why should home gardeners have to settle for the same high-test hybrids as the large commercial growers, who expect so much more (and so much less) from their vegetables? Yet since the late 1940s these hybrid varieties, growable in all areas of the country but adapted to none, have been the ones most aggressively marketed to home gardeners in a sort of "one size fits all" sales effort. With millions of Americans now growing a part of their own food each year, we home gardeners deserve better.

Fortunately, heirlooms provide small gardeners with a choice. Does this mean that F_1 hybrids have no place in the garden? Of course not; many hybrids are well suited to growing at home and deserve a place at the table. But gardeners who want more variety will want to consider heirloom and OP varieties equally when making their seed choices.

Of course, for gardeners who want to save their own seeds, OPs are the only real choice (see "Seed-Saving Basics," page 7). Growing your own vegetable seeds and sharing them with friends and family is one of the most rewarding aspects of gardening with OP varieties. And selecting heirloom varieties makes starting your own seedlings in the spring an even more important and worthwhile pursuit; you are raising unique plants, most of which can't be found in flats or pots at the local nursery. For instance, over the past few years I have won over many friends, family members, and coworkers to the merits of the 'De Milpa' tomatillo, a marble-sized "ground cherry" (also known as husk tomato) that varies in color from green to deep purple and makes some of the best salsa you can imagine. Needless to say, one does not find flats of purple tomatillo plants for sale in New Hampshire nurseries. Not yet. So the sharing of heirloom seeds or seedlings from your own garden offers a unique and valued gift for anyone you know who gardens.

Delving into the histories of specific varieties is another part of our modern fascination with heirloom gardening. The search can lead us to a deeper understanding of our own traditions and to a greater appreciation of other cultures. Because most cultivated vegetables have been selected and developed by humans over hundreds, even thousands of years, heirlooms represent an interwoven fabric of both natural and human history. That history imbues these seeds with meaning and importance; when we grow heirloom varieties we are linking ourselves in a very tangible way to our ancestors. To many people, the true value of heirloom vegetables transcends the simple pleasures of growing and eating them. The seeds become living windows to the past.

Biodiversity and the Backyard Gardener

Some modern champions of biodiversity have drawn up battle lines between open-pollinated (OP) varieties and hybrids, with the former represented as the garden good guys and the latter scorned as crossbred villains. As with most political arguments, this issue is not nearly so simple. The fact of the matter is that hybrid crops have contributed greatly to the world's food-producing capacity. The real danger lies not so much in planting hybrids for large-scale cash crops but in losing or neglecting the broad genetic base of both wild and cultivated plants that have made these productive hybrids possible.

The importance of crop plant diversity was demonstrated dramatically in 1970, when a disastrous corn blight wiped out more than 15 percent of the entire U.S. corn crop. The culprit was a single gene that plant breeders had inserted into all of the common commercial corn varieties, one that proved highly susceptible to the blight. In the words of Kent Whealy, director of Seed Savers Exchange, it was as if a burglar had stolen the key to a single apartment, then found that all the other apartments in the building could be opened with the same key. And corn is not the only vegetable with a dangerously narrow genetic base: across the board, commercial farmers raise only a handful of highly bred, genetically similar hybrid varieties. Clearly, maintaining as diverse a genetic base as possible is in everyone's best interest, since little-known or little-grown varieties of plants may someday provide the genes needed to create tomorrow's drought-tolerant, disease-resistant, or high-yielding hybrids.

What makes the preservation of the heirloom and OP varieties so important? Surely, the loss of a single strain of seed can't be equated with the daily extinction of plants and animals, some of which disappear before they have even been "discovered" by mankind. Or can it? While it is true that the disappearance of a single cultivated variety of bean (let's say 'Swedish Brown') won't immediately threaten the survival of the huge and varied species we know as "common beans" *(Phaseolus vulgaris)*, the loss of even that one variety deprives all future gardeners and plant breeders of a unique genetic package, one that has evolved through years (perhaps even thousands of years) of cultivation and careful human selection. To not perpetuate a particular variety, even one that is currently out of fashion, means throwing away irreplaceable genetic material that may be needed in the future to protect our food supply against climate change and global warming, pesticide-resistant bugs, or diseases and challenges as yet unknown to us.

Various governments around the world have established about 120 seed banks that are dedicated to preserving the genetic material, or *germplasm,* of important food crops. Many of these repositories, however, including the National Seed Storage Laboratory in Colorado, are woefully underfunded. The truth is that we cannot always depend on governments or multinational seed companies to husband and preserve our valuable genetic resources. Simply storing seeds is not enough; even frozen in liquid hydrogen, a seed still has a metabolism like any other living thing, and it comes with a built-in "expiration date." That date can be extended, but not indefinitely.

Fortunately, by growing out and maintaining heirloom varieties, a whole host of private seed trusts is beginning to assume some of the responsibility for keeping the old strains alive; not just the ones we currently think of as the prettiest, the biggest, or the best varieties, but plants of all kinds. Many of these seed-saving networks, such as Seed Savers Exchange in Decorah, Iowa, make these old-time varieties available to interested breeders and backyard gardeners alike. Even in your home garden, you can become a small but significant link in the chain: by growing, saving, increasing, and sharing your own heirloom seeds; by patronizing the seed companies that carry these varieties; and by supporting the work of organizations (see page 314) that are helping to preserve these irreplaceable plants for future generations to enjoy.

Seed-Saving Basics

Because almost all heirloom vegetable varieties are, by definition, open-pollinated (reproduce true to type from seed), they hold a special appeal for home seed savers. You certainly don't have to save seeds from your heirloom plants to enjoy growing them in your garden, but there are a number of reasons you may want to learn basic seed-saving practices:

• Adaptation. Once you've identified a favorite variety that seems well adapted to your general climate or growing region, you can save seeds of that vegetable over several generations, making it even better suited to your own garden's growing conditions. Once adapted to a specific site, most varieties will tend to grow better, healthier plants with less intensive care by the gardener.

• Preservation. According to Seed Savers Exchange, nearly 45 percent of the open-pollinated vegetable varieties available to home gardeners in 1984 had disappeared from mail-order seed catalogs by 1991. In other words, you shouldn't assume that the company that has sold seed for a particular tomato or lima bean this year will necessarily list the variety next season. The best way to ensure the availability of your favorite varieties from year to year is to save seed from your own plants.

• Sharing Seeds. One of the real joys of saving seeds is sharing them with friends and family members. For a fellow gardener, nothing makes a better holiday gift than home-grown seeds from your prize vegetables. And the rarer and more unusual the variety, the better; folks who receive 'Jenny Lind' melons or 'Blue Pod Capucjiner' peas from me at Christmastime appreciate the fact that they're getting a unique and personal gift. Also, by saving more seed than you need of these endangered varieties, then spreading them around, either to friends or through a seed savers network (see page 314), you are helping to ensure that these excellent plants will be around for future gardeners to discover and enjoy.

• Frugality. Garden seeds represent a splendid investment, returning more for the money than almost any other commodity. Still, if you have a big garden, spending $1 or $2 per packet every year adds up. Saving some of your own seed can help save money, even if, like me, you then turn around and spend the savings on new varieties or garden gadgets.

General Seed-Saving Information

For the most part, saving seeds from garden vegetables is a simple matter. The only reason it seems so daunting today is that, in our restless culture, we have lost our connection to the land, and with it much of our "plant literacy." Fortunately, you don't have to be a latter-day Luther Burbank to save seeds from most vegetables. All you need is a little basic information to get started.

Consider the following tips only as basic ground rules. For complete information on more advanced seed-saving techniques such as hand pollination, or for advice on how to save seed of specific types of vegetables, refer to the books listed under Seed Saving and Plant Breeding on page 320.

Types of Plants

Like ornamental plants, vegetables can be classified as annuals, biennials, or perennials. For growing purposes, home gardeners don't worry much about these distinctions, since most vegetables are treated as annuals — grown for only one season and harvested. However, when you want to save seed from a particular vegetable, it's crucial to know whether the plant is an annual (flowers and sets seed in the same season) or a biennial (flowers and sets seed in its second season, sometimes after a period of dormancy).

Perennials don't really concern us here, since they are generally propagated vegetatively (by root division, cuttings, or layering) rather than from seed. Also, seed saved from certain perennial plants, such as rhubarb, does not come true to type; in other words, if you want a new plant like the parent plant, it's easier to divide the rhubarb crown and replant it than to save and plant seeds and then discard (or "rogue out") all the plants you don't want. Asparagus, another perennial vegetable, is fairly easy to grow and save for seed, so long as you have the patience of Job; it takes three to five years to grow harvestable asparagus spears from seed.

Annuals, on the other hand, are generally the easiest plants from which to save seeds, since they flower and set seed in the course of one growing season. Of these, the best vegetables for beginning seed savers are *self-pollinating annuals* like beans, peas, lettuce, tomatoes, peppers, and eggplant. Each of these self-pollinating plants bears "perfect" flowers that have both male and female reproductive parts. The fact that these plants are self-fertile (don't require cross-pollination by insects or wind to set seeds) means that you don't need to separate two different varieties of the same vegetable by a great distance to avoid unwanted crosses and ensure pure seed strains. Beans and peas are the classic example; for home garden purposes, planting different varieties 20 to 30 feet apart is usually sufficient to maintain pure strains.

Cross-pollinating annuals are plants that require some help in pollinating and setting seed; this help is usually provided by insects, the wind, or humans (through *hand pollination*). Many of these plants will also cross-pollinate readily with different varieties of the same vegetable or even with wild plants (members of the mustard family are notorious for doing this), and so must be isolated from other varieties by a great distance or grown inside mesh "cages," away from insect pollinators. Vegetables pollinated by the wind, like spinach, can be even trickier to isolate, since the plant's small pollen grains can be carried up to a mile away.

These cross-pollinating annuals pose more of a challenge to seed savers than self-pollinators like beans and tomatoes. Yet the seeds of many popular vegetables such as squash, cucumbers, melons, and corn are easy to save by practicing hand pollination. (For complete information on hand-pollinating plants, consult one of the seed-saving books listed in "Further Reading.") While hand pollination does involve keeping tabs on growing plants and following a number of simple steps, there is really nothing magical or arcane about it. You don't need a degree in botany to try it, and once you've seen just how straightforward it is, you'll wonder why more home gardeners don't do it.

Finally, biennials are those plants that require more than one growing season to flower and set seed. Common garden biennials include carrots, beets, turnips, onions, cabbage, cauliflower, celery, parsley, parsnips, Swiss chard, and many other plants. As a seed saver, your success with various biennial vegetables will depend very much on your climate and growing zone and the hardiness of the particular vegetable you are growing. In colder regions, many plants such as onions or cabbage will need to be pulled up, roots and all, then cured and stored in a root cellar over the winter. The following spring, the overwintered plants get planted back in the garden and are left to blossom and mature seed. Without a doubt, the hardest plant to winter over in this way is cauliflower; cold-climate gardeners who can raise seed successfully from this crop deserve a gold medal.

In most growing areas, cold-hardy biennials such as carrots, parsnips, leeks, endive, kale, collards, and Swiss chard can be heavily mulched following the first hard frosts in the fall and wintered over successfully in the garden. The following spring, simply pull back the mulch and select the best plants to save for seed-growing, harvesting and eating the remainder of the crop.

Building Confidence

If you've never saved seeds before, start with one easy crop in your first growing year. It's very hard to go wrong with self-pollinating annuals such as peas, beans, tomatoes, or peppers. Concentrate on saving seed from only one variety of each vegetable at a time, and plant other varieties of the same vegetable far enough away to lessen the chances of accidental cross-pollination.

Once you've saved seeds successfully from these plants, you can then move on to plants that require more advanced techniques such as hand pollination or caging.

Selecting the Best Plants

Save seed from only the healthiest, best-looking individual plants. If you like, you can also begin selecting plants based on specific qualities that you'd like to perpetuate: earliness, disease resistance, drought tolerance, and so on. Mark all plants you've set aside for seed saving with a brightly colored piece of yarn, tape, or ribbon. For individual fruits like squash, tomatoes, or melons, wrap the marker around the plant stem near the fruits you plan to harvest for seed.

If you aren't selecting for a single characteristic (for instance, the earliest-ripening tomatoes), save seeds from several different fruits or plants, then mix them together once you've processed and dried them. This practice helps to preserve the genetic diversity of a particular open-pollinated variety, which in turn helps future crops respond to a wider range of climate and growing conditions. If you plan to offer seed to other gardeners through a seed exchange, you will probably be required to save seed from as many healthy plants or fruits as possible to ensure broad diversity. Try to select plants based on a variety of good characteristics, not just for the size or quality of the vegetable's edible parts: vigorous growth, abundant flowering, heat or cold tolerance, and insect and disease resistance are all important qualities to carry on.

Harvesting and Storing Seeds

The right time to harvest seeds depends on the type of vegetable and the length of its growing season. For most vegetables, though, the seeds will not be fully mature until after the plant or its fruits have passed through the stage at which you would normally pick them for table use. Snap beans should be left on the plant until the seeds swell and the pods begin to dry. Eggplants, melons, squash, and other fruits intended for seed production should ideally be left on the vine or plant until they are very ripe and almost ready to fall off. There are exceptions to every rule, however, and a few varieties of heirloom tomatoes come to mind. Several of these old-timers will actually begin to sprout their seeds if the fruits are left too long on the plant. To be safe, pick tomatoes you are saving for seed at the same stage of ripeness as those you bring inside for eating.

Some vegetables, like corn, require a rather long growing season to dry seeds sufficiently; sweet corn varieties, for instance, should stand in the field for at least a month beyond the fresh-eating stage. Mature, mostly dry ears of corn can withstand a few light frosts in the fall, but if heavy frosts threaten, or if the autumn season is particularly damp and rainy, it's best to pick the ears, strip back the husks, tie or braid them together, and hang them up inside to finish drying. Harvest other long-season vegetables such as winter squash or onions around the time of the first fall frosts and cure them in the sun to prepare them for storage. Since onions are biennials, they will be planted out the following season; corn and squash seeds can be processed anytime throughout the winter.

Different vegetables require different seed-processing techniques. The seeds of melons and cucumbers, for instance, should be scraped out of the seed cavity into a bowl, covered with a little water, and left to ferment for four or five days. At the end of that time, pour off the floating pulp and immature seeds. Rinse the good seeds, then dry them on screens or paper towels. Tomato seeds and pulp undergo the same fermentation process, except that it is best done outside the house because of the strong and unpleasant smell. Don't let seed from heirloom tomatoes soak for more than four days, since some old-time varieties will begin to sprout quite easily, thus ruining the seeds for storage. For information on processing other types of vegetable seeds, refer to the seed-saving books listed in the appendix.

Drying garden seeds properly and storing them in good conditions (dry, cool, and dark) are the most important steps in ensuring their long life and good germination. Seeds dry best in a place that's warm and dry and that allows for good air circulation. Use simple, fine-mesh screen frames (store-bought or homemade) to dry many seeds outside in the warm, sunny days of late summer and fall. Another alternative, one that I use, is to place seeds in an envelope and put them in a canning jar or other airtight container with an equal weight of silica gel. Silica gel is a fine particulate material that draws excess moisture out of the seeds. Several mail-order seed companies sell silica gel, either in sealed packets or in bulk powder. If you buy bulk, look for the kind tinted with blue particles. When the gel absorbs a certain amount of moisture, the blue particles turn pink, and the gel should then be redried by spreading it out on a tray and placing it in a 200°F oven until it turns blue again.

Remove the seed packets from the silica jars after they have dried for a few days to a week; overdrying can harm seeds. Place the seeds in airtight containers (for small seeds, I use old plastic film containers) and store them in a cool, dry, dark location. A freezer or refrigerator is ideal if you have the space, but any location where the temperature doesn't vary much will do.

Seed Viability and Germination

Most vegetable seeds remain viable for at least three to five years in good storage conditions. Notable exceptions are alliums (onions, leeks, etc.) and parsnips. Still, if you store onion seed in ideal conditions in a freezer, don't toss out seed that's more than one year old. It's always a good idea to perform a germination test before planting time to determine how viable your seed is and therefore how thickly you'll need to sow it.

Testing germination is easy. As a sample, pick some fractional portion of 100 (10, 25, or 50), then place that number of seeds on a double thickness of dampened paper towel. Roll up the paper towel, put it inside a plastic bag, place a slip of paper with the variety name inside, seal the bag with a twist tie, then place the bag in a warm location — on top of the refrigerator is good. Check the bag after four or five days and see if the seeds have sprouted; slower-germinating seeds may take seven to ten days or more to sprout.

Count the number of seeds that actually germinate. If nine of ten seeds sprout, your germination rate would be 90 percent. If 21 of 25 sprout, the germination rate would be 84 percent. Knowing the germination rate of your seed varieties not only helps you plan for your own garden needs, but it is an important step in record-keeping if you plan to offer seed to other gardeners through a seed exchange program.

One final note: never plant all your seed of a given variety. Every year seed catalogs stamp the words "Crop Failure" across varieties that for whatever reason (poor germination, hail, drought, grazing deer, etc.) didn't produce enough seed to offer for sale. Given the unpredictable weather extremes that seem to affect different parts of the U.S. every summer, it's wise to keep a "strategic reserve" of your favorite seeds on hand in case of disaster.

Organic Control of Pests and Diseases

One of the main criticisms leveled against open-pollinated vegetables in general, and heirloom varieties in particular, is that they are much more susceptible to disease and insect damage than modern hybrid vegetables. This argument always strikes me as both oversimplistic and counterintuitive. After all, the much-vaunted disease resistance that has been bred into many high-tech hybrids comes ultimately from the genetic traits of those supposedly "inferior" plants used as parent strains. What's more, some of the newer hybrids are bred not so much to be *resistant* to certain pests and diseases, but to be *tolerant* of the agrichemicals (herbicides, fungicides, and insecticides) that are so freely applied to most of our commercially grown vegetables in an ultimately futile attempt to control these pests and diseases.

Fortunately, for the swelling ranks of backyard gardeners and small-scale growers who have jumped off the chemical bandwagon and returned to more sustainable, organic methods, heirloom vegetables as a group present no greater challenges than any other varieties, hybrid or otherwise. It is true that most heirlooms are less widely adapted than hybrids and may demand more specific climate, soil, or growing conditions to reach their full potential. But while it may take you awhile to discover the varieties best suited to your own growing area, the rewards are well worth the effort. In fact, most home gardeners I know consider this yearly experimentation with different varieties part of the fun of gardening.

Once you've identified your favorite vegetables, the ones that grow consistently well in your garden, you can begin saving seed from the healthiest, most robust plants each year — selecting, improving, and adapting the variety even more closely to your specific garden site and microclimate. That's a process difficult or even impossible to accomplish with F_1 hybrid "mules," which are typically one-season wonders whose seeds do not come true to type.

Timely Prevention Is the Best Defense

Controlling pests and disease in an organic garden is more a matter of preventing problems rather than waiting for symptoms to show up and then spraying or dusting with a quick-fix chemical "solution." The following recommendations will be a familiar refrain to most organic gardeners. Yet I am always amazed at how easy it is for all of us, novices and experts alike, to forget these simple, common-sense ways to discourage garden pests and diseases, even before they strike.

1. Select varieties that are already adapted to your growing region. Most backyard gardeners are naturally curious and like to experiment with seeds purchased from a number of different suppliers. That's great, but all things being equal, you are most likely to obtain seed that will perform well in your particular garden from a seed company based in your own region of the country. (See "Mail-Order Seed Sources" starting on page 307 for the names and addresses of seed companies that specialize in heirloom vegetables.)

There's one important corollary to this rule: almost all mail-order companies buy the seed they offer from other suppliers or contract growers instead of growing out the crop themselves. If this is the case, make sure that the varieties have been thoroughly tested by the company and proven successful in their own growing region. Seed catalogs generally describe the company's operation and regional climate right up front; if they don't, call or write them and ask.

2. Practice crop rotation. This is the most basic and effective means of preventing pests and disease, or at least making sure that they do not affect the same vegetable crop year after year. For all gardeners, organic or otherwise, I recommend a three-year crop rotation plan. This involves drawing up a garden map every spring, then saving it to refer to in future years. (It's amazing just how quickly one forgets what grew where and when.)

Don't grow the same vegetable in the same place two years running if you can avoid it. Rotating crops means that any pests or diseases that affected the crop this growing season won't be able to pick up where they left off next spring. Also, think in terms of plant families, not individual vegetables. For instance, if you've grown tomatoes in one spot this year, try not to follow them next year with another closely related member of the nightshade family (Solanaceae), such as eggplant, peppers, or potatoes. Closely related plants tend to attract similar pests.

The bigger your garden, the easier it is to plan and effect rotations. Yet, even with good crop rotation, some backyard gardeners will be unable to avoid the return of some insect travelers from year to year. My home garden is rather small, and a few Colorado potato beetles always seem to find my tomato plants, no matter where I move them. But even a small shift is better than none at all. Keep the bugs guessing.

Another related strategy involves interplanting certain vegetables with herbs or flowers. Many gardeners swear by this kind of *companion planting*, but whether it actually helps prevent insect damage is a subject of much debate. To my mind, companion planting is one of the many "chicken soup" practices in gardening — while it may not make a great difference, it certainly can't hurt. And it definitely adds color interest and diversity to any backyard vegetable patch.

3. Erect physical barriers. Use whatever means necessary to keep unwanted bugs and critters out of your garden. To prevent flying insects from chewing up, say, salad or cole crops, the best strategy is to place a floating row cover over the plants, digging in the edges on either side of the row or bed. This will allow sunlight, air, and rainwater in but will exclude airborne nibblers. Once the plants have grown larger, and the insect's main season has ended, you can remove the row cover and use it on other young crops. (To determine the main season for various insect pests in your area, contact your state or county Agricultural Extension Service office.)

Well-built walls and fences are the best way to discourage most four-legged interlopers. Helen and Scott Nearing, the celebrated homesteaders who wrote *Living the Good Life*, once built a formidable five-foot-high wall of stone and mortar 420 feet around their garden, which they claimed kept out everything that didn't have wings. An easier (though more expensive) solution is to buy one of the new portable electric fences used for pasture rotation and sold at most garden centers and animal feed-and-supply stores. For maximum protection, design your own electric fence with three lower strands of wire at 3- to 4-inch intervals above the ground. Then add two upper wires or electric tapes at 3 and 4 feet above the ground to discourage larger animals. Hook the whole thing up to a solar fence charger. This upper and lower spacing of wires is usually sufficient to discourage most animals. Be sure to keep any grass growing under the fence mowed short, or, better yet, run a black plastic mulch underneath the fence lines.

4. Give plants what they need, when they need it. Just like the human body, when a plant is stressed its natural defenses are weakened. As a result, it becomes much more susceptible to disease and much less able to use whatever "immune system" it has to fight off insects and disease.

One of the most common stress factors in plants is water, or more specifically the lack of it. But the answer is not necessarily to water all the time during hot, dry weather. Many vegetables, such as tomatoes, need above all a *consistent* supply of moisture, neither too much nor too little. One way to conserve soil moisture is by mulching with well-rotted hay, dried grass clippings, or some other organic material; this organic mulch will also help feed the soil as it decomposes. Another technique, commonly used with mulch, is drip irrigation, which delivers a small, steady volume of water to the root zones of plants, where it is needed most. Drip irrigation systems can be as fancy as an expensive fixed array of hoses and valves running up and down garden rows or as simple as a single leaky "soaker" hose that you move around as needed.

In addition to water, plants need nutrients. A comprehensive laboratory soil test will indicate which natural amendments (lime, rock phosphate, greensand, composted manures, etc.) you should add to your garden to optimize plant growth. A home soil test can tell you the relative pH of your soil and other useful details, but it is really no substitute for a professional lab test, especially if you've never had one done. The usual place to have a soil test done is at the Extension Service at your state's land-grant college. However, organic growers and people who want to get more extensive tests (as for trace minerals) might want to consider using a private soil-testing service. One excellent company is Timberleaf Soil Testing, 5569 State Street, Albany, OH 45710; contact them to receive more information on services and rates.

A soil that is nutritionally well balanced and at the proper pH level is one more factor that greatly influences a plant's overall health and disease resistance. Applying natural fertilizers during the growing season helps. Master gardener Eliot Coleman claims (and I heartily agree) that heirloom varieties seem to respond even better than other plants to a little extra tender loving care. And, since heirlooms are usually grown as special varieties, most gardeners don't begrudge them that extra spadeful of compost or the occasional drink of fish emulsion.

5. Keep the garden clean. Remove any diseased or insect-infested plants or plant parts from the garden as soon as you notice them. Mulching around plants can help avoid or at least mitigate certain soil-borne diseases, such as alternaria (early) blight in tomatoes. Space or thin seedlings to maintain the recommended growing distance between plants and to ensure good air circulation. Nearly everyone recommends staying out of the bean patch when there's any dew or rain on the plants, to avoid spreading disease. In general I try to avoid working in the rest of the garden, too, when plants are wet, though of course this is sometimes unavoidable.

Other Strategies

Carrying out the simple steps outlined above will give your plants a distinct advantage in the battle against insects, diseases, and animal pests. If a problem still occurs, and the damage caused is more than merely cosmetic, your next option should be one of the pest-specific biological controls like Bt (*Bacillus thuringiensis,* sold commercially under brand names like Dipel), beneficial nematodes, or milky spore disease. The advantage of these biological products is that they target a fairly small range of pests and do not harm beneficial insects at work in the garden.

Remember too that there are other natural "controls" that cost even less than Bt and other products. For people who garden organically, building bird or bat houses in the vicinity around the garden may be one of the most cost-effective (and satisfying) ways to deal with insect populations. Simple nesting boxes can attract many birds, such as bluebirds, chickadees, house wrens, and nuthatches. Building a box without a perch and with a narrow diamond-shaped entrance hole will help attract the birds you want and discourage nuisance birds such as starlings from moving in.

Growing "trap plants" as companion crops to vegetables is another common strategy for foiling insects. The theory is that the bugs will find the trap plants so tasty that they will chew on them first, allowing you to observe and pull up the infested plants, bugs and all, and burn or dispose of them safely away from the garden. In practice, though, trap crops tend to work more effectively in larger gardens; in my back-yard plot, the bugs simply eat cafeteria-style, sampling both the trap plants and the vegetables at the same time.

Many interesting folk remedies claim to foil animal pests, ranging from sprinkling blood meal or black pepper on greens to discourage rabbits to spritzing lion (or, less exotically, human) urine around to discourage big game such as deer. I'm sorry to say that none of these highly logical and intellectually appealing solutions has ever worked well for me. That's not to say, though, that you shouldn't give them a try.

Very occasionally I use a homemade or commercial insecticidal soap or dust my bean or basil plants with rotenone, one of the class of botanical insecticides that also includes sabadilla and pyrethrum. Some people consider such products organic, while others do not. Organic or not, these natural insecticides pack quite a wallop and should always be used judiciously and carefully, according to the manufacturer's directions. If you feel you have to resort to them in order to save a crop, treat them as you would any other potent chemical. Then, once the immediate problem is over, examine what you might do differently in the future to avoid a similar episode.

Further information on specific pests and diseases can be found in the encyclopedia section under the individual vegetable entries. For books on the organic control of pests and diseases, refer to page 320.

The Plant Gallery

The plant portraits that follow will help you put a "face" to some of the variety names found in the essays and encyclopedia section. They are organized alphabetically by type of vegetable. A short description accompanies each plate, giving the botanical name for each plant and other key information where known, such as height, days to maturity, country or region of origin, and date of introduction. Page numbers correspond to the plant's encyclopedia entry.

A Word About Color

Color, more than many other visual attributes, is in the eye of the beholder. What one person describes as blue, another may call lavender or even purple. And it's not just the names that vary. Light and shade, time of day, and other colors nearby can all affect what we actually see. A leaf that appears rich red in the midday sun may be a deep lavender in late-afternoon shade.

As you look at the photos on the following pages, remember that the camera, no less than the eye, captures the color as it appears at a certain moment. Add to that the natural variation among plants and the difficulties of printing colors precisely, and you'll see why your plant may not have exactly the same color you see in the photograph.

Amaranth
'Joseph's Coat'

Amaranthus
gangeticus
(A. tricolor)
Southeast Asia
Plant height: 3 ft.
Ornamental annual

p. 127

Amaranth
'Love-Lies-
Bleeding'

Amaranthus
caudatus
South America
Plant height: 3 ft.
Ornamental annual

p. 127

**Amaranth
'Merah'**

*Amaranthus
gangeticus
Southeast Asia
Plant height: 2 ft.
Ornamental annual
65–80 days*

p. 127

**Amaranth
'Molten Fire'**

*Amaranthus
gangeticus
California
1920s
Plant height: 4 ft.
Ornamental annual*

p. 128

**Artichoke, Globe
'Green Globe'**

*Cynara scolymus
Mediterranean
region
Before 1863
Tender perennial*

p. 129

Asparagus

*Asparagus
officinalis
Eurasia
Hardy perennial
3 yrs. from seed to
harvest*

p. 129

**Snap Pole Bean
'Hickman'**

*Phaseolus vulgaris
America
10–12-ft. climbing
vines
6–8-in. pods
75–90 days
Snap and dry use*

p. 135

**Snap Pole Bean
'Kentucky
Wonder'**

*Phaseolus vulgaris
United States
1850s
7–10-in. pods
58–72 days*

p. 135

Snap Pole Bean   *Phaseolus vulgaris*   *p. 135*
'Romano Pole'   *Italy*
                            60–70 days

Snap Pole Bean
'Trionfo Violetto'

Phaseolus vulgaris
Italy
7-in. pods
60–65 days
Ornamental

p. 135

**Wax Bush Bean
'Buerre de
Rocquencourt'**

*Phaseolus vulgaris
France
5–6-in. pods
48–54 days
Recommended for
the North*

p. 135

**Wax Bush Bean
'Dragon Langerie'
('Dragon's
Tongue')**

*Phaseolus vulgaris
Netherlands
Plant height:
12–15 in.
57–65 days
Ornamental*

p. 136

**Wax Pole Bean
'Kentucky Wonder
Wax'**

*Phaseolus vulgaris
Southern California
1901
6–9-in. pods
61–68 days
Snap and shell use*

p. 136

**Wax Pole Bean
'Yellow Annelino'**   *Phaseolus vulgaris
Italy
75–85 days*   *p. 136*

**Horticultural
Bush Bean
'Dwarf
Horticultural'**

*Phaseolus vulgaris
Italy
Before 1800
53–56 days
Recommended for
cool-climate and
coastal areas*

p. 137

**Horticultural
Bush Bean
'Tongue of Fire'**

*Phaseolus vulgaris
South America and
Italy
70–75 days
Snap, shell, and dry
use*

p. 137

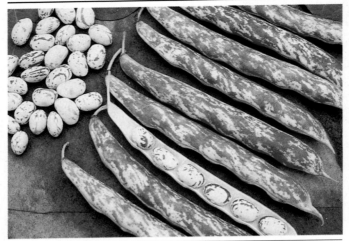

**Horticultural
Bush Bean
'Vermont
Cranberry Bush'**

*Phaseolus vulgaris
New England
Before 1800
60–85 days
Shell and dry use*

p. 138

**Horticultural Pole
Bean
'Lazy Wife'**

*Phaseolus vulgaris
Germany and
Pennsylvania
1810
80 days*

p. 138

Horticultural Pole Bean 'Wren's Egg' ('London Horticultural')

Phaseolus vulgaris
Chile
1825
65 days

p. 138

Dry Bush Bean 'Black Turtle'

Phaseolus vulgaris
South America
Before 1806
85–105 days
Recommended for the South

p. 140

Dry Bush Bean
'Hutterite'

Phaseolus vulgaris   *p. 140*
Austria and
Canada
1750s
75–85 days

Dry Bush Bean
'Jacob's Cattle'
('Trout')

Phaseolus vulgaris   *p. 140*
New England and
Southwest U.S.
80–100 days
Native American

Dry Bush Bean
'Low's Champion'

Phaseolus vulgaris   *p. 140*
New England
1884
70–80 days
Snap, shell, and dry
use
Native American

Dry Bush Bean
'Soldier'

Phaseolus vulgaris   *p. 141*
New England
80–90 days
Drought-tolerant
Recommended for
cool climates

Dry Bush Bean   *Phaseolus vulgaris*   *p. 141*
'Sulphur'   *America*
                       Before 1870
                       90–95 days
                       Soup and baking
                       use

Dry Bush Bean   *Phaseolus vulgaris*   *p. 141*
'Swedish Brown'   *Sweden and Upper*
                       Mississippi Valley
                       1890
                       85–95 days
                       Recommended for
                       the North

**Dry Pole Bean
'Mostoller's Wild
Goose'**

*Phaseolus vulgaris
Western
Pennsylvania
1865
90–100 days
Native American*

p. 141

**Dry Pole Bean
'Ruth Bible'**

*Phaseolus vulgaris
Kentucky
1832
80–95 days
Snap and dry use*

p. 142

Fava Bean
'Broad Windsor'

*Vicia faba
Africa and Middle
East; England
Before 1863
65–85 days
Recommended for
cool-season areas
or early planting*

p. 143

Lima Bush Bean   *Phaseolus lunatus*   *p. 145*
'Hopi Orange'   *Southwest U.S.
                          Plant height: 3 ft.
                          90 days
                          Drought-tolerant
                          Shell and dry use*

Lima Bush Bean　　*Phaseolus lunatus*　　*p. 145*
'Jackson Wonder'　　*Georgia*
　　　　　　　　　　　1888
　　　　　　　　　　　65–75 days
　　　　　　　　　　　Drought-tolerant
　　　　　　　　　　　Recommended for
　　　　　　　　　　　the South

Lima Pole Bean　　*Phaseolus lunatus*　　*p. 145*
'Black'　　　　　　*America*
　　　　　　　　　　　1892
　　　　　　　　　　　80–90 days
　　　　　　　　　　　Recommended for
　　　　　　　　　　　the North

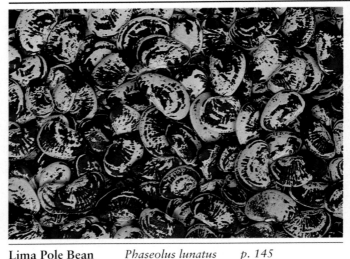

**Lima Pole Bean
'Christmas'**

*Phaseolus lunatus
America; 1840s
10-ft. climbing
vines
80–100 days
Recommended for
the Southeast*

p. 145

**Lima Pole Bean
'King of the
Garden'**

*Phaseolus lunatus
America
1883
85–95 days*

p. 146

Lima Pole Bean
Left: 'Willow Leaf White'
Center: 'Red Calico'
Right: 'Black'

Phaseolus lunatus
Left: America;
1891; 65–80 days;
ornamental
Center: 1790;
South Carolina;
90 days; drought-

tolerant
Right: 1892;
80–90 days

p. 145–146

Runner Bean
Left: 'Aztec Dwarf White'
Right: 'Scarlet Runner'

Phaseolus coccineus
Left: Southwest
U.S.; before 1890;
55–75 days;
drought-tolerant
Right: America;
before 1750;

65–90 days;
ornamental;
recommended for
cool climates

p. 147–148

**Runner Bean
'Painted Lady'**

*Phaseolus
coccineus
America
1827
68–130 days
Bicolored flowers
Ornamental*

*Snap and shell use
Recommended for
cool climates*

p. 147

**Runner Bean
'Scarlet Runner'
(blossom)**

*Phaseolus
coccineus
America
Before 1750
65–90 days
6–18-ft. climbing
vines*

*Ornamental
Snap and shell use
Recommended for
cool climates*

p. 148

Soybean
Left: 'Agate'
Right: 'Lammer's
Black'

Glycine max
Left: Japan; 1929;
90–95 days
Right: Asia; 104
days; recommended
for short-season
areas

p. 149

Tepary Bean
(various strains)

Phaseolus
acutifolius
Mexico and
Southwest U.S.
Plant height: 2–3 ft.
Dry use

p. 149

Beet
'Chiogga'

Beta vulgaris,
Crassa group
Italy
55 days

p. 152

Beet
'Cylindra'

Beta vulgaris,
Crassa group
Denmark
1880s
55–60 days
6–8-in.-long roots

p. 152

**Beet
'Detroit Dark Red'**

*Beta vulgaris,
Crassa group
United States
1892
55–60 days
Dark green tops*

p. 152

**Beet
'Golden Beet'**

*Beta vulgaris,
Crassa group
Europe
Before 1828
55–60 days
Nonbleeding roots*

p. 152

Beet
'Lutz Green Leaf'

Beta vulgaris,
Crassa group
Europe
60–80 days
14–18-in. tops with
pink midribs
Long storage

p. 152

Beet
'MacGregor's
Favorite'
('Dracena Beet')

Beta vulgaris,
Crassa group
Scotland
60 days
Ornamental
Grown for purple-
red leaves

p. 153

**Broccoli
'Romanesco'**

*Brassica oleracea
Northern Italy
85 days
Ornamental
Recommended for
the North*

p. 155

**Brussels Sprouts
'Rubine Red'**

*Brassica oleracea,
Gemmifera group
Europe
1930s
Plant height: 3 ft.
100–125 days
Ornamental*

*Extremely frost-
hardy*

p. 156

Cabbage
'Danish Ballhead'

Brassica oleracea,
Capitata group
Europe
1887
5–7-lb. heads
85–110 days
Bolt-resistant

Recommended for
cool, short-season
areas

p. 159

Cabbage
'Early Jersey
Wakefield'

Brassica oleracea,
Capitata group
England and New
Jersey; 1840s
2–4-lb. heads
60–75 days
Disease-resistant

p. 159

Cabbage, Red 'Mammoth Red Rock'

Brassica oleracea, Capitata group
Europe
Before 1906
5–8-lb. heads
90–100 days
Long storage

p. 160

Cabbage, Savoy 'January King'

Brassica oleracea, Capitata group
England
Before 1885
3–5-lb. heads
140–160 days

p. 160

**Carrot
'Chantenay Red
Cored'**

*Daucus carota var.
sativus
France
Before 1929
5–7-in.-long roots
60–75 days
Long storage
Suitable for heavier
soils*

p. 162

Carrot
'Danvers Half
Long'

*Daucus carota var.
sativus
Massachusetts
1871
6–8-in.-long roots
75 days*

*Long storage
Widely adapted*

p. 162

**Carrot
'Imperator'**

*Daucus carota var.
sativus*
United States
AAS 1928
8–9-in.-long
coreless roots
70–75 days
Light or deeply
worked soil

p. 163

**Cauliflower
'Early Snowball'**

*Brassica oleracea,
Botrytis group*
United States
1898
6-in. head
55–60 days

*Adapted to warm
and cool climates*

p. 165

**Cauliflower
'Purple Cape'**

*Brassica oleracea,
Botrytis group
Europe
1834
120 days
Winter-hardy to
Zone 6 with
protection*

p. 165

**Celeriac
'Giant Prague'**

*Apium graveolens
var. rapaceum
Europe
1871
110–120 days
Fertile soil;
pH 7.0–7.5*

p. 167

**Celery
'Golden Self-
Blanching'**

*Apium graveolens
var. dulce
France
Before 1885
Plant height:
18–30 in.
80–85 days
Stringless ribs
Disease-resistant*

p. 168

**Chicory
'Sugar Loaf'**

*Chicorium intybus
Europe
80–90 days
Self-blanching
heads
Grow in cool
weather; mid to
late fall harvest*

p. 171

**Corn, Sweet
'Golden Bantam'**

*Zea mays
Western
Massachusetts
1902
Plant height: 5–6 ft.
2 ears per stalk
5–7 in., 8-rowed
ears
70–85 days*

p. 177

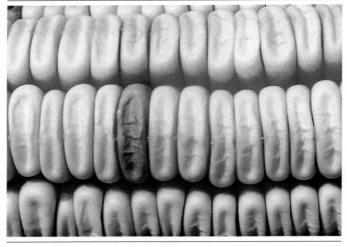

Corn, Dent	*Zea mays*	*8–9-in. ears*
'Hickory King'	*Southern U.S.*	*85–100 days*
	Before 1900	
	Plant height:	*p. 178*
	8–12 ft.	
	2 ears per stalk	

Corn, Dent   *Zea mays*   *p. 178*
'Nothstine Dent' *Michigan*
Plant height: 7 ft.
7–8-in. ears
95–100 days
Recommended for
the North

Corn, Flour   *Zea mays*   *Ornamental*
'Mandan Bride' *Northern Plains* *Not recommended*
Plant height: *for the South*
5–6 ft.
7–8-in. ears;   *p. 179*
multicolored
kernels

Popcorn 'Strawberry' (left)

Zea mays
America
Plant height:
4–5 ft.
2–4 ears per stalk
2–3-in. ears

80–110 days
Ornamental

p. 180

Popcorn 'Tom Thumb Yellow'

Zea mays
New Hampshire
Plant height: 3½ ft.
2–4 ears per stalk
3–4-in. ears
105 days

Recommended for the North

p. 180

**Corn Salad
(Mâche)
'Coquille de
Louviers'**

*Valerianella locusta
var. olitoria
France
45–60 days
Frost-hardy
Recommended for
short-season areas*

p. 181

**Cucumber
'Boothby's
Blonde'**

*Cucumis sativus
Maine
6–8-in.-long fruit
60–65 days*

p. 185

**Cucumber
'Lemon'**

*Cucumis sativus
United States
1894
2–3-in.-long fruit
60–70 days
Widely adapted;
disease-resistant*

p. 185

**Cucumber
'Suyo Long'**

*Cucumis sativus
Northern China
10–18-in.-long fruit
60–70 days
Heat-tolerant;
disease-resistant*

p. 186

**Cucumber
'White Wonder'**

*Cucumis sativus
Western New York
Before 1890
6–9-in.-long fruit
57–60 days
Heat-tolerant*

p. 186

**Eggplant
'Black Beauty'**

*Solanum
melongena
United States
1902
Plant height:
24–30 in.
6–7-in.-long fruit
72–85 days
Widely adapted*

p. 188

| Eggplant 'Listada de Gandia' | *Solanum melongena* *Italy* *Plant height: 14–16 in.* *5–6-in.-long fruit* *75 days* | *Drought-tolerant* *Ornamental* *p. 188* |

| Eggplant 'Pintong Long' | *Solanum melongena* *Taiwan* *Plant height: 12 in.* *10–14-in.-long fruit* *90 days (from seed)* *Disease-resistant* | *p. 189* |

Eggplant   *Solanum*   *p. 189*
'Rosa Bianca'   *melongena*
     Italy
     4–6-in.-long fruit
     75 days
     Ornamental

Eggplant
'Turkish Orange'

Solanum
integrifolium
Turkey
Plant height: 3–4 ft.
2-oz. fruits
95 days
Ornamental

p. 189

**Endive
'Green Curled
Ruffec'**

*Chicorium endivia
Europe
Before 1863
16–18-in.-rosette
75–100 days
Tolerates cold and
wet conditions*

p. 191

**Endive
'Tres Fine
Marachiere'
('Frisée')**

*Chicorium endivia
France
Before 1900
6-in.-rosette
60 days
Bolt-resistant*

p. 191

**Florence Fennel
'Romy'**

*Foeniculum vulgare
var. azoricum
Italy
90 days
Fertile, well-
drained soil*

p. 192

**Garlic
'Carpathian'**

*Allium sativum var.
ophioscorodon
Southeast Poland
Hardneck type
6–10 cloves per
bulb
Late season*

p. 195

Garlic 'German Red'

Allium sativum var. ophioscorodon
Idaho
10–15 cloves per bulb
Hardneck type
Midseason

p. 195

Garlic
'Spanish Roja'

Allium sativum var. ophioscorodon
Northwest U.S.
6–13 cloves per bulb
Hardneck type
Midseason

Medium storage
Recommended for the North

p. 196

Garlic
'Inchelium Red'

Allium sativum var.
sativum
Washington
8–20 cloves per
bulb
Softneck type
Midseason

p. 196

Garlic
'Lorz Italian'

Allium sativum var.
sativum
Italy and
Northwest U.S.
Before 1900
12–19 cloves per
bulb

Softneck type
Midseason
Heat-tolerant

p. 196

Garlic
'Nootka Rose'

Allium sativum var.   *p. 197*
sativum
Washington
15–24 cloves per
bulb
Softneck type
Very late season

Jerusalem
Artichoke
(plants in bloom)

Helianthus
tuberosus
North America
Hardy perennial
Plant height: 6–8 ft.
3–4-in. flowers
Ornamental

p. 197

Jerusalem Artichoke 'Smooth Garnet' (shown at right, with other strains)

Helianthus tuberosus North America Hardy perennial Short to medium storage

p. 199

Kale 'Dwarf Blue Curled Scotch'

Brassica oleracea, Acephala group Europe Plant height: 12–15 in.

55–65 days Extremely frost-hardy

p. 201

**Kale
'Lacinato'**

*Brassica oleracea,
Acephala group
Italy
Before 1885
Plant height: 2 ft.
62 days*

*Heat- and cold-
tolerant
Ornamental*

p. 201

**Kale
'Red Russian'
('Ragged Jack')**

*Brassica oleracea,
Acephala group
Eastern Europe
and Canada
Before 1863
Plant height:
2–3 ft.*

*50–55 days
Ornamental*

p. 201

**Kohlrabi
'Early Purple
Vienna'**

*Brassica oleracea,
Gongylodes group
Central Europe
Before 1860
55–60 days
Crack-resistant
Ornamental*

p. 204

**Kohlrabi
'Early White
Vienna'**

*Brassica oleracea,
Gongylodes group
Central Europe
Before 1860
Plant height:
10–12 in.
50–55 days*

p. 204

| Leek 'Blue Solaise' | *Allium ampeloprasum var. porrum* *France* *100–105 days* *Frost-hardy* *Ornamental* | *Recommended for short-season areas* *p. 206* |

| Leek 'Giant Musselburgh' ('American Flag') | *Allium ampeloprasum var. porrum* *Europe* *1870* *9–15-in. stalks* *100–120 days* | *Extremely frost-hardy; overwinters with protection* *Widely adapted* *p. 206* |

**Lettuce
'Black-Seeded
Simpson'**

*Lactuca sativa
United States
1850
Loosehead type
40–55 days
Slow-bolting*

*Heat- and drought-
tolerant*

p. 208

**Lettuce
'Deer Tongue'
('Matchless')**

*Lactuca sativa
United States
1740s
Loosehead type
55–65 days
Ornamental*

p. 209

Lettuce
'Oak Leaf'

Lactuca sativa
United States
Before 1900
Loosehead type
40–60 days

Heat-tolerant;
long-standing
Ornamental

p. 209

Lettuce
'Iceberg'

Lactuca sativa
United States
1894
Crisphead type
50–85 days
Heat-tolerant;
disease-resistant

Recommended for
short-season areas

p. 210

| Lettuce 'Limestone Bibb' | *Lactuca sativa* Kentucky 1850 Bibb/butterhead type 55–75 days | *Plant in early spring; bolts readily in hot weather* p. 210 |

| Lettuce 'Merveille des Quatre Saisons' ('Four Seasons') | *Lactuca sativa* France Bibb/butterhead type 6–10-in. heads 55–70 days | *Bolts readily in hot weather* p. 210 |

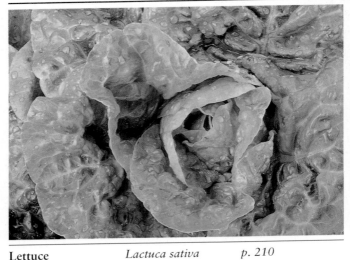

**Lettuce
'Mescher'**

*Lactuca sativa
Austria
Before 1800
Bibb/butterhead
type
50 days
Cold-hardy*

p. 210

**Lettuce
'Pirat'**

*Lactuca sativa
Germany
Bibb/butterhead
type
55–65 days*

p. 210

| Lettuce 'Speckled' | *Lactuca sativa* *Germany* *Bibb/butterhead* *type* *90 days* *Ornamental* | *p. 210* |

| Lettuce 'Tom Thumb' | *Lactuca sativa* *England* *1830* *Miniature* *bibb/butterhead* *type* *Plant spread: 5 in.* | *48–55 days* *Good for frames or* *containers* *p. 210* |

Lettuce
'Paris White Cos'

Lactuca sativa
France
Before 1868
Romaine/cos type
8–10-in.-tall heads
50–83 days

Recommended for
the North

p. 211

Lettuce
'Rouge d'Hiver'
('Red Winter')

Lactuca sativa
France
1840s
Romaine/cos type
60 days

Heat-tolerant and
cold-hardy
Ornamental

p. 211

**Melon
'Casaba'**

*Cucumis melo,
Inodorus group
Asia Minor
Before 1850
7–8-lb. fruit
110–120 days*

*Heat- and drought-
tolerant
Long storage*

p. 213

**Melon
'Collective
Farmwoman'**

*Cucumis melo
Ukraine
6-in. fruit
80–85 days
Recommended for
short-season areas*

p. 213

| Melon
'Hale's Best' | *Cucumis melo,*
Reticulatus group
California
Before 1923
2–3-lb. fruit
75–88 days | *Drought-tolerant;*
disease-resistant

p. 214 |

| Melon
'Jenny Lind' | *Cucumis melo,*
Reticulatus group
Armenia
Before 1846
1–2-lb. fruit
70–85 days
Disease-resistant | *Recommended for*
short-season areas

p. 214 |

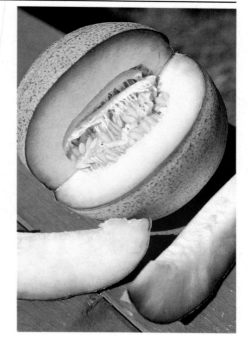

**Melon
'Rocky Ford'
('Eden Gem')**

*Cucumis melo,
Reticulatus group
Colorado
1881
2–3-lb. fruit
85–95 days
Disease-resistant*

p. 215

**Mustard and
Oriental Greens
'Michihili'**

*Brassica rapa,
Pekinensis group
East Asia
1870s
14–24-in.-tall heads
70 days*

p. 217

Mustard and Oriental Greens 'Mizuna' ('Kyona')

Brassica rapa, Japonica group Japan Plant height: 12–24 in. 40–65 days

Cold-hardy and heat-tolerant Ornamental

p. 217

Mustard and Oriental Greens 'Osaka Purple'

Brassica juncea Japan 70–80 days Savoyed leaves Ornamental

p. 217

**Mustard and
Oriental Greens
'Red Giant'
(shown at left)**

*Brassica juncea
East Asia
90 days
Frost-hardy; slow-
    bolting
Savoyed leaves
Ornamental*

p. 218

**Okra
'Cow Horn'**

*Abelmoschus
esculentus
Southern U.S.
Plant height:
6–7 ft.
10–12-in. pods
55–65 days*

p. 219

**Okra
'Louisiana Green
Velvet'**

*Abelmoschus
esculentus
Southern U.S.
1930s
Plant height: 6 ft.
6–7-in. pods
57–65 days*

p. 220

**Okra
'Red Okra'
('Purple Okra')**

*Abelmoschus
esculentus
Southern U.S.
Plant height: 3–4 ft.
55–65 days
Heat- and drought-
tolerant
Ornamental*

p. 220

**Okra
'Star of David'**

*Abelmoschus
esculentus
Israel
Plant height:
6–8 ft.
5–9-in. pods
60–70 days*

p. 220

Onion
'Red Torpedo'
('Italian Red
Bottle')

*Allium cepa, Cepa
group
Europe
Before 1900
6–8-in.-long,
spindle-shaped
bulbs
95–120 days
Recommended for
the South*

p. 223

Onion
'Ailsa Craig
Exhibition'

*Allium cepa, Cepa
group
England
Large 3-lb. bulbs
105–110 days
Medium storage*

*Recommended for
the North*

p. 223

**Bunching Onion
(Welsh Onion)**

*Allium fistulosum
Siberia
Before 1629
Hardy perennial
60–80 days
Full sun to partial
shade*

p. 225

**Bunching Onion
'Evergreen White
Bunching'
('He-Shi-Ko')**

*Allium fistulosum
Japan
1880s
Hardy perennial
Plant height:
12–14 in.
Slow-bolting;
insect- and disease-
resistant*

p. 225

**Egyptian Onion
(Topset Onion,
Walking Onion)**

*Allium cepa,
Proliferum group
North America
Before 1700
Hardy perennial*

p. 226

**Multiplier Onion
'Yellow Potato
Onion'**

*Allium cepa,
Aggregatum group
Europe
Before 1828
Multiple 3-in. bulbs
Drought-tolerant;
winter-hardy;
disease-resistant
Widely adapted;
not recommended
for Zones 9–10*

p. 228

Parsley
'Gigante d'Italia'   *Petroselinum   p. 230
crispum var.
neapolitanum
Northern Italy
Plant height:
2–3 ft.
75–80 days*

**Parsley
'Hamburg Root'**

*Petroselinum
crispum var.
tuberosum
Germany
Before 1600
8–10-in.-long roots
85–95 days
Frost-hardy;
overwinters well
with protection
Long storage
Loose, fertile soil*

p. 230

**Parsnip
'Hollow Crown'**

*Pastinaca sativa
Europe
1850
10–15-in.-long
roots
95–135 days
Frost-hardy;*

*overwinters well
with protection
Long storage*

p. 231

**Pea
'Blue Pod
Capucijners'**

*Pisum sativum var.
arvense
Netherlands
Before 1600
4–5-ft. climbing
vines
3-in. pods*

*85–90 days
Ornamental*

p. 235

**Pea, Edible-
Podded
'Golden Sweet'**

*Pisum sativum var.
macrocarpon
India
4–5-ft. climbing
vines
3-in. pods
70 days*

*Heat- and drought-
tolerant*

p. 237

Pea, Edible-Podded 'Mammoth Melting Sugar'

Pisum sativum var. macrocarpon
Eurasia
Before 1906
4–5-ft. climbing vines
4–5-in. stringless pods
65–75 days
Disease-resistant

p. 237

Cowpea 'Papago'

Vigna unguiculata
Southwest U.S. and Mexico
Native American
70 days
Drought-tolerant; widely adapted

Recommended for the North

p. 239

Cowpea   *Vigna unguiculata*   p. 239
'Susanne'   *Alabama*
                    12-in. pods
                    85–90 days

Cowpea   *Vigna unguiculata*   p. 239
'Whipporwill'   *Southern U.S.*
                    10-in. pods
                    75–90 days

**Cowpea
'Zipper'**

*Vigna unguiculata
Southern U.S.
70–75 days
Insect- and disease-
resistant*

p. 239

**Pepper, Hot
'Chiltepine'**

*Capsicum annuum
var. aviculare
Southwest U.S. and
Mexico
Plant height:
1–3 ft.
¹/₄–¹/₂-in. fruit*

*120–150 days
(from seed)*

p. 242

**Pepper, Hot
'Chimayo'**

*Capsicum annuum
Northern New
Mexico
Plant height:
24–30 in.
4–5-in.-long fruit
95 days*

p. 242

**Pepper, Hot
'Grandpa's Home
Pepper'**

*Capsicum annuum
Siberia
Plant height: 1 ft.
70 days
Excellent
houseplant;*

*produces in low
light conditions*

p. 243

Pepper, Hot 'Karlo'

Capsicum annuum
Romania
50–55 days

p. 243

Pepper, Hot 'Long Red Cayenne'

Capsicum annuum
America
Before 1827
Plant height:
20–30 in.
4–6-in.-long fruit
70–75 days

p. 243

**Pepper, Hot
'Red Squash'
('Mushroom
Pepper')**

*Capsicum sp.
South America
Before 1888
Plant height:
24–30 in.
2-in. fruit*

*100–110 days
(from seed)*

p. 243

**Pepper, Sweet
'Aconcagua'**

*Capsicum annuum
Argentina
Nonbell type
Plant height:
28–30 in.
7–11-in.-long fruit
70–75 days*

p. 244

**Pepper, Sweet
'Cherry Sweet'**

*Capsicum annuum
America
Before 1860
Nonbell type
Plant height: 20 in.
1-in. fruit
70–80 days
Salad and pickling
use*

p. 244

**Pepper, Sweet
'Corno di Toro'
(red strain shown)**

*Capsicum annuum
Italy
Nonbell type
Plant height: 3 ft.
8-in.-long fruit
70–80 days
Red and yellow
strains*

p. 244

**Pepper, Sweet
'Golden Summit'**

*Capsicum annuum
Yugoslavia
Before 1800
Bell type
65 days
Recommended for
short-season areas*

p. 244

**Pepper, Sweet
'Merrimack
Wonder'**

*Capsicum annuum
New Hampshire
1942
Bell type
3½ x 3½-in. fruit
60 days
Recommended for
short-season areas*

p. 244

**Pepper, Sweet
'Quadrato d'Asti
Giallo Rosa'**

Capsicum annuum
Italy
Bell type
4 x 5-in. fruit
70–80 days
Mixed red and
yellow fruits

p. 245

**Pepper, Sweet
'Sweet Banana'
('Hungarian Wax
Sweet')**

Capsicum annuum
Hungary
1941
Nonbell type
Plant height:
16–24 in.
6-in.-long fruit
60–75 days

p. 245

**Potato
'All Blue'
(shown at center)**

*Solanum
tuberosum
Western South
America
Disease-resistant
Midseason; over 80
days*

p. 249

**Potato
'Russian Banana'**

*Solanum
tuberosum
Russia and British
Columbia
Fingerling type
Disease-resistant*

*Late season; over
90 days*

p. 251

**Radish
'French Breakfast'**

*Raphanus sativus
Europe
1879
2-in.-long roots
20–30 days*

p. 253

**Radish
'Long Black
Spanish'**

*Raphanus sativus
Europe
Before 1828
7–10-in.-long roots
55–60 days
Long storage*

p. 253

**Radish
'White Icicle'**

*Raphanus sativus
Europe
Before 1896
4–5-in.-long roots
30 days
Heat-tolerant*

p. 254

**Rhubarb
'Victoria'**

*Rheum
rhabarbarum
England
Before 1863
Hardy perennial
3 yrs. from seed to
harvest*

p. 257

**Rutabaga
'Laurentian'**

*Brassica napus,
Napobrassica
group
Canada
Before 1920
4–6-in. roots
90–120 days
Long storage*

p. 259

**Salsify
'Mammoth
Sandwich Island'**

*Tragopogon
porrifolius
Europe
1860s
8–9-in.-long roots
120–150 days
Harvest after frost;
overwinters well
with protection*

p. 261

**Spinach
'Bloomsdale Long
Standing'**

*Spinacia oleracea
Europe
1925
40–60 days
Savoyed leaves
Heat-tolerant;
slow-bolting*

p. 263

**Squash, Winter
'Blue Banana'**   *Cucurbita maxima   p. 267
South America
Circa 1893
18–30-in.-long fruit
105–120 days*

Squash, Winter
'Boston Marrow'

Cucurbita maxima   p. 267
South America
Before 1831
10–20-lb. fruit
95–100 days
Native American

Squash, Winter
'Buttercup'

Cucurbita maxima
North Dakota
1925
3–5-lb. fruit
90–110 days
Long storage

p. 268

**Squash, Winter
'Hubbard'**

*Cucurbita maxima
South America or
West Indies
1798
10–15-lb. fruit
100–115 days
Long storage*

p. 268

**Squash, Winter
'North Georgia
Candy Roaster'**

*Cucurbita maxima
Southern U.S.
30–36-in.-long fruit
Rampant and
prolific vines
100–110 days*

p. 268

**Squash, Winter
'Red Kuri'**

*Cucurbita maxima
Japan
4–7-lb. fruit
90–95 days*

p. 269

**Squash (Pumpkin)
'Rouge Vif
d'Etampes'**

*Cucurbita maxima
France
Before 1850
105–130 days
Ornamental and
decorative use*

p. 269

Squash, Winter 'Turk's Turban'	*Cucurbita maxima Europe and America Before 1818 5-lb. fruit 90–120 days*	*Ornamental and decorative use* *p. 269*

Squash, Winter 'Green-Striped Cushaw'	*Cucurbita mixta West Indies 1820s 10–12-lb. fruit 110 days Recommended for the South*	*p. 269*

**Squash, Winter
'Butternut'**

*Cucurbita
moschata
United States
1944
3–5-lb. fruit
75–110 days
Long storage*

p. 270

**Squash (Pumpkin)
'Cheese Pumpkin'**

*Cucurbita
moschata
America
1824
110 days
Short keeper*

p. 270

**Squash, Summer
'Cocozelle'**

*Cucurbita pepo
Italy
1934
10–12-in.-long fruit
55–65 days*

p. 272

**Squash (Pumpkin)
'Connecticut
Field'**

*Cucurbita pepo
America
Before 1700
15–25-lb. fruit
100–120 days
Native American
Decorative use*

p. 272

Squash, Winter   *Cucurbita pepo*   *p. 272*
'Delicata'   *America*
                        1894
                        7–9-in.-long fruit
                        95–100 days
                        Long storage

Squash, Summer
'Early Yellow
Summer
Crookneck'

Cucurbita pepo
America
Circa 1700
8–10-in.-long fruit
42–60 days

p. 272

Squash, Summer
'Ronde de Nice'
Cucurbita pepo
France
Before 1900
1–4-in. round fruit
45–65 days
p. 272

Sunflower
'Arikara'
Helianthus annuus
Northern Plains
Native American
Plant height:
6–8 ft.
Single- and
polyheaded plants
Ornamental annual

p. 275

**Sunflower
'Italian White'**

*Helianthus debilis
var. cucumerifolius
Texas (native)
Plant height: 6 ft.
Polyheaded plants
4–5-in., chocolate-
scented flowers
80–100 days
Ornamental annual*

p. 275

**Sunflower
'Mammoth
Russian'**

*Helianthus annuus
Russia
Circa 1875
Plant height:
7–12 ft.
10–15-in. single
heads
90–110 days
Disease-resistant
Ornamental annual*

p. 276

Sweet Potato (various heirloom strains shown)

Ipomoea batatas
Central and South
America
110–120 days
Warm, loose, well-drained soil
Medium storage

Recommended for the South

p. 276

Swiss Chard 'Rainbow Chard' ('Five Color Silver Beet')

Beta vulgaris,
Cicla group
Europe
50–60 days
Ornamental

p. 280

Swiss Chard　　*Beta vulgaris,*　　*p. 280*
'Rhubarb Chard'　*Cicla group*
　　　　　　　　　Europe
　　　　　　　　　1857
　　　　　　　　　50–60 days
　　　　　　　　　Ornamental

Tomatillo　　　*Physalis ixocarpa*　*p. 283*
'Purple de Milpa'　*Mexico*
　　　　　　　　　1–2-in. fruit
　　　　　　　　　Medium storage

| Tomato 'Chadwick's Cherry' | *Lycopersicon lycopersicum England and California Indeterminate plants* | *1½-in. fruit 85–90 days* *p. 287* |

| Tomato 'Costoluto Genovese' | *Lycopersicon lycopersicum Italy Indeterminate plants 80 days Drought-tolerant* | *Recommended for warm climates* *p. 287* |

**Tomato
'Gardener's
Delight'**

*Lycopersicon
lycopersicum
Europe
Indeterminate
plants
65 days*

p. 288

**Tomato
'Super Italian
Paste'**

*Lycopersicon
lycopersicum
Italy
Indeterminate
plants
6-in.-long fruit
65–75 days*

*Recommended for
long-season areas*

p. 289

**Tomato
'Anna Russian'**

*Lycopersicon
lycopersicum
Russia and United
States
Indeterminate
plants
65 days*

p. 289

| **Tomato 'Brandywine' (pink and yellow strains shown)** | *Lycopersicon lycopersicum United States 1885 Indeterminate plants* | *1–2-lb. fruit 80 days* *p. 289* |

Tomato
'Cherokee Purple'

Lycopersicon
lycopersicum
Tennessee
Before 1890
Native American
Indeterminate
plants

10–12-oz. fruit
70–75 days

p. 290

Tomato
'Oxheart'

Lycopersicon
lycopersicum
United States
Circa 1925
Indeterminate
plants
7-oz. fruit

80–95 days
Recommended for
the Southeast

p. 290

**Tomato
'Zapotec Ribbed'**

*Lycopersicon
lycopersicum
Mexico
Indeterminate
plants
4–8-oz. fruit
80–85 days*

p. 291

**Tomato
'Banana Legs'**

*Lycopersicon
lycopersicum
America
Determinate plants
3–4-in.-long fruit
Paste type
85–90 days*

p. 291

**Tomato
'Golden Queen'**

*Lycopersicon
lycopersicum
America
1882
Indeterminate
plants*

*4–6-oz. fruit
75–80 days*

p. 292

**Tomato
'Goldie'**

*Lycopersicon
lycopersicum
America
1870s
Indeterminate
plants*

*1–2-lb. fruit
85–95 days*

p. 292

**Tomato
'Verna Orange'**

*Lycopersicon
lycopersicum
Indiana
Indeterminate
plants
1½-lb. fruit
75–85 days*

p. 292

**Tomato
'Yellow Pear'**

*Lycopersicon
lycopersicum
America
Before 1805
Indeterminate
plants
1-oz. fruit
70–80 days
Disease-resistant*

p. 292

Tomato	*Lycopersicon*	*Recommended for*
'Black Krim'	*lycopersicum*	*warm, long-season*
	Ukraine	*areas*
	Indeterminate	
	plants	*p. 292*
	80–95 days	

Tomato	*Lycopersicon*	*Disease-resistant*
'Tigerella'	*lycopersicum*	*Ornamental*
('Mr. Stripey')	*England*	
	Indeterminate	*p. 293*
	plants	
	2-in. fruit	
	55–65 days	

**Tomato
'Yellow Currant'**

*Lycopersicon
pimpinellifolium
South America
Indeterminate
plants
½-in. fruit
65 days
Disease-resistant;
prolific*

p. 293

**Turnip
'Gilfeather'™**

*Brassica rapa,
Rapifera group
Southern Vermont
Before 1900
3-in. roots
60–75 days*

p. 295

**Turnip
'Purple Top White
Globe'**

*Brassica rapa,
Rapifera group
Europe
Before 1880
14–22-in. greens
3–4-in. roots
45–65 days*

p. 295

**Turnip
'Red Milan'
('De Milan
Rouge')**

*Brassica rapa,
Rapifera group
Europe
Before 1885
35 days
Plant in early
spring*

p. 295

Watermelon
'Georgia
Rattlesnake'

Citrullus lanatus
Southern U.S.
25–30-lb. fruit
Rose-red flesh
90 days
Recommended for
the South

p. 298

Watermelon
'Moon & Stars'

Citrullus lanatus
Russia and United
States
Before 1910
25–30-lb. fruit
Pinkish red flesh
95–105 days

Ornamental
Recommended for
warm, long-season
areas

p. 298

**Watermelon
'Red-Seeded
Citron'**

*Citrullus lanatus
var. citroides
Africa and America
Before 1863
10–12-lb. fruit
80–100 days*

*Preserves and
pickling use*

p. 299

Encyclopedia of Plants

A Note on the Varieties

With the current interest in heirloom vegetables, many old varieties are reappearing, while others continue to vanish from the seed trade every year. Almost all of the heirloom vegetables included as Recommended Varieties in the following entries are available from at least one supplier (for addresses and catalog information, see "Mail-Order Seed Sources," p. 307).

However, seed companies, like other businesses, come and go. Over the past 25 years or so, several fine smaller seed companies have emerged (many of them specializing in open-pollinated seeds that are well adapted to a particular bioregion). Unfortunately, over the same period, many more seed houses have changed hands or succumbed to the pressure to "get big or get out."

For this reason, names of specific suppliers have not been given for the recommended varieties. Readers wishing to find the specific companies that carry a particular variety should refer to the *Garden Seed Inventory*, a "catalog of catalogs" that lists all nonhybrid varieties for sale by U.S. and Canadian seed suppliers. Seed Savers Exchange publishes and updates the inventory regularly (see "Seed Trusts and Historic Seed Programs," p. 314), and it is a valuable resource for anyone interested in finding and growing heirloom vegetables.

Dates of introduction for the recommended varieties appear in the entries wherever they could be determined. Almost all of the following varieties qualify as true heirlooms (open-pollinated and more than 50 years old), but a few more recent entries have also been included if they happen to represent a superior or important type of vegetable that is "in the heirloom spirit."

Amaranth
Amaranthus spp.
Amaranth is a beautiful and valuable food plant, grown since ancient times in Southeast Asia, India, and the Americas. Some types of amaranth are prized for their edible leaves, which are harvested and used in salads or steamed lightly like spinach; other species produce colorful heads filled with small seeds, which are popped or cooked as a cereal grain or ground to make a high-protein flour.

But most American gardeners know amaranth, first and foremost, as an ornamental plant, particularly the popular 'Love-Lies-Bleeding' *(A. caudatus),* whose graceful, trailing reddish pink tassels lend a delightfully old-fashioned air to an annual bed or border. Other varieties of amaranth are equally useful as ornamentals and vegetables; several cultivars have multicolored leaves splashed in shades of red, green, and gold.

How to Grow
Amaranth is easy to grow and tolerates a wide range of soil conditions; in fact, it is said that plants grown on poor or normal soil produce leaves with a more vivid color than those raised in rich soil.

Varieties specifically grown for greens are known by many names, including Chinese spinach, tampala, calaloo, and hinn choy. All of them benefit from even moisture, full sun, and a nitrogen-rich soil. By the end of the season, the plants can reach 3–6 ft. in height. Direct-seed ⅛ in. deep after the last spring frost date; thin seedlings to 6 in. apart and use the thinnings for salad or cooked greens.

Amaranths grown for grain typically grow into tall, handsome plants, reaching 5–9 ft. in height depending on the richness of the soil. Direct-seed ¼ in. deep after the last spring frost date in rows spaced 12 in. apart, and keep the seedbed watered until plants germinate. Thin seedlings to 6 in. apart. Grain amaranths tolerate drought but benefit from deep watering during prolonged dry spells. To ripen seed, amaranth requires a long growing season (100 days or more), so it's not suitable for the coldest regions of the country.

A tender annual, amaranth will often self-sow if the plants are left to mature in the garden.

Harvest
Pick the edible leaves from amaranth throughout the growing season in cooler growing regions; in the South, gardeners can plant succession crops every few weeks to have a continuous supply of young greens. Larger leaves are edible but most people find the younger leaves more tender and deli-

cately flavored. The taste is difficult to describe; some people compare it to artichokes, others to more sharply flavored spinach.

Harvest amaranth for grain before the first expected frost in the North. Cut off the plant tassels and set them out on a waterproof tarp to dry until brittle in the sun, covering them with plastic to guard against rain and nightly dew. In areas with later frost dates, plants can remain standing in the garden until the tops dry further and begin to drop seeds. Rub seedheads over a screen to release the dense seeds, then winnow with a fan or the wind to separate the seeds from the chaff.

■ RECOMMENDED VARIETIES

'Elephant Head' (1880s) *A. gangeticus*
Without a doubt the most unusual flowering amaranth, this variety comes from German immigrants. Each plant sports a huge (36–40 in.), dark red flower head with many protuberances and an 18–24-in. "trunk" that makes it look like a trumpeting elephant. Mainly grown as an ornamental "prodigy" plant, but the shiny black seeds make a nutritious grain and are also attractive to birds; 80–100 days.

'Hopi Red Dye' ('Komo') *A. cruentus*
Reddish purple plant, to 5 ft., used traditionally by Hopi Indians as a ceremonial dye plant. Both the tiny black seeds and the greens are edible; 100–120 days.

'Joseph's Coat' *A. gangeticus (A. tricolor)* p. 22
A classic ornamental plant, originally from India; to 4 ft., bearing tricolored leaves or red, green, and yellow. Good for salad greens when young; 70 days.

'Love-Lies-Bleeding' *A. caudatus* p. 22
Originally from South America, this is perhaps the most commonly grown ornamental amaranth. Plants to 3 ft., with showy, reddish pink tassels that droop down in ropes. Both seeds and leaves are edible; 110 days.

'Merah' ('Coleus Leaf Salad') *A. gangeticus* p. 23
Round brilliant magenta leaves with yellow trim, resembling coleus leaves; plants to 2 ft. Leaves have a pleasant nutty taste that's good in salads; 65–80 days.

'Mercado' ('Dreadicus') *A. hypochondriacus*
A traditional grain amaranth from southern Mexico. Plants 7–9 ft., with green coxcomblike heads that bear tasty orange-

gold seeds that are ground for flour or popped; in Mexico, the popped seeds are mixed with molasses to make a popular candy called *alegrias,* or "joy bars"[1]; 125–130 days.

'**Molten Fire**' ('Summer Poinsettia') *A. gangeticus* p. 23
One of the excellent ornamental varieties developed in the 1920s by Luther Burbank. Plants to 4 ft., with scarlet and green edible leaves and a dark red seedhead.

Artichoke, Globe

Cynara scolymus
Native to the Mediterranean region, the globe artichoke is a large, coarse-leaved thistlelike perennial. The edible part of the "choke" itself is actually only the fleshy bases of the plant's unopened flower bracts. If left to open and blossom, the artichoke's flowers are very beautiful and useful in dried flower arrangements; the gray-green foliage remains attractive all season long in the garden.

How to Grow
In warmer zones, such as the California coast, artichokes can be treated as true perennials, grown in the same bed or row planting for 6 or 7 years before they need to be renewed and replanted. Like other perennials, they do not necessarily come true to type from seed and are best propagated by root division from parent plants. Plant the divided crowns 6–8 in. deep and 6 ft. apart in a well-drained soil rich in organic matter; space rows 8 ft. apart to allow for the spread of the mature plants. Artichoke roots cannot tolerate a prolonged freeze, so mulch heavily at the end of the season to protect the crowns. Mulch should be pulled back early the following spring to prevent crown rot.

In colder regions, where winter protection is not possible, artichokes can be treated as annuals, grown from seed to harvest in one long season. To accomplish this, the seeds must be started early, about 12 weeks before the last spring frost date. I use Eliot Coleman's method from his book *Four-Season Harvest:* Start the seeds inside the house or in a heated greenhouse; after about 6 weeks, move the seedlings to a cold frame, keeping the glazing open during the daytime if temperatures allow; finally, after 6 more weeks, transplant to the garden, spacing the plants about 24 in. apart.

The time spent in the cooler temperatures of the unheated cold frame supposedly fools the artichoke seedlings into thinking they have gone through a winter season. Artichokes grown as annuals will take up less room in the garden, hence

the closer spacing between plants. Gardeners starting artichokes from seed should rogue out any undesirable plants before transplanting to the cold frame or garden. Northern
growers should at least try to overwinter artichokes in the
garden by mulching heavily; if successful, the plants should
yield more heavily in their second year of growth; in this case,
follow the 6-ft. spacing guideline.

Harvest
Artichoke buds mature late in the summer and should be cut
off just before the leathery bracts begin to open. One plant,
if well fertilized and watered during the season, will yield a
number of chokes. The smaller, purple varieties of artichokes,
popular in France and Italy, can be eaten *cru,* or raw, when
the buds are young.

■ RECOMMENDED VARIETIES

'Green Globe' p. 24
The standard main-crop variety, listed by Burr in 1863. Plants
3–6 ft., bearing 3–4-in. chokes with thick green bracts. Grown
as a perennial from crowns, requires 18 months to harvest.

'Purple Sicilian'
Perhaps not an heirloom itself, but one of the modern de-
scendants of the purple type, listed by Burr in 1863. Produces
fairly early, bearing small, bronzy purple buds.

'Violetto'
Another recent purple variety that bears a midsummer crop
if started inside in midwinter. In warmer climates, start in
spring and transplant in autumn. Purple chokes are more conical and elongated than 'Green Globe'.

Asparagus
Asparagus officinalis p. 24
Asparagus has been the star of the spring table since ancient
times. In fact, Roman chefs valued asparagus so much that
they dehydrated the finest stalks and kept them on hand to
cook as needed. One of the emperor Augustus's favorite say-
ings was *Citius quam asparagi coquentur,* "Do it quicker than
you can cook asparagus" — a delightful expression that
proves the Romans knew how to treat this noble vegetable.
In addition to its culinary virtues, the ancients also valued asparagus for its supposed medicinal properties. Among other
things, it was thought that if a person smeared on an as-

paragus-and-oil liniment, bees would not sting or even approach him.[2]

As late as 1869, the famous American seedsman Peter Henderson maintained that there were in fact no truly separate varieties of asparagus and that any apparent differences were the result of growing the crop in different localities on different kinds of soils.[3] Although he later changed his mind, Henderson's opinion illustrates the importance of local conditions and good cultivation in the quality of asparagus.

A hardy perennial, asparagus is usually propagated and grown from roots, or crowns, which generally yield a harvestable crop beginning in the second year after planting. Since asparagus beds can remain productive for 10 to 20 years or longer, they are typically sited outside the annual vegetable garden.

In recent years, the disease-resistant Washington strains ('Mary Washington', 'Martha Washington', etc.) have come to dominate the U.S. market. The heirloom varieties listed below are not often sold as crowns and will have to be grown from seed, which can be done successfully, though it requires patience — at least 4 years from sowing to first harvest. It is also possible to save seeds from your established asparagus plants by harvesting the red berries from female plants in the fall.

How to Grow

Asparagus grows well in most regions of the country, except the Deep South and other areas that have mild winters.

The easiest way to grow asparagus is to purchase 1- or 2-year-old roots. Dig a planting trench 12–15 in. deep, allowing 4 ft. between beds. Mound up a mixture of soil and compost or aged manure and drape the fleshy roots of an asparagus plant over the mound, spacing crowns 18 in. apart in the trench. The top of the crown should be 3–5 in. below the soil surface. Fill in the trench, burying the crowns about 1 in. deep at first; as the shoots emerge add more soil to the trench, until the bed is level. Keep the bed well weeded and watered and let the plants grow undisturbed into ferns through the first season. Dress the bed with dried cow manure and cut off the ferny top growth in the fall. In the second year, harvest only a few shoots. In the third year, begin regular harvesting of asparagus spears.

To grow asparagus from seed, soak the seed in lukewarm water for 48 hours before sowing, replenishing with warm water periodically. Direct-seed in well-drained garden soil 3–5 in. apart in rows spaced 12 in. apart, and thin plants to 12 in. apart; or start seeds indoors 6 to 8 weeks before the last spring frost date and transplant 12 in. apart in rows or a cold frame. Mulch plants heavily at the end of the first growing season. The following spring you'll transplant the roots to a permanent bed. Select for the larger (male) roots, but be sure to transplant some female roots as well. Plant and care for as described under the root method, above.

Pests and Diseases
Asparagus is susceptible to various diseases, the most serious being rust, blight, gray mold, and especially fusarium wilt. The best way to avoid these diseases is to establish the asparagus bed in a well-drained location and remove all dead stalks and other plant material in the fall. This is also a good time to fertilize the bed and to make a shallow cultivation, being careful not to damage the crowns. Such cultivation helps prevent problems with the spotted asparagus beetle, a common insect pest. One often-recommended way to discourage insects is to plant tomatoes or other plants with strongly scented foliage (basil, parsley, marigolds) in or around the asparagus bed.

■ RECOMMENDED VARIETIES

'Argenteuil Early'
Listed by Vilmorin-Andrieux (1885) as a selection from 'Giant Dutch Purple', this is one of three subvarieties of 'Argenteuil' (early, intermediate, and late). Argenteuil is a town just northwest of Paris that was for centuries an important asparagus-growing district; at one time several thousand persons were employed in cultivating the crop there. This variety has thick stalks with purple tips; in good conditions the stalks are 3–6 in. in circumference.

'Conover's Colossal' (1870)
An American variety developed by Abraham Van Siclen on Long Island and introduced by S. B. Conover of New York City. This variety was once widely grown and deemed superior to other varieties of its day. Bountiful Gardens describes it as "the best variety for general use and for raising from seed." Vilmorin considered it similar to Argenteuil.

BEANS

So ubiquitous is the cultivation of beans around the world today that it comes as something of a surprise to realize that the common or kidney bean, *Phaseolus vulgaris*, was not "discovered" by Europeans until the time of Columbus. Common, lima, runner, and tepary beans, all members of the large genus *Phaseolus,* are all native to the Americas. Other popular garden beans include the broad bean or fava bean *(Vicia faba)* and the soybean *(Glycine max),* each of which is discussed separately below.

Easy to grow, self-pollinating, and with large, often colorful seeds, beans of all types are the perfect "starter kit" for budding seed savers. Many of the great old heirloom beans that still survive today have been preserved over the years by immigrants, by families, or simply by popular demand.

Snap Beans
Phaseolus vulgaris

Snap beans constitute part of the diverse and wonderful species known variously as common beans, kidney beans, French beans, garden beans, and filet beans. The "snap" refers more to how the beans are used (young pods harvested for fresh eating) than to any botanical distinction, though over the years both amateur and professional plant breeders have selected for beans that are "stringless," at least in their immature stage, and that contain little or no tough fiber (or parchment) in the young pods. Whereas the wild form of the common bean has hard-coated seeds and grows all over creation by means of lateral runners, the growing habit of cultivated common beans is more restrained. Domesticated pole bean varieties grow in a roughly pyramidal fashion, perfect for climbing up cornstalks or trellises. Dwarf or determinate bush varieties probably arose as consciously selected mutants once beans became an important agricultural crop; not having to compete with other plants for nutrients and light, the beans could quit sending out all those leaves and tendrils and concentrate on setting pods.[4]

Many American home gardeners (and nearly all growers) prefer those varieties of snap beans that remain stringless for a long time on the bush or remain fresh in the refrigerator for a long time after picking. In contrast, the French prefer the long, skinny filet beans that have to be picked early and often to ensure tenderness and optimum flavor. I like both kinds, and in fact there's really no need to choose; good heirloom varieties of both types are readily available.

How to Grow
Beans grow best in full sun on normal, well-drained garden soil. All common beans need warm soil temperatures (65° to 80° F) to germinate and grow, so wait to plant seed until after the last spring frost date. Before planting, moisten seeds and coat them with a legume inoculant powder, which will en-

courage good nitrogen fixation on roots. Bacterial inoculant now also comes in granular form, which you can sprinkle right in the planting furrow.

For bush varieties, plant seeds 1 in. deep and about 4 in. apart in rows or beds spaced 24–36 in. apart. To ensure a continuous harvest throughout the season, make succession plantings every 2–3 weeks.

Plant pole beans 3–4 in. apart in a row to grow up heavy-duty wire or mesh trellises strung between posts; or plant 6–7 seeds at the base of four 12-ft. poles driven into the ground and tied at the top to form "teepees." (To maximize garden space, you can also sow a quick-growing salad crop inside the teepee base at the same time; the beans will shade the greens in hot weather.)

Harvest
Pick snap beans when they are young and tender and keep picking them regularly to encourage the plants to produce new pods. It is especially important to pick the long, skinny French or filet beans frequently (every 2–3 days, especially during hot weather) to prevent the pods from becoming fibrous and unpalatable.

Pests and Diseases
Beans are subject to a number of diseases, including anthracnose, bean mosaic virus, downy mildew, rust, and blight. You can avoid most of these through good cultural practices such as rotating crops, leaving enough space between plants to allow for good air circulation, and removing bean plants from the garden at the end of the season. Most important, though, is to avoid working around your beans whenever rain or dew is on the plants; you can easily spread disease from plant to plant in this manner.

Mexican bean beetles and other beetles eat holes in bean leaves. Handpick and destroy the insect and their eggs when you see them, or dust with rotenone or pyrethrum to control.

■ RECOMMENDED VARIETIES

Snap Bush Beans

'Black Valentine' (before 1850)
An almost legendary bean among American gardeners. The original strain was stringy and tough, but 'Stringless Black Valentine' is back and better than ever; matures early as a snap bean (48 days) and is also good as a dry black soup bean (70 days). Distinctive flavor.

'Bountiful' (1898)

Developed by D. G. Burlingame of Genesee, New York. Early and productive; bears straight, broad, flat 6–7-in. pods on 18-in. plants; light tan seeds; 41–52 days.

'Burpee's Stringless Green Pod' (1894)

Developed by the great bean breeder, Calvin Keeney, of LeRoy, New York, who was known as the Father of the Stringless Bean. Early, hardy, and productive; fleshy, round, curved 5–6-in. pods on 20-in. plants; tolerates heat and drought; coffee brown seed; 50–55 days.

'Canadian Wonder' (1873)

Vigorous, hardy, prolific; flat-oval 7–8-in. pods; dark red to deep purple seeds; unique flavor; 65 days.

'Fin des Bagnols'

Also known as 'Shoestring Bean'. From the 1800s, the old standard variety for French filet beans; pick every 2–3 days before pods become fibrous; 55 days.

'Masterpiece' (1907)

Early, prolific, and reliable; long, straight, semiflat 8–10-in. pods on 15–18-in. plants; 56 days.

'Red Valentine' (1832)

An old American variety, first listed by Landreth Seed Co.; strong plants, very productive; 5-in. curved pods are thick, tender, and crisp; 47 days.

'Tendergreen' (1922)

Probably developed by Calvin Keeney. Vigorous, 18–20-in. plants with meaty, 5–6-in. pods; disease-resistant and heat-tolerant; early, heavy yields; excellent flavor, tender, and stringless; 45–57 days.

'Triomphe de Farcy' (1892)

Another heirloom French filet bean, slightly later than 'Fin des Bagnols'; long, thin, straight green pods lightly striped with purple; pick frequently to avoid toughness; 60–65 days.

Snap Pole Beans

'Blue Coco' (1775)

French heirloom; 5–6-in. purple curved pods; heat- and drought-tolerant; meaty flavor; tan flat seeds; good as snap, shell, or dry bean; 60 days.

'Cherokee Trail of Tears'
Reportedly grown by the Cherokee Nation and transported with them when they left their homeland in the 1800s; prolific; 6-in. creasebacked green pods turning reddish purple; good as snap or dry soup bean; shiny black seeds; 60–70 days for snaps, 85–95 days for dry beans. Lawrence Hollander of CRESS describes this bean as "one of the best — tender, tasty, and high-yielding."

'Hickman' ('Hickman's Soup') p. 25
A vigorous climber, 10–12 ft.; 6–8-in. flat, wide, velvety green pods; stringless and very tasty; 75 days for snaps, 90 days for dry beans, which are good for soup; seed color varies.

'Kentucky Wonder' ('Old Homestead'; 1850s) p. 25
Still the most popular and widely available pole bean; flattened oval 7–10-in. pods in clusters; rust-resistant; both white- and brown-seeded strains available; 58–72 days.

'Oregon Giant' ('Paul Bunyan')
Listed by U. P. Hedrick in *Beans of New York* (1931). A popular variety in the Pacific Northwest; pods 7–9 in., slightly curved, stringless, light green mottled with purple; thrives in cool, wet soils; 63–70 days.

'Romano Pole' p. 26
The classic Italian gourmet bean, with thick, meaty, tender, flat, stringless pods; mosaic-resistant; unique flavor; 60–70 days.

'Trionfo Violetto' p. 26
Another Italian heirloom, and my favorite purple-podded variety. Pretty, with purple-veined leaves, purple stems, and lavender flowers; pods 7 in., oval-round; extended harvest if kept picked; excellent flavor; 62 days.

Wax Bush Beans

'Brittle Wax' ('Round Pod Kidney Wax'; 1900)
Home garden and canning variety. Pods 6–7 in. long, slightly curved, round, fleshy; high yields and long harvest period; also a good shelling bean; white seed with black eye; 52 days.

'Buerre de Rocquencourt' p. 27
Old French variety with straight, 5–6-in. yellow pods; productive if kept picked; good for regions where summers or night temperatures are cool; 48–54 days.

'Dragon Langerie' ('Dragon's Tongue') p. 27
A beautiful wax bean from the Netherlands. Plants are compact and stocky, 12–15 in. high. Pods are long and flat; color is creamy yellow covered with purple streaks; excellent flavor. Plants are productive and rust-resistant; 57–65 days.

'Golden Wax' (1871)
Hedrick says this variety "represents a distinctive group of wax beans, one of our oldest known cultivated types." Pods are 4–6 in. long, golden yellow, and stringless, with a nice buttery flavor; good for northern climates; disease-resistant; for fresh use, canning, or freezing; 45–60 days. Many variations and improved strains are available.

'Mont D'Or' (1880s)
French heirloom; oval pods with delicate flavor; disease-resistant; 57 days.

'Pencil Pod Black Wax' (1900)
Another outstanding bean developed by Calvin Keeney; Hedrick says it was "by many considered the highest quality bean in the entire list [of wax beans]." Pods round-oval, dull golden-yellow, curved, stringless and fiberless, with a fine texture and excellent eating quality; 50–65 days.

Wax Pole Beans

'Kentucky Wonder Wax' (1901) p. 28
Originated in the garden of a Miss Callahan of Los Angeles, California, in 1898. Used as both a snap and shelling bean. Slightly curved, flattened oval, golden yellow 6–9-in. pods; productive and everbearing, especially in cooler climates; light brown seed; 61–68 days.

'Meraviglia di Venezia' ('Wonder of Venice')
Broad, flat, stringless Italian slicing bean. Vigorous climber, to 11 ft.; light yellow pods turn golden as they mature; use as snap or shelling bean; seed black; 75 days. Rare, but according to Rob Johnston a similar variety named 'Goldmarie' has been selected from 'Meraviglia di Venezia' and recently introduced in the seed trade.

'Yellow Annelino' p. 28
An Italian heirloom, and one of my favorite pole beans. Pale yellow pods curve into semicircles, making them somewhat hard to pick (it's worth the effort). Very productive and flavorful; 75–85 days. I like to steam these beans briefly and toss with just a hint of butter, white pepper, and nutmeg.

Horticultural or Shell Beans

Phaseolus vulgaris

Horticultural beans differ from snap beans only in the stage at which they are generally harvested. Pick them when the pods have swelled but before the beans inside have begun to dry. This is known as the "green shell" stage, and the beans, once shelled, are ready to be steamed, cooked, or baked in a variety of dishes.

Until recently most produce markets in the U.S. did not carry shelling beans, even in season, and they were the sole province of the home gardener or local farmstand grower. Today, they have become a more common sight, often appearing under the title of "cranberry beans," regardless of their variety.

As with the other categories of beans, some shelling varieties make good snap beans when picked very young, or good soup or baking beans if left in the pod to dry. The best shelling varieties develop leathery pods with a suture that "pops" or opens easily.

How to Grow
See Snap Bean, p. 132, for growing information.

Harvest
Pick pods in the green shell stage, after the beans have swelled and filled out the pods completely, but before the pods have dried.

■ RECOMMENDED VARIETIES

Horticultural Bush Beans

'Chevrier Vert' (1880)
The classic flageolet bean from France; used young as snap beans, cooked like peas in the green shell stage, or dried as a baking bean; matures in 50–68 days; pods contain 6–7 beans.

'Dwarf Horticultural' (late 1700s) p. 29
May have originated in Italy. Medium to large seeds, oval, plump, and pinkish buff drying to light brown and streaked with maroon; good for cool climate and coastal areas; 53–56 days.

'Tongue of Fire' ('Horto') p. 29
Apparently there are two different strains of this excellent bean, one from Tierra del Fuego in South America, and the other from Italy. Attractive pods are streaked with red and useful as snap beans when picked at 5 in. (56 days) or later

in the green shell stage (70–75 days). Seeds are large, round, and flavorful; buff-colored with red splashes; good for fresh use, canning, freezing, or as a dry baked bean. Rob Johnston says 'Tongue of Fire' "always rates tops in cooking tests of bush shell beans."

'Vermont Cranberry Bush' (1700s)   p. 30
An old-time New England heirloom useful as either a green shell or dry bean. Pods open easily and yield 5–6 cranberry-colored beans that have an excellent, sweet flavor; 60–85 days.

Horticultural Pole Beans

'Lazy Wife' ('White Cranberry'; 1810)   p. 30
First noticed in America growing in Bucks Co., Pennsylvania, where it was brought by German immigrants. The name refers to the fact that the beans when used as snaps did not require destringing. Hedrick claims that "as a shell bean it is probably unsurpassed." Plants are late to mature (around 80 days), but bear continuously until frost. Pods are 5–6 in. long; seeds are white with gray patterns.

'Vermont Cranberry Pole'
Very old heirloom that is the climbing form of 'Vermont Cranberry Bush'. Useful as a green shell bean (60 days), but also good as a dry baking bean (90 days). Productive, flavorful, and grows well in all climates.

'Wren's Egg' ('London Horticultural'; 1825)   p. 31
Hedrick describes this as "probably one of our earliest horticultural type beans," and suggests that it may be the Arancauo bean of Chile. Pods are dark green in the snap stage and almost stringless; pick when 5 in. long for fresh use. Pods are streaked with purplish red in green shell stage (65 days). Seeds are large, broad, oval, and buff-colored, streaked with dark red. Productive, with a long harvest period; the largest of the horticultural beans.

Dry or Field Beans

Phaseolus vulgaris
The oldest archaeological evidence of common beans comes from Tehuacan in Mexico, where radiocarbon dating suggests they were grown as early as 7000 B.C.[5] Almost certainly, ancient farmers harvested and consumed dried beans, not only because the "stringless" bean had not yet been developed, but

because dried beans could be stored and used over an extended period of time as an excellent and nutritious food.

Today, the distinctions between snap, shell, and dry bean varieties are muddy, while many heirloom beans remain tasty and useful at all three stages. What most characterizes dried bean varieties, though, are their tough mature pods, which get stringy and fibrous and break open readily when the seeds are ripe (a characteristic botanists refer to as being "strongly dehiscent").

It is also in their dry, mature stage that beans become fascinating to the seed saver or collector, mostly for their wide range of colors and markings. Four main color groups — white, black, red, and brown — form the basic background color of the seed coat, or *testa*.[6] But all sorts of complex patterns and markings, from streaks to splotches to rings around the hilum, or "eye," of the bean, distinguish many heirloom varieties from one another and make them living works of art.

How to Grow
See Snap Beans, p. 132, for growing information.

Harvest
Pull plants out by the roots when the pods are dry and at least 90 percent of the leaves have fallen. Complete drying under cover if the weather is wet.

To thresh out dried beans from the pod, you can shell them by hand if the crop is small, hold a few plants upside down inside a large trash can and whack them from side to side, or put the plants in a large burlap sack and step on them or beat them with a wooden flail. Dry beans thoroughly before storing.

Pests and Diseases
After threshing and drying bean seed, examine the seeds for small holes in their coats. This indicates the presence of bean weevils. If you find evidence of this kind, place the beans in a lidded glass jar and put in the freezer for up to a week before storing. This freezing step helps protect home-saved seeds and ensures that weevils will not survive to affect next year's bean plants.

■ RECOMMENDED VARIETIES

Dry Bush Beans

'Arikara Yellow'
An ancient American Indian variety, introduced by Oscar H. Will to the seed trade in the late 1800s. Hardy and drought-

tolerant; seed golden brown with reddish brown eye ring; an excellent baking bean; 85 days.

'Black Coco'
Vigorous and widely adapted heirloom; young pods make good snap beans; dry beans cook quickly and make good re-fried beans; 85 days.

'Black Turtle' ('Turtle Soup'; before 1806) p. 31
A very old variety, originally from South America. Late variety; 85–105 days; not for short-season areas. Vigorous growing habit, with sprawling half-runners; disease-resistant and heat-tolerant; excellent for the South. Dry beans have a unique taste and make great soup that has a greenish cast (hence the turtle soup name).

'Cannellini' ('Cannelone'; before 1900)
Classic Italian white shelling bean, with large kidney-shaped white seeds; does well in cool weather; 90 days.

'Great Northern' ('Montana White')
A very old variety originally grown by the Mandan Indians of the Dakotas; introduced by Will in 1907. Hardier, earlier, larger, more productive, and quicker-cooking than the common navy bean. Pods straight, flat, 5 in. long with 5–6 long, thin-skinned white seeds. Grows well in northern areas; 65–90 days.

'Hutterite' (1750s) p. 32
I was first turned on to these little pale green beans by Alan Kapuler, the research director for Seeds of Change. Now they are one of my favorite dried beans, since they cook down beautifully to make a thick, delicious soup. The Hutterites are a religious sect from Austria that moved to Canada in the 1750s, presumably bringing these tasty beans along with them. Compact, vigorous plants; 75–85 days.

'Jacob's Cattle' ('Trout') p. 32
This popular New England baking bean is of ancient origin; it is very similar in appearance to a bean called 'Anasazi' from the Southwest. It's also one of the most attractive beans, with white seeds speckled reddish brown. Pods contain 5 seeds; 80–100 days.

'Low's Champion' ('Dwarf Red Cranberry') p. 33
Another one of my favorites, this bean belongs under dried beans only because of its beautiful mahogany red seeds; it is as useful as a green shell bean or a snap, with its broad,

meaty, stringless pods. Introduced in 1884 by the Aaron Low Seed Co., Hedrick considered it "one of the oldest varieties in cultivation," probably grown by Native Americans. Stands for a long time in the snap stage; hardy, vigorous, and compact plants; 70–80 days.

'Santa Maria Pinquito'
A terrific little bean grown by early Spanish settlers in California's Santa Maria Valley. Small, slender pods hold 6–10 small pink dry beans, almost the size of lentils. David Cavagnaro has grown this bean for years and describes it as "incredible . . . the best-tasting baking bean." Plants are small; 75–90 days.

'Soldier' ('Johnson Bean') p. 33
Another New England heirloom, named for the brownish red markings around the eye that look like a colonial soldier. Hardy, drought-tolerant plants; pods contain 6 long, large beans. Does well in cool climates; an excellent and popular soup and baking bean; 80–90 days.

'Sulphur' ('China Yellow'; before 1870) p. 34
An old variety that was rediscovered and introduced in 1893 by the Ford Seed Co. under the apt name 'Eureka'. Small, plump, pale sulphur yellow seeds with a good, distinctive flavor for soups or baking; makes a rich gravy; can also be used young as a snap bean. Not very productive; 90–95 days.

'Swedish Brown' (1890) p. 34
Originated with Swedish immigrants in the Upper Mississippi Valley, where it is still popular as a nutty-flavored bean. Small to medium seeds are oval, plump, and golden brown; plants are compact, bushy, and very productive. Good for northern areas; 85–95 days.

'Yellow Eye' ('Molasses Face')
The most popular dry baking bean in Maine, this variety is very old and has many different strains, which have developed based on regional growing conditions, breeding, and selection. Plump, oval, white seeds have a butterscotch yellow marking around the eye; 80–95 days.

Dry Pole Beans

'Mostoller's Wild Goose' (1865) p. 35
A family heirloom from western Pennsylvania, these beans (so the story goes) were discovered by the Mostoller family in the crop of a goose and planted out the following spring.

Lawrence Hollander believes that the bean has Seneca origins and may have been grown by American Indians living on the Cornplanter Reservation on the Upper Allegheny River. A tall climbing variety, this bean makes a good baker or soup bean and can also be used in the snap or green shell stage. Seeds are white with a light orange-tan marking around the eye that is flecked with darker reddish brown. Heavy producer; 90–100 days. These beans were maintained in the Mostoller family for 117 years and are now preserved by Seed Savers Exchange (see p. 316).

'Ruth Bible' (1832) p. 35
A very productive "cutshort" variety from Kentucky with flat, green 5-in. pods that contain 6–7 small round seeds. Seed is brownish tan with an orange eye ring. Use for snap beans when young or dried in soups; 80–95 days.

Fava or Broad Beans
Vicia faba
A legume related to vetch, fava beans are one of the oldest cultivated plants. E. Lewis Sturtevant in his *Notes on Edible Plants* mentions archaeological evidence of favas found in Bronze Age deposits in Switzerland. These beans were also eaten by the ancient Egyptians, Greeks, and Romans; in fact, one noble Roman family, the Fabii, derived its name from the plant.[7] Before Columbus's voyage to the Americas, favas were the only beans known in Europe.

Probably native to Africa and the Middle East, favas (also known as broad beans, Windsor beans, horse beans, and Scotch beans) are not very widely grown in America but are popular as snaps and green or dry shelling beans in southern European countries and in England, where unlike most common beans they grow well in the cool, moderate climate. A small number of people, usually of southern European ancestry, have a hereditary allergic reaction to favas.

Favas make an excellent substitute for lima beans in cold, short-season areas where the latter cannot be grown successfully. Their taste has been described as somewhere between a garden pea and lima bean, often with rich, nutty overtones. They are nutritious and deserve a more prominent place in American home gardens.

How to Grow
Favas germinate in cool soil temperatures and should be planted as early as the ground can be worked in the spring, at the same time you would plant peas. They prefer well-

drained fertile soil. Mix seeds with a legume inoculant and plant 1 in. deep and 4–6 in. apart in rows spaced 18–36 in. apart (closer spacing will keep pod-laden plants from drooping over). Unlike other beans, favas tolerate some frost and grow best in cool, rainy weather. Hot weather can inhibit flowering and pod-setting; plant favas early enough so that they flower before daytime temperatures exceed 70°F. To encourage pod-setting, pinch back the tops of plants after the first 4–5 flower clusters have appeared. In southern and mild coastal regions, plant favas from October to December for harvest the following March.

Fava plants are large and bushy, to 4 ft., with strong, nonbranching stems that do not require trellising or support.

Harvest
For snap beans, pick young pods when they are 2–3 in. long. Harvest for green shell use when pods are 5–8 in. long and filled out with the large beans. Cook like peas or shell beans.

Pests and Diseases
Aphids can transfer viruses from plant to plant, resulting in blackened leaves, particularly during hot weather. Control aphids with an insecticidal soap spray.

■ RECOMMENDED VARIETIES

'Aquadulce Claudia'
Vilmorin-Andrieux listed 'Agua-Dulce Long-Podded' in 1885, as an improved strain of 'Seville Long-Pod'. Plants to 3 ft.; pods are 2 in. wide and 12–16 in. long; quarter-sized seeds are listed as either brown or white. Extremely cold-tolerant, reportedly to 12°F. Susceptible to aphids if spring-sown; sow in fall for a spring crop in southern or mild coastal areas; 90–140 days (spring-sown); 240 days (fall-sown and over-wintered).

'Broad Windsor'   p. 36
A classic variety, listed simply as 'Windsor' by Burr in 1863, but under its present name by Vilmorin-Andrieux in 1885. Glossy green pods contain 4–7 oblong, flat, pale green shell beans; 65–85 days.

'Castillo Franco'
An outstanding heirloom once grown by Spanish farmers in New Mexico; plants 3–4 ft.; tolerates hot weather in spring better than other varieties; delicious, dark brown beans; 85–100 days.

'Crimson-Flowered' (1778)
In 1863 Fearing Burr listed a 'Red or Scarlet Blossomed' fava
bean that may be similar to this variety, which is rare but well
worth growing for its ornamental qualities. Pods are smaller
than those of other varieties, but well filled with small, bright
green, tasty beans; 100 days.

Lima or Butter Beans

Phaseolus lunatus
Lima beans come in both large-seeded and small-seeded
types. The small-seeded type, often called sieva or Carolina
bean, originated in Mexico, while the large-seeded type was
domesticated independently in South America. In fact, the
word "lima," though pronounced with a long vowel, comes
directly from Lima, the name of Peru's capital city; radiocarbon dating indicates that limas were being grown around
5300 B.C. at Chilca in Peru.[8] Today's gardeners are most familiar with the large-seeded limas, but one can find many
beautiful and productive varieties of both types.

How to Grow
Plant lima beans in a warm, well-drained garden soil, waiting to sow seeds until at least two weeks after the last spring
frost date. Plant bush limas 1–2 in. deep and about 4–6 in.
apart in rows spaced 36 in. apart; treat pole limas like other
pole beans, growing them on strong wire trellises in rows or
at the base of four 12-ft. poles lashed at the top to form
"teepees."
   Limas require a long growing season, having roughly the
same period to maturity as dried common beans. Because of
their preference for hot weather and their long season, limas
are better suited to the South, though several varieties are
fairly well adapted to northern growing conditions.

Harvest
Pick limas for green shell use when the beans have filled out
the pods, or let the pods dry and then thresh out the beans
as described under Dry Beans, p. 139.

Pests and Diseases
Limas are subject to the same diseases and pests as common
snap beans; follow the preventive measures outlined on p.
133, and be sure not to work near your limas when rain or
dew is on the plants.

■ RECOMMENDED VARIETIES

Bush Limas

'Henderson' (1885)
In 1883 a passing pedestrian discovered the original plant growing along a road near Lynchburg, Virginia; today this lima and its improved strain are still very popular as a home garden and market variety. Early, hardy, productive, drought-tolerant, and bears over a long season. Small green seeds come 3–4 to a pod and dry to a creamy white color; 60–75 days.

'Hopi Orange' p. 36
A rare and beautiful variety that grows about 3 ft. in height and is actually a weak climber rather than a true bush type; very drought-tolerant; seeds are mottled orange and black and are good for shell or dry use; 90 days.

'Jackson Wonder' (1888) p. 37
Originated with Thomas Jackson, a farmer from Atlanta, Georgia. One of the best varieties for the South; hardy and drought-tolerant; very productive. Pods can be used as snap beans when very young. Seeds are small, 3–5 per pod, and buff-colored with purple-black mottling; 65–75 days.

Pole Limas

'Black' (1892) p. 37
Little known today, but a good lima for northern areas. Hedrick lists it in *Beans of New York* (1931) and suggests that this variety may be a strain of 'Florida Butter'. Vigorous climber, needs strong support; very productive and disease-resistant, even in wet weather. Seeds are medium size, 3–4 per pod, and very dark purple to black; 80–90 days.

'Christmas' (1840s) p. 38
Strong climber, to 10 ft.; 4–6-in. pods contain 4–5 quarter-sized white seeds spotted with maroon; good flavor. Productive; likes hot, humid weather; 80–100 days. Rosalind Creasy describes this variety as "a beautiful bean."

'Civil War' (1860s)
A Kentucky family heirloom, reportedly brought home by a Civil War veteran. Vigorous climber, productive; seeds are small to medium size, 3–4 per pod, and come in three color variations: pure white, maroon-white, and maroon-black; good nutty flavor; 100 days.

'Dr. Martin'

The largest-seeded lima available; pods contain 2–3 plump, light green beans that are 2–3 times the size of other large limas; excellent flavor. Plants climb to 7–8 ft. and need strong support. Requires a long, hot season; 90–100 days.

'King of the Garden' (1883) p. 38

Popular large-seeded variety; vigorous climber; 4–6 creamy white seeds per pod; excellent flavor; bears over a long period; 85–95 days.

'Red Calico' (1790)

A Thweat family heirloom from South Carolina; hardy, productive, disease-resistant, and drought-tolerant. Pods contain 2–3 medium-size seeds that are a pretty dark red speckled with black; 90 days.

'Willow Leaf White' (1891) p. 39

Unique and highly ornamental variety, with very dark, glossy green foliage that resembles the leaves of a willow. Hedrick says it originated as a sport of the small-seeded Carolina or sieva type that grows wild in the South. Flowers freely with small, white blossoms. Pods contain 3–4 small white seeds; 65–80 days. Came to Seed Savers Exchange via the famous bean collector, John Withee.

Runner Beans

Phaseolus coccineus

The runner bean is native to Mexico and Central America, where it thrives in cool and humid upland terrain. Unlike other beans, runner beans form tuberous (and poisonous) perennial roots, though gardeners in temperate regions treat them as an annual. Also, while other *Phaseolus* beans have two common flower variations, lilac pink and white, runner bean blossoms are typically either white or bright scarlet red. The showy flowers appear prominently above the leaves, attracting hummingbirds to the garden. For this reason runner beans are grown primarily for their ornamental, cottage-garden qualities; though in northern Europe they're also used as a vegetable bean, either as snaps when very young or at the green shell stage.

How to Grow

Most runner beans have a climbing habit: unless noted as a bush variety, grow on a strong trellis or support as you would pole beans; space seeds 6–12 in. apart in a row. Runner beans are equally at home outside the vegetable garden, looking very ornamental when trained up a fence or wooden lattice. Runners tolerate hot summer weather, but temperatures above 90°F may inhibit the plant's ability to set pods. In the mid-Atlantic states and the South, pod production will resume in late summer and fall as temperatures moderate. Finally, although runner beans tolerate cool temperatures better than other beans, they are just as sensitive to frost.

Harvest
Pick young pods for use as green snaps. Harvest pods when the beans have filled out for green shell use, or let the pods dry if you intend to harvest beans for dry use or seed-saving. See harvesting instructions under Dry Beans, p. 139.

■ RECOMMENDED VARIETIES

'Aztec Dwarf White' p. 39
An ancient variety that Hedrick lists in *Beans of New York* as 'Barteldes Bush Lima', from the seed company that introduced it in 1890. Luther Burbank reported that seeds of this strains were discovered in a sealed vase in an ancient New Mexican settlement, dating the bean to the time of the Anasazi (Navaho, meaning "ancient ones"), if not definitively to the Aztecs. Growing 3–4 ft. in height, this is not a true bush bean but has short runners; however, it does not need staking or support. Bears masses of pure white flowers; coarse green pods contain 3–4 football-shaped plump white seeds. Hardy, drought-tolerant; 55–75 days.

'Blackcoat' ('Black Runner')
One of the oldest varieties known; described by Titus in 1654 as one of the rarest and most beautiful beans; plants climb to 6 ft., bearing deep scarlet flowers; good green shell bean; seeds are large and coal black when mature; 65–90 days.

'Czar'
A white-flowered runner bean with long, flattish pods and large, creamy white seeds; good quality and flavor as a snap, shell, or dry bean; 110 days.

'Painted Lady' (1855) p. 40
An old bicolored variety, described as early as 1827; flowers have red wings and pinkish white standards. Vigorous climber; 9–12-in. pods contain large brown and white seeds; good for snap or shell use and for freezing; pods mature slowly; 68–130 days. Rosalind Creasy says this is the best variety in her northern California climate.

'Scarlet Runner' (before 1750) p. 40
The most famous and widely grown runner bean, popular in England as a snap bean or for shelling. Blossoms are very large and bright scarlet, borne in masses of 20–40 on each long flower stalk. A tall, vigorous climber, growing 6–18 ft. Young pods almost stringless; seeds very large and usually shiny black mottled with purple; 65–90 days.

'Seneca Indian Bear Paw'
A rare variety recommended by David Cavagnaro of Seed Savers Exchange in Decorah, Iowa, where the strain is being maintained. A good climbing type and very free flowering, with attractive scarlet blossoms borne high above the leaves. Seed color is mixed: some are black and purple like typical 'Scarlet Runner' seeds, while others are pinkish purple with a few black flecks.

'White Dutch Runner' (before 1825)
Very tall climber, to 10 ft. or more; hardy and productive; thick, long, meaty pods are good as young snaps or for shell or dry use; attractive white flowers and very large, pure white seeds; 90–100 days.

Soybeans

Glycine max
Valued for its nutritional properties, the soybean is native to tropical Asia. It was listed in a Chinese writing from the 2nd century B.C. as one of the "five cereals" sown by Shen nung around 2800 B.C. In 1854 Commodore Matthew Perry returned from his Japanese expedition bearing soybeans, which were then distributed by the U.S. Patent Office.[9]

Dried soybeans contain about 40 percent protein and 18 percent oil. In addition to being cooked and eaten in the green shell or dry stage, soybeans are processed into a number of food products, including tofu, tempeh, miso, soy sauce, soy flour, and soy milk and cheese. In Japan, green-seeded soybeans are steamed in the pod and then shelled out as a kind of "beer nut." Black soybeans are preferred for dry use; dry soybeans require a lot of cooking time, so be sure to presoak them overnight.

How to Grow
After the last spring frost date, plant soybeans 1 in. deep and 4–6 in. apart in rows spaced 24–30 in. apart. Soybeans require a long season, but the heirloom varieties listed below will

mature soon enough to grow in most areas. Soybean plants are compact and bushy and do not require staking or support.

Harvest
For green vegetable types, harvest when the pods have filled out; harvest whole pods and steam briefly, then shell and complete cooking as needed. For black vegetable soybeans, harvest in the dry stage, following instructions for harvesting and threshing under Dry Beans, p. 139.

■ RECOMMENDED VARIETIES

'Agate' (1929) p. 41
Introduced to the U.S. from Sapporo, Japan. An early-maturing variety with unique olive-gold and brown color; compact plants; 65–70 days (green shell), 90–95 days (dry).

'Lammer's Black'
This heirloom is one of the best for short-season areas; large 2-ft. plants are high-yielding; black beans are thin-skinned and cook faster than green soybeans; good for making tofu and tempeh; 104 days.

Tepary Beans
Phaseolus acutifolius p. 41
A little-known crop outside the Desert Southwest, teparies are another bean species native to the Americas; archaeological evidence shows that they were being grown around 5000 B.C. at Tehuacan in Mexico.[10] The small dried beans have a unique flavor and are good for soup or baking. Many traditional varieties grow well in the Sonoran Desert or other hot, arid regions, but are either too late, too disease-prone, or too daylength-sensitive for some climates, particularly in the Northeast. The recommended varieties are the most widely adapted heirlooms now available.

How to Grow
Tepary beans thrive in hot, arid conditions, growing into a viney, sprawling bush that covers the ground and conserves any available moisture. In nondesert regions, teparies grow best in full sun on sharply drained sandy loam; if you have such a spot where almost nothing else will grow, it's worth giving teparies a try. In temperate or humid areas of the country plant tepary seeds farther apart in the row than you would other beans, both to accommodate their rambling ways and to lessen the chances of disease.

Harvest

To harvest as dry beans, cut or pull tepary plants when the pods are fully developed and at least two-thirds of the pods are dry. Spread out on tarps to dry completely, covering with plastic if necessary to protect from rain or dew. Follow threshing directions under Dry Beans, p. 139. Tepary pods are bitter and not useful as snap beans.

■ RECOMMENDED VARIETIES

'Mitla Black'

A traditional variety from Oaxaca, Mexico; dense, vigorous plant with short runners; easy to grow, productive. Thin, delicate pods contain 5–6 small, round, flattened black seeds. Has been grown successfully in the Pacific Northwest, Midwest, and northern Great Plains; perhaps the most adaptable variety; 75–90 days.

'Sonoran Gold Bush'

Delicious dry soup bean; seeds are golden brown in color, somewhat flattened, and larger than 'Mitla Black'. Sprawling 2–3-ft. bush produces 3–4 in. pods; 85 days. Recommended for the Midwest, South, and Pacific Northwest.

Beet

Beta vulgaris, Crassa group

Beets belong to the same species as Swiss chard, though no written reference to the red, turnip-rooted vegetable we know as garden beets exists before the 16th century. Before that time beets were grown and eaten mainly for their greens, and a few heirloom varieties are still valued more for their foliage than their roots. Another form of beet, called mangels or mangel-wurzels, have large roots with white flesh and over the years have been used more for stock feeding and sugar production than for table food.

How to Grow

Beets like full sun and somewhat cool conditions on loose, loamy garden soil; they thrive in even temperatures and rainfall rather than extremes of heat and moisture, which often causes "zoning," or white rings inside the roots. Plant two crops of beets per season: one in the early spring, 2–4 weeks before the last frost date; another 6–8 weeks before the first frost date in the fall.

Presoak beet seeds overnight before planting. Prepare the planting bed by working in compost, dried manure, or organic fertilizer, along with a sprinkling of bone meal to encourage good root development. Sow seeds about ½ in. deep and 1–2 in. apart in rows spaced 18–24 in. apart. Thin to 3 in. apart when the greens are big enough to eat, but before roots develop. Provide consistent moisture to keep roots from becoming woody.

Harvest

Pull up thinnings to use as cooked or raw greens. After the roots have developed to at least half-size, cut and harvest the leafy tops for greens, or thin further and use both the greens and baby beets, leaving more elbow room for the remaining beets. To prevent beets from bleeding, leave on skins and at least ½ in. of the tops when boiling, or bake in a 350°F oven until tender.

Beets tolerate light frosts, and fall crops will taste sweeter and store better if harvested after the first frost of the season. Before the first hard freeze, either harvest the remaining crop or mulch heavily in the garden. Beets store well in a root cellar or overwinter in the garden under a heavy mulch in regions with mild winters. Since beets are biennials, you will need to store the roots in one of these two ways if you plan to grow them for seed next season. In the spring, replant overwintered beets 18 in. apart. Cut off the seed stalk once the seeds have ripened.

Pests and Diseases

Beets are affected, though usually not seriously, by a variety of diseases and insect pests. Both black heart, a dark or hollow center, and brown scab, found on the outside of mature beets, indicate a boron deficiency in the soil. Beetles can be controlled with rotenone or sabadilla; aphids with insecticidal soap. Weevils can sometimes pose a problem in the South; to prevent future infestations, remove affected roots, clean out all plant debris at the end of the season, and practice crop rotation.

■ RECOMMENDED VARIETIES

'Albina Vereduna'

A Dutch variety; pure white, globular roots; thick skin; very sweet, potato-like texture; bright green curly tops; stores well in ground and can grow large without losing its tenderness; 55–60 days.

'Bull's Blood'

An old variety, now rare; recommended by Rosalind Creasy for its spectacular red-purple foliage; no edible root.

'Chiogga'   p. 42
Italian heirloom; one of the prettiest slicers, with alternating pink and white concentric "candystripe" rings; tops are green with pink-striped stems; very ornamental; fast-growing, and long-standing in fall; sweet flavor; becoming very popular in American specialty markets; 55 days.

'Crosby's Egyptian'   (1880)
The old standard in early bunching beets; uniform, flattened, round to heart-shaped roots and dark red flesh; smooth skin; bright, glossy green tops; 50–60 days.

'Cylindra'   ('Formanova'; 1880s)   p. 42
Dark red, cylindrical, 6–8-in. carrotlike roots are good for slicing or canning; sweet; easy to peel; attractive red-veined tops. Plant closer together than turnip-rooted beets and keep soil hilled up over root crowns; 56–60 days.

'Detroit Dark Red'   (1892)   p. 43
Old all-purpose variety for table use and home canning; 3-in. globular red roots are solid and have little zoning; fine-grained flesh, sweet and tender; tasty dark green tops. Still the most popular standard variety; 55–60 days.

'Early Wonder'   (1911)
One of the best varieties for early greens, with flavorful 16–18-in. tops; quick growing; half-flat, smooth-skinned, 3-in. roots are bright red with light zones; 50–60 days.

'Golden Beet'   (before 1828)   p. 43
An outstanding beet whose 1–2-in. mild-tasting roots don't bleed, making them perfect for salad use. Roots are globe-shaped and orange, turning golden yellow when cooked; they remain tender and mild even when pulled at an older stage. Tops are green, sweet, and tasty. Seeds of 'Golden' have a lower germination rate than other beets, so plant more thickly than other varieties and thin young plants in the row; 55–60 days.

'Lutz Green Leaf'   ('Winter Keeper')   p. 44
One of the best heirlooms for fall harvest and winter storage; smooth-skinned, reddish purple roots are shaped like a top, with a half-long tap root. Can grow very large without losing its sweetness or getting woody. Tall, 14–18-in. tops have pink midribs. Overwinter in damp sand in the root cellar, like carrots; 60–80 days.

'MacGregor's Favorite' ('Dracena Beet') p. 44
Scottish heirloom variety grown specifically for its narrow,
spear-shaped metallic purple leaves, which are excellent-
tasting and highly ornamental. Long, dark red roots; 60 days.

'Yellow Intermediate Mangel' ('Yellow Mangel')
Listed by Vilmorin-Andrieux in 1885 and referred to by Burr
in 1863 as a recent introduction. This mangel-type beet can
grow very large, 8–10 lb., without losing its delicious, sweet
flavor. Roots are tapering, with orange-yellow skin and white
flesh. Large leaves can be steamed and used like Swiss chard;
70 days.

Broccoli

Brassica oleracea

Broccoli comes in two distinct types. The first, and much
older, variety (called sprouting broccoli or asparagus broccoli)
belongs to the Italica group. It developed around 2,000 years
ago from the European wild cabbage through both natural
and human selection. Sprouting broccolis produce many
small, tender shoots instead of one large head.

Standard broccoli belongs to the Botrytis group. This is the
green vegetable with the single, large, compact heads that we
see at the market. A further refinement on the old sprouting
forms, this familiar type of broccoli is identical in nearly all
respects to cauliflower; the difference is mainly in the
blanched whiteness of the cauliflower's head and the fact that
cauliflower is more commonly grown as a summer crop,
while broccoli prefers the cooler temperatures of fall.

In recent years, broccoli has been found to contain an en-
zyme called sulforaphane that scientists believe is a cancer-
preventing agent. If broccoli indeed proves to be one of our
future "miracle foods," we have the Italians to thank for it.
The ancient Italians were probably the first to select sprouting broccolis for their tasty, tender shoots. What's more, Italian immigrants brought broccoli with them to America and
helped to popularize it here.

How to Grow

Like other members of the cabbage family, broccoli likes a
rich, loamy soil that retains moisture; if your soil is sandy or
sharply drained, build it up with lots of organic matter.

Start broccoli seeds inside in flats or cells 6 weeks before
the last spring frost date (for spring crops) or in early to midsummer (for fall crops). Sow seeds ¼–½ in. deep and tamp

down lightly. When the seedlings have sprouted 4–5 leaves, transplant into 3–4-in. pots or soil blocks. After hardening off, set out seedlings 12–18 in. apart in rows spaced 24–30 in. apart.

You can also direct-seed broccoli, but the seeds require warm soil temperatures (70–75°F) to germinate, so it's better to start seeds indoors for spring crops and direct-seed in mid- to late summer if desired for fall crops, thinning plants to 15–18 in. apart in the row.

Broccoli needs abundant water and nutrients to grow well. Side-dress plants with compost or dried manure, or water with a liquid fish or seaweed emulsion.

Harvest
Cut the large central heads when they have grown to about two-thirds of their mature size, before the tiny yellow flower buds open. This encourages the plant to send out smaller side buds along the stem, which can be harvested throughout the season.

Pests and Diseases
Most diseases can be avoided through good garden hygiene and crop rotation — by not growing members of the cabbage family in the same spot from year to year. To guard against cutworms, place a heavy paper collar around the stem of plants when setting them out.

Insect pests include flea beetles, cabbage worms and loopers, aphids, and root maggots. Cover crop with a floating row cover to foil the beetles and maggots. For cabbage worms and loopers, use Dipel (the commercial name for Bt, a biological pest control) as directed. Control aphids with insecticidal soap spray.

■ **RECOMMENDED VARIETIES**

'Calabrese' (1880s)
This good home garden variety came to the U.S. with Italian immigrants. Dark green plants, 18–30 in. high, produce 3–6-in. blue-green central heads, followed by many side shoots that appear until frost; for fresh use or freezing; 60–90 days.

'De Cicco' (1890)
Another Italian heirloom that is slightly earlier than 'Calabrese'; light green plants, 24–36 in. high, produce 3–4-in. blue-green central heads, then a long harvest of medium-size side shoots. More variable, more productive, and with a longer harvest period than hybrids; excellent flavor; use fresh or freeze; 48–85 days.

'Early Purple Sprouting' (before 1835)
Listed by Burr in 1863, this sprouting variety grows into a 2–3-ft. bush and is extremely frost-hardy; in cool regions, transplant in spring for a late fall harvest; in areas where it can overwinter, it will grow slowly and put out abundant shoots the following spring; leaves are purple-green and flower buds deep purple; somewhat susceptible to aphids; 125 days (spring-sown); 220 days (fall-sown).

'Romanesco' p. 45
A beautiful and unusual cauliflower-like type, with a pale green, 4–5-in., whorled, spiraling head that comes to a point like the top of a seashell; widely grown in northern Italy; good texture and flavor for salads and dips; good for northern areas; sow early summer for fall crop; 85 days.

Brussels Sprouts

Brassica oleracea, Gemmifera group

For years I never understood how the Brussels sprout could have earned its unfortunate reputation as the food kids love to hate. Never, that is, until I accidentally overcooked some sprouts. There are few things more unappetizing (to children or adults) than a mushy, soggy, malodorous Brussels sprout. On the other hand, there is nothing better than the sweet, nutty flavor of a freshly picked, properly steamed sprout, dressed with just a dab of garlic butter or (damn the diet) a dollop of hollandaise sauce.

As its name suggests, the Brussels sprout was first cultivated around the 14th century in the vicinity of Brussels, Belgium, from kalelike forms of wild cabbage.[11] However, the Brussels sprout didn't make much of an impression in English or American gardens until the early 1800s.

Today's hybrid varieties of Brussels sprouts are bred to be *big*. If you're more concerned with taste than neighborhood bragging rights, the heirloom varieties listed below are the way to go. The "bigger is better" school, though, has been around for years. In *The Vegetable Garden* (1885), Vilmorin-Andrieux wrote that the Belgians preferred the smaller-sized sprouts, while the French liked their sprouts "as big as a good-sized walnut." However, the authors added, "the smallest and hardest Brussels Sprouts are certainly the most delicate in flavour."[12]

How to Grow
Brussels sprouts require a long growing season, but the mature plants are extremely frost-hardy, usually among the lat-

est green vegetables (along with kale and collards) to survive in northern gardens. For a late fall crop, start seeds in flats or cells in early spring and transplant 4–6 weeks later, spacing plants 18 in. apart in rows spaced 24–30 in. apart. You can also direct-seed Brussels sprouts in the garden about 4 months before the first fall frost date; sow thinly, covering seeds with ¼–½ in. of soil; thin seedlings to 18 in. apart in the row.

When setting out plants, add a little compost or dried manure mixed with bone meal to the planting hole. Mulch around the base of the plants to conserve soil moisture, and water during dry periods. Water with a fish or seaweed emulsion solution once or twice during the season.

Once the sprouts begin to form along the stem, pinch off the growing tip of the plant to encourage the sprouts to swell.

Harvest
Sprouts mature from the bottom of the plant upward. Pick sprouts when they are firm and about 1–2 in. in diameter. Break off the leaf below the sprout and then snap off the sprout; this will help the higher sprouts to mature.

Brussels sprouts develop their sweet flavor only after a frost, so try to schedule your spring planting so that sprouts will mature late enough in the season. In the North, it is not uncommon for Brussels sprouts to keep producing until early December. In milder winter climates, start plants in late summer and overwinter them with mulch protection, picking sprouts from November through March.

Pests and Diseases
Similar to other members of the cabbage family. Use Dipel to control cabbage worms and loopers or cover young plants with a floating row cover.

■ RECOMMENDED VARIETIES

'Bedford Fillbasket'
Plants are 3–4 ft. high and produce good yields of large, solid sprouts; 85–100 days.

'Long Island Improved' (1890s)
Sometimes associated with the 'Catskill' strain developed by Arthur White of Arkport, New York, in 1941. The two varieties are very similar; both semidwarf plants, 20–24 in. high, with good yields of 1–2-in. sprouts; 85–115 days.

'Rubine Red'   p. 45
A beautiful plant, to 3 ft., with reddish purple foliage and sprouts; very ornamental; matures late but is extremely frost-

hardy. Elwyn Meader, the eminent plant breeder, reports that red types were available in the 1930s and '40s, and this variety is a handsome example; 100–125 days.

Cabbage

Brassica oleracea, Capitata group
The head-forming types of cabbage arise — as do all related forms such as kale, collards, broccoli, Brussels sprouts, and cauliflower — from the wild cabbage, *Brassica oleracea,* whose cultivation spread from the Middle East into both Europe and Asia many thousands of years ago. On this time scale, the smooth, solid-headed cabbages we know today are a fairly recent development; the ancient Romans, for instance, probably grew a more loose-headed variety similar to the form with blistered leaves that we now call Savoy cabbage.[13]

Cabbage varieties are usually classified by the shape of their heads as, for instance, flat, round, oval, or pointed. Subvarieties differ in terms of keeping qualities, length of growing season, and color. The red-purple forms of cabbage are very old, with examples mentioned as early as the 16th century.[14]

A friend of mine from Seoul, South Korea, tells me that in her native country employers traditionally give a "cabbage bonus" to workers every autumn. People go to the market to select cabbage heads from a towering heap, ·then take them home to prepare and ferment in crocks to make *kim chee,* a spicy vegetable relish that is a Korean national delicacy (though an acquired taste for most Western palates). American business leaders, take note — an occasional "vegetable bonus" might well boost workers' morale, and it is definitely the cheapest form of preventive health care.

How to Grow
Cabbage needs cool weather to form good heads, and plants will tolerate light frosts. Early varieties will mature heads some 8 weeks or more after transplanting; late varieties can require twice that time.

Like other members of its family (broccoli, cauliflower, etc.), cabbage is a heavy feeder and likes a rich soil with a balanced pH (over 6.0). It also requires consistent moisture throughout its growing season.

Start seeds for early and midseason varieties in flats, 4–6 weeks before transplanting to the garden. Thin seedlings in the flats and transplant once into individual cells or pots. Harden off seedlings and set out 15–18 in. apart in rows spaced 24–30 in. apart. Mix a little compost or dried manure into the bottom of each planting hole to give seedlings a slow, steady nutrient boost. Surround the stems of seedlings with heavy paper collars to guard against cutworm damage. Mulch underneath plants to help conserve soil moisture. Cabbages like a consistent supply of moisture, and the heads of early varieties can split open if the plants receive a lot of rain or water after a prolonged dry spell. If these conditions occur, you can sometimes avoid head-splitting by grasping the plant and twisting it a quarter turn; this will break off some of the roots.

You can also direct-seed cabbages in rows; sow seed thinly, about 3–4 per foot, ¼–½ in. deep; thin seedlings to 15–18 in. apart in the row. Direct-seeding is most successful for fall crops, and it adds about 14 days to the maturation dates listed below for the recommended varieties.

For a fall crop, start seeds of midseason or storage varieties in late spring and transplant to the garden around midsummer in the North, later in the South. Schedule your planting so that the heads will mature before the first hard frosts of the year.

Harvest

For early and midseason varieties, cut heads off about 1 in. above ground level; this will encourage a second crop of small heads to form around the cut stem of the plant.

For winter storage, grow late storage varieties and select only the most solid, perfect heads to place in the root cellar; eat other heads first. Leave heads in the garden as long as possible; cabbage can withstand a couple of light frosts. Be careful not to bruise heads when harvesting them; trim off the bottom stem and all loose outer leaves before storing.

Cabbage stores well in cool temperatures, slightly above freezing, and in humid conditions. Wrap heads in sheets of newspaper and store on shelves or slatted boxes up off the floor to ensure good air circulation.

Pests and Diseases

Cabbage can sometimes suffer from a disease called "the yellows," which is also known as fusarium root rot. This generally occurs when soil temperatures are high (above 65°F); applying an organic mulch around the base of plants and keeping them well watered will help avoid this.

Aphids can transmit viral disease to cabbage; control them by using insecticidal soap spray. Flea beetles chewing on young seedlings can be controlled by dusting with rotenone or pyrethrum or by covering plants with floating row fabric. To control cabbage worms or loopers, spray plants with Bt (Dipel) or cover with floating row fabric. For cutworms, see the How to Grow section, above.

■ RECOMMENDED VARIETIES

Green Cabbage

'Brunswick' (before 1880)
A mid- to late-season variety; flat "drumhead" type with uniform, 6-lb. heads; dependable in a wide range of growing conditions; 85–90 days.

'Christmas Drumhead' (1903)
Solid, flattened heads on dwarf, compact plants; hardy and productive; good late variety; sow in June in northern gardens for late fall harvest; 110 days.

'Couve de Tronchuda' (before 1877)
Also known as Braganza, Portuguese, or Sea Kale Cabbage. An old European variety that doesn't form a solid head and is similar to the kalelike ancestral wild cabbage. Plants grow 3 ft. high with a short stem; bears large, light green, spoon-shaped leaves with thick white midribs; succulent, sweet flavor; good for soups; tolerates heat better than any other cabbage; transplant 2 ft. apart in row.

'Danish Ballhead' (1887)   p. 46
The standard long-stemmed storage variety; heads are round, blue-green, and 5–7 lb.; does well in cool and short-season areas; not resistant to yellows; heads resist bolting and splitting; 85–110 days.

'Early Jersey Wakefield' (1840s)   p. 46
According to seedsman Peter Henderson, this excellent heirloom was first grown in America by Mr. Francis Brill of Jersey City, New Jersey, and it remains one of the most popular early cabbages for the home garden. Small, compact plants form small, 2–4-lb., pale green pointed heads that have a delicious flavor; few outer leaves; can be planted close; yellows-resistant; heads resistant to splitting; 60–75 days.

'Glory of Enkhuizen'
This midseason variety dates back to the 1800s and is named after a coastal town on Holland's Zuiderzee. Heads are round, 6–10 lb., and dark blue-green; spreading, vigorous plants with few outer leaves; 75–80 days.

'Late Flat Dutch' ('Premium Late Flat Dutch'; before 1840)
Described by Burr in 1863. One of the best late fall and winter cabbages, first grown in America by early European settlers. Short-stemmed plant bears large, firm, flattened oval

head (10–15 lb.) that is blue-green with a crisp, white interior; space plants 18 in. apart in row for largest heads; good eating and storage qualities; few outer leaves; 100–110 days.

Red Cabbage

'Mammoth Red Rock' ('Red Danish'; before 1906)   p. 47
A large, late storage cabbage with firm, flattened round heads that weigh 5–8 lb.; red-purple color is consistent to the core; good quality for pickling and boiling; excellent winter keeper, better than many green varieties; 90–100 days.

Savoy Cabbage

'Drumhead Savoy' (before 1885)
Vilmorin-Andrieux describes this variety as having been grown on the Plain of Aubervilliers and says that "mountains of this Cabbage are sent to the Central Market of Paris during a considerable part of the winter." Large, coarsely crumpled compact heads on 6–8-in. stems; outer leaves numerous, so space out plants in row; hardy; crisp and tender, excellent quality and flavor; 90 days.

'January King' (before 1885)   p. 47
One of the hardiest and most popular winter cabbages; a semisavoy type with solid, flat, light green heads weighing 3–5 lb.; savoyed wrapper leaves have a purple flush; stands well without splitting; outstanding flavor; sow May–July, harvest November–January; 140–160 days.

Carrot

Daucus carota var. *sativus*
Compared to other vegetables, the familiar orange-rooted carrot that we know today is a recent innovation. Although ancient peoples from the Mediterranean Sea to the Orient undoubtedly knew about various forms of wild carrots and to some extent cultivated them as both food and medicine (carrots and ginseng are kissing cousins), not much was written about them specifically until the 16th century.[15] In the wild, carrot roots vary in color from the dominant white to shades of yellow, orange, red, and purple. The pretty meadow wildflower known as Queen-Anne's-lace is simply a wild form of *Daucus carota* and has white roots that are perfectly edible, though they contain a woody central core.

For today's sweet, orange-red, improved varieties, we can largely thank the French, who early on became the most enthusiastic carrot-boosters. In the latter half of the 19th century, the famous French seed house of Vilmorin developed many of the strains we still grow today, including 'Chantenay', 'Nantes', and 'Oxheart' (or 'Guerande').[16]

How to Grow
Carrots like a loose soil, either sandy or silty loam. If your soil is clayey or stony, use a hand fork or broadfork to loosen it; pick out any large stones, and work in a lot of compost or well-rotted manure, plus a little bone meal for good root development. Living in New Hampshire (which is not called "the Granite State" for nothing), I am an old hand at this preplanting ritual, which I usually perform a week or two before seeding. I mound up soil from either side of the carrot patch to form a raised planting bed, which improves drainage and gives the carrot roots some vertical growing space.

Even after hand-digging, some garden soils may be too heavy or shallow to get good results from the longer-rooted varieties of carrot. In this case, select one of the many good half-long, stump-rooted, or round "forcing" varieties.

Presoak carrot seeds overnight to hasten germination, then drain through a fine sieve and mix with a little soil or wood ashes to separate the seeds. Some seed companies now offer pelletized carrot seed, which has a clay coating that makes both seeding (and later thinning) much easier.

Rake the ground before planting to ensure a flat, smooth seedbed. Sow carrot seed thinly and cover with ¼–½ in. of soil. Carrot seeds take about 2 weeks to germinate, so I generally mix them with radish seeds to mark the planted area and facilitate weeding and thinning. The radishes will be up and out of the bed long before they begin to compete with the carrots.

Thin carrot seedlings twice. On the first pass, thin the young plants to about 1 in. apart and remove the thinnings. On your second thinning pass, the roots you pull should be large enough to use as "baby carrots"; thin until the remaining carrots are spaced about 3 in. apart in the bed or row.

Harvest
Leave carrots in the ground until you need them. Carrots will tolerate light frosts unprotected but should be mulched before heavy freezes occur. Even in cold-climate areas, carrots can overwinter in the ground given adequate protection, such as a deep layer of mulch. In snowy regions, mark the carrot patch with a stake to make it easy to find for winter or early spring harvest; pull the mulch away and dig the carrots as needed.

Another alternative for storing carrots is to dig or pull them up in the late fall, break off the greens and store them in layers in a box of moistened sand or sawdust in the root cellar. As with all vegetables, pick only the healthiest-looking carrots for long-term storage; store the rest in the refrigerator and eat them first.

Pests and Diseases

Carrot weevils and wireworms can usually be avoided by tilling the ground thoroughly; by not planting in new, soddy areas; and by rotating crops yearly. The larvae of carrot rust flies can also destroy carrots. Pull up and destroy infected plants, sprinkle rock phosphate on the row or bed, and practice good crop rotation by not planting other carrot family members (parsnips, celery, or parsley) in the same spot following carrots. To prevent adult flies from laying eggs, use a floating row cover.

■ Recommended Varieties

'Belgium White' (before 1863)
Probably the best cultivated white carrot, praised by Burr in 1863 as "remarkable for its productiveness . . . even on poor soils." In the past it was valued more as a stock feed than for table use, but I like its mild flavor and crisp, crunchy texture, either raw or in soups or stews. Green shoulders poke above the ground; roots are pure white and 8–10 in. long; 75 days.

'Chantenay Red Cored' (1929) p. 48
One of the best of the improved Chantenay type, which first came to America in the late 1800s. The roots are deep red-orange to the core, 5–7 in. long, cone-shaped, and with wide shoulders; crisp, tender, and good flavor; sweetest of the Chantenay varieties; suitable for growing on heavier soils; becomes sweeter in storage; 60–75 days.

'Danvers Half Long' (1871) p. 48
A true-blue American heirloom that originated among market gardeners near Danvers, Massachusetts. Deep orange, tapered roots, 6–8 in. long; bright orange flesh, nearly coreless; widely adapted to many different soil types; stores well; 75 days.

'Dragon'
A bicolored variety from China with purple exterior flesh that surrounds an orange or sometimes yellow core; roots are smooth, 5–6 in. long, with a blunt, rounded tip; unique spicy

flavor is good either raw or cooked, especially in soups and stews. Garden City Seeds has recently refined this Chinese heirloom and introduced it under its new name; GCS Research Director John Navazio considers 'Dragon' far superior to the more common 'Afghan Purple' carrot; 65 days.

'Early Scarlet Horn' (before 1610)
The oldest cultivated carrot still available; named not for its shape, but for the Dutch town of Hoorn. Short, stump-rooted carrots are 2–6 in. long and good as baby carrots or for greenhouse forcing; sow in successions for early to late summer crops; excellent flavor; 65–70 days.

'Imperator' (1928) p. 49
A popular variety and former All-America Selection; deep red-orange skin and orange flesh; 8–9-in. coreless roots; tender, brittle flesh; requires a loose or deeply worked soil to grow well; 70–75 days.

'Long Orange Improved' (1850)
An improvement on 'Long Orange', an old variety that dates back to the 1600s. Deep orange-red roots, 11–12 in. long, tapering to a point; visible core; good taste and keeps well; grow on loose or well-worked soils; 85 days.

'Oxheart' ('Guerande'; 1884)
Blunt, heart-shaped orange roots, 5–6 in. long and weighing more than 1 lb.; orange flesh and yellow core; very good flavor, though less sweet than other varieties; easy to pull and will not corkscrew; excellent keeper; good for northern gardens; 70–80 days.

'Rondo' ('Paris Market')
The standard in round carrots since the 19th century, and one of the best varieties for greenhouse growing or on heavy soils. Roots are small, round, 1–2 in. in diameter, orange-red to the core, and very sweet; 65–70 days.

'St. Valery' (1885)
An improved 'Long Orange' type that has large, 10-in. roots that are fine-grained, sweet, and tender; adaptable to most soils; sow early spring to midsummer; excellent storage type; rare; 60–80 days.

'Topweight' (1750s)
A large, 10–12-in. carrot from England; bright orange roots; very hardy, overwinters well with protection; very good flavor; grow on loose or deeply worked soil; 80 days.

'Touchon'
My favorite carrot of the blunt-rooted Nantes type; bright orange-red roots are 6–8 in. long, cylindrical, coreless, and very smooth; sweet flavor; prefers a loose, humus-rich soil; 65–70 days.

Cauliflower

Brassica oleracea, Botrytis group

In *Pudd'nhead Wilson* (1894), Mark Twain wrote that "cauliflower is nothing but cabbage with a college education." Almost identical to broccoli, cauliflower differs mainly in that, once the main head has been harvested, the plant develops no smaller heads or side sprouts. Most cauliflowers sold in the market are white, a color that is usually achieved by blanching the developing head — tying the outer (wrapper) leaves of the plant around the head and shading it from the sun. Without blanching, the head can turn yellow or purple in the hot summer sun and become "ricey." However, a few open-pollinated and hybrid varieties with intentionally green or purple heads are also available to home gardeners.

The first primitive forms of cauliflower were cultivated more than 2,000 years ago in the eastern Mediterranean. During the Middle Ages, selections were made in the cooler climate of Europe, resulting in the familiar white-headed type we know today.[17]

How to Grow
Start cauliflower seed in flats in late winter or early spring, thinning to 2 in. apart and transplanting to individual cells or pots. Harden off plants gradually and transplant to the garden 4–6 weeks after seeding, spacing 18 in. apart in rows spaced 24–30 in. apart. You can also try direct-seeding cauliflower; if you do, add about 21 days to the maturity dates listed in Recommended Varieties, below, which refer to transplanted seedlings.

Cauliflower grows quickly in cool to mild weather; excessively hot weather can cause tiny heads to form. The plant is also rather fussy about soil conditions, requiring a fertile, well-drained soil with a neutral pH to perform well. Mix in compost, dried manure, or a balanced organic fertilizer before transplanting seedlings. Water with fish or seaweed emulsion during early growth, and use an organic mulch under plants to help conserve soil moisture. Cauliflower needs a consistent supply of moisture.

Unless you are growing a self-blanching variety, on which the wrapper leaves shade the head naturally, you will need to blanch as soon as the small white heads become visible. Draw the outer leaves up over the head and fasten them together loosely with a rubber band or garden twine. An alternative method is to break the midribs of the wrapper leaves and fold them over the top of the plant.

Harvest
Unfasten the wrapper leaves periodically and examine the heads. Cut when the heads have reached their mature size but before the white "curd" becomes loose or begins to show signs of browning.

Pests and Diseases
Cauliflower is subject to the same pests and diseases as broccoli and cabbage. To prevent cutworm damage, place heavy paper collars in a circle around stems when transplanting seedlings to the garden. For cabbage worms and loopers, use Bt (Dipel) or protect young seedlings with a floating row cover. For flea beetles, dust with rotenone or pyrethrum or use a floating row cover. Practice crop rotation by not growing any members of the cabbage family in the same spot in succession.

Soil that is too acidic (below 6.5 on the pH scale) can cause clubroot, a fungal disease that causes plants to wilt and yellow in hot weather. To prevent this, raise the pH of acidic soil gradually by adding lime, wood ashes, and organic matter.

■ RECOMMENDED VARIETIES

'Early Snowball' (1888) p. 49
Introduced by Peter Henderson & Co. and for many years the standard early variety of cauliflower; dwarf plants with short stems; solid, round, 6-in., pure white heads; adapted to warm climates; reliable and uniform; can be grown as a fall crop in short-season areas; matures over 2–3-week period; 55–60 days.

'Purple Cape' (1834) p. 50
A beautiful purple-headed variety that is hardy to Zone 6, where it can winter over with protection; plant out in fall and harvest late winter or early spring; excellent flavor; popular in Europe but rare in the U.S.; around 120 days.

'Veitch's Autumn Giant' (before 1885)
Vigorous 3-ft. plants with long stems and upright leaves; large white heads are 8–10-in. in diameter and very firm; one of

the best varieties to grow for fall cutting and winter storage; start seed in April for fall harvest; 75 days (from transplants) to 130 days (from seed).

Celery and Celeriac

Apium graveolens var. *dulce* and *rapaceum*

Wild celery, often referred to as "smallage" by early writers, is probably native to the Mediterranean region, though according to Sturtevant its natural range includes marshy habitats from Sweden to North Africa and eastward to the Himalayas. Apparently ignored as a food plant until at least the 16th century, celery gradually became cultivated for table use in Italian and French gardens.[18] Market growers have traditionally blanched celery by hilling soil around the plants, leaving only the top leaves exposed. Home gardeners can do the same, although several varieties are self-blanching, with pale, tasty hearts. Left unblanched, celery gets darker green and develops a stronger, but not unpleasant, flavor. The term "cutting celery" refers to those varieties grown specifically as an herb or seasoning; the leaves are harvested and used, much like parsley, in soups, stews, and salads.

Celeriac, or celery root, is an odd-looking type of celery most often seen in markets in the fall. The knobby, ball-shaped, buff-colored roots can grow about as big as a fist and have white flesh that looks like a turnip but tastes like mild celery.

How to Grow

Sow celery seed in flats, 10–12 weeks before planting outside in the garden. Since the seeds are so small, sow thinly on top of the potting soil and then tamp down lightly, to avoid planting too deep. Germination takes 2–3 weeks. When seedlings show two true leaves, transplant to individual cells. Harden off seedlings by cutting back on water, but do not expose the young plants to temperatures below 55°F; prolonged exposure to cold causes them to bolt. Transplant to the garden after the last spring frost date, setting out plants 6–8 in. apart in rows spaced 24–36 in. apart.

Celery needs a constantly moist, well-drained, fertile soil to grow well. Water and fertilize regularly throughout the growing season, and mulch the row or bed to conserve moisture, suppress weeds, and keep the soil cool. Weed celery carefully and preferably by hand, because the plant's roots grow near the surface and can be damaged by deep cultivation.

The acidity of your garden soil is also an issue, since celery likes a neutral or slightly sweet soil (pH 7.0–7.5). Gardeners, especially those living east of the Mississippi, should check soil pH and correct it if necessary by applying calcitic lime in advance or working in a small amount of wood ashes just before planting. Celery needs both calcium and potassium, and the lime and wood ashes provide both, in addition to reducing soil acidity.

The traditional method of planting celery — digging trenches or furrows, setting out plants in the bottom, and pulling soil up around the plants as they grow — requires far too much work, in my opinion. Simply hilling soil around the plants in the early fall, to just below the top leaves, is enough to blanch the plants. This technique has the added benefit of protecting the plants against the first light frosts.

Celeriac requires the same fertile soil as celery, though once it's established in the garden it doesn't need the same kind of constant watering. Start and set out plants as described above; water seedlings well when transplanting to the garden. Celeriac has a longer growing season than most varieties of celery.

Harvest
Celery can remain in the garden through the first frosts of the fall, especially if you pull up soil or mulch around the plants. In milder climates, celery can even be overwintered in the ground by hilling with soil and mulching heavily. In more northern areas, store heads of celery in a cool, moist root cellar, removing any rotten outer stalks during the winter.

Celeriac roots are usually harvested in the fall and stored like carrots, in a box of moistened sand in the root cellar. In many regions, the roots can also overwinter in the garden under a heavy mulch. For fresh use, harvest roots when about 2 in. in diameter; for storage dig up 2–4 in. roots.

Pests and Diseases
Black heart is a disease caused by a calcium deficiency in the soil. It can also occur if you do not provide celery with consistent moisture throughout the season. Celery mosaic is spread by aphids, which can be controlled using an insecticidal soap spray. Maintaining a good crop rotation prevents most other diseases.

■ RECOMMENDED VARIETIES

Celeriac

'Giant Prague' (1871)   p. 50
The best of the older types of celeriac; thick, white, globe-shaped roots are evenly shaped, 2–4 in. in diameter, and with

few side rootlets; use in soups and stews, gratinéed, or steamed and sliced cold for salads; 110–120 days.

Celery

'Golden Self-Blanching' (before 1885)   p. 51
An old variety of French origin, listed by Vilmorin-Andrieux as 'Golden Yellow'. Several tall or dwarf strains are available; plants are 18–30 in. high and have 9-in. ribs; yellow-green foliage and outer stalks; well-formed hearts blanch to a waxy, creamy yellow; tender, stringless, delicate flavor; disease-resistant and easy to grow from seed; 80–85 days.

'Red Stalk'
An heirloom with dark maroon stalks that remain red even after cooking; plants to 2 ft.; more cold-hardy than green varieties; strong celery flavor that's good for soups or cooking; one of the best types to overwinter and grow for seed; abundant crop of spicy-flavored seeds produced in second growing season for seasoning or seed-saving; 120 days.

In 1863 Fearing Burr listed another old variety, 'Solid Red', which is also still available; stalks blanch well to either lighter red or white.

'Solid Pink' (1894)
Similar to the red varieties in its cold-hardiness; frosts bring out color; blanches easily and quickly; set out plants 12 in. apart in row; from England.

'Zwolsche Krul'
A Dutch heirloom variety of "cutting celery," this plant is much less fussy than stalk celeries and is grown for its leaves, which give a strong celery flavor to soups, stews, and garnishes. Fine, curly, dark green leaves with thin, hollow stems. Spring-sow and harvest like parsley into early winter; 60 days.

Chicory

Chicorium intybus
Several years ago, with the sudden rise of "California cuisine," chicory burst onto the American food scene. Before that time, most folks thought of chicory as a minor crop grown chiefly for its roots, which were dried, roasted, ground, and used as a coffee substitute or additive. Anyone who has ever drunk coffee in the French Quarter of New Orleans has probably tasted chicory in his cup of joe.

But the latest incarnation of chicory is as a colorful and tasty salad ingredient. Italians refer to all chicories that form a head as *radicchio,* but in America we restrict that term to mean the small, bitter, and pricey red-and-white heads that have become such a gourmet salad fixture.

Although new to most American palates, both the wild and cultivated forms of chicory have been eaten by Europeans for centuries as a salad green. The *spring* or *cutting chicories* are harvested young for their leaves; "Italian dandelion" is another name for some varieties, because the narrow, lancelike leaves resemble dandelion greens. *Radicchio,* the red Italian type of chicory, forms its baseball-sized heads as a second growth, after its top leaves have been cut back in the fall. The *sugarloaf* type of chicory looks just like romaine lettuce, though because of its bitter outer leaves only the heart is eaten. *Witloof chicory* (also known as Belgian endive) is grown for its roots; however, unlike other large-rooted varieties that are ground as a coffee substitute, these roots are dug up in the fall and then forced in darkness. From the roots sprout the tender little cylindrical heads that we call Belgian endive and that the French call *chicons* or *barbe de capuchin* (monk's beard), after the Capuchin order of friars.

How to Grow

Chicory grows best in cool weather and on a rich, slightly acidic soil (around pH 6.0). To grow cutting chicory, direct-seed in the garden as early in the spring as the ground can be worked; direct-seed a fall crop about 8 weeks before the first frost date in the fall. Sow seeds ¼ in. deep, and thin young plants to 6–8 in. apart in the row or bed.

To grow radicchio and other heading varieties, direct-seed or transplant to the garden in late spring. In southern and coastal areas (Zone 8 or higher), radicchio can be planted in the fall for a winter or spring harvest, especially if mulched lightly with straw or leaves. Thin or transplant to 8–10 in. apart in the row. Cut back plants around Labor Day for spring-sown crops, leaving about 1 in. of stem; plants will sprout small round heads that are ready to harvest in 4–6 weeks. Mulching the heads will blanch them and make them milder-tasting.

Direct-seed or transplant sugarloaf chicory in the late summer or early fall, to mature before the first hard frosts. Thin or transplant to 12 in. apart in the row.

For witloof and other large-rooted chicories, sow seeds ½ in. deep in rows spaced 12–18 in. apart, from midsummer through early fall in milder zones. After the first light frosts of fall, dig up the roots, which should be about 10 in. long. Bring the roots inside for forcing or drying.

Harvest

Cut spring or cutting chicory with scissors when the plants are young and the leaves are 4–8 in. long; use lightly cooked or in salads. Cutting chicory is also good to mix with the seeds of other cool-weather greens to create your own "cut-and-come-again" planting of mesclun for salads. The seed stalks are also edible when about 6 in. tall and can be harvested and cooked like asparagus.

Cut back and harvest radicchio as described in How to Grow, above. Radicchio roots, like those of witloof, can be dug up in the fall and brought inside for forcing. Forced in darkness, the radicchio heads will form small round or conical heads as they would if grown outside, but the head color will be lighter.

My friend Shep Ogden of the Cook's Garden describes a good way to force Belgian endive heads *(chicons)* from witloof roots for midwinter eating:

Dig the roots of witloof chicory and store in a cool root cellar or other location at 35–40°F in a box of moist sand, sawdust, or peat moss, as you would carrots or other root vegetables. During the winter, trim the roots to 8–10 in. in length, stand them upright, neck to neck in the boxes of moistened sand or other material, and move into a completely dark, warmer location (around 50–60°F). Begin watering lightly and regularly. The object is to keep the humidity high, around 95 percent; Shep suggests enclosing the roots in a plastic bag with one or two holes punched in it.

Harvest the endive sprouts when they are 4–6 in. high by cutting them just above the crown. With proper care, the roots should provide you with a second and even a third crop of *chicons*.

Pests

Slugs represent the biggest pest problem for chicory. To control, set out shallow saucers of beer near the garden to attract slugs, which will then drown in the beer. Another antislug strategy is to sprinkle a sharp-edged substance such as wood ashes or diatomaceous earth (not the kind used for swimming pools) around the plants. If aphids present a problem, control with insecticidal soap spray.

■ RECOMMENDED VARIETIES

Spring or Cutting Chicory

'Catalogna' ('Italian Dandelion', 'Asparagus Chicory')
Leaves are lancelike and deeply cut like dandelion greens; seed stalks are cooked like asparagus; tender leaves are good

cut and used young for salads, cooked greens, or as part of a mesclun planting; 55–75 days.

Radicchio and Heading Chicory

'Castelfranco'
An heirloom Italian radicchio with heads marbled red and white; this is a "self-heading" variety that does not need cutting back to form good heads; 83 days.

'Rossa di Treviso'
A beautiful, elongated variety of radicchio from Treviso, Italy; shape resembles Belgian endive or small romaine lettuce; leaves are green in summer and turn burgundy red with white veins in fall; taste is tart and slightly bitter; 80–100 days.

'Rossa di Verona'
After cutting back in fall, this variety grows the classic baseball-sized radicchio head; bright red, heart-shaped leaves; used sparingly in salads, the taste is pleasantly bitter; hardier than 'Rossa di Treviso'; 85–100 days.

'Sugar Loaf' ('Pain de Sucre', 'Pan di Zucchero') p. 51
Large, elongated green heads look like romaine lettuce; self-blanching; outer leaves are bitter, but hearts are tender and crisp with a mild flavor; 80–90 days.

Witloof and Root Chicory

'Large-Rooted Magdeburg' ('Coffee Chicory')
Described by Burr in 1863; 15-in.-tall plants with dandelion-like foliage can be harvested for greens; 12–16-in. roots are harvested and roasted as a coffee substitute; needs a rich, well-worked soil to grow well; 100–110 days.

'Witloof' ('Belgian Endive')
Discovered in Belgium in the mid-1800s and considered by Vilmorin-Andrieux (1885) to be a subvariety of 'Large-Rooted Magdeburg'. This is the variety used to force tender new growth in winter storage for *chicons*, or Belgian endive. Plants grow to 18 in. tall in season with long green leaves; harvest inner leaves and hearts for salads before digging up roots for forcing. *Witloof* means "white leaf" in Flemish; 60 days (for greens); 150 days (for forced *chicons*).

Chinese Cabbage. *See* Mustard and Oriental Greens

Corn

Zea mays

On October 16, 1492, Christopher Columbus's crew saw fields of maize, or corn, growing on the island of Hispaniola (the island now shared by Haiti and the Dominican Republic).[19] Yet long before Europeans ever sailed to the New World, various races of corn were already being grown over a vast geographic area, stretching from Brazil and Chile to southern Canada. The cultivation of corn helped sustain the Aztec, Maya, Inca, and other civilizations. American Indians considered corn, along with squash and beans, one of the "Three Sisters," and they commonly interplanted all three crops on hills or mounds, a growing method that still has merit. Today, people around the world plant and eat corn, and it has become one of humankind's most important, adaptable, and productive food crops.

Most plant researchers believe that a wild grass called teosinte (literally, "God's corn") is the original ancestor of our modern corn. Teosinte still grows wild in parts of Mexico, Honduras, and Guatemala, and it has remained genetically so similar to primitive types of maize that the two plants still cross-fertilize freely when grown in close proximity.[20] Through thousands of years of intensive selection and improvement by indigenous farmers, teosinte and primitive kinds of maize were gradually transformed from wispy, loose-headed, grassy forms resembling other grains such as wheat and rye to the large-eared varieties of corn we know today, with their seeds packed tightly together on a cob that is fully invested within a tight-fitting husk. In fact, modern corn has become so highly specialized as a food plant that it can no longer survive unless cultivated and cared for by humans.

The fact that corn is pollinated by the wind, and that its tiny pollen grains can be carried a mile or more from the plant, means that different varieties cross readily, ensuring great genetic diversity even in a relatively small area. Plant researcher Edgar Anderson lived for a time in a small town outside Guadalajara, Mexico, and reported that there was more genetic variation among the corn in that one suburb than in the entire United States, with corn varying not only from field to field, but often from plant to plant.[21] Commercial farmers in the U.S. still rely on a perilously small number of high-performance hybrids; in contrast, home gardeners can grow a rainbow of corn colors and discover historic varieties that are specially adapted to almost any location, or any use.

Corn varieties fall into several types, which are based on the shape of the seed, or kernel. *Flint corn* has very hard kernels that are tough to grind when dry. *Dent corn* kernels have an indentation on top and contain soft, starchy corn under their hard tops. In *flour corn* varieties, the entire kernel is soft and easy to grind. *Popcorn* kernels, of course, burst open when heated; in fact, popcorns were probably one of the earliest cultivated types of corn.

Another ancient variety of corn, called *pod corn,* is seldom grown today. The ears of pod corn contain multicolored kernels that are individually wrapped in little husks called "glumes." Pod corn makes an unusual and interesting ornamental plant but isn't much of a vegetable.

Sweet corn, the kind most often grown by home gardeners, differs from other types of corn in that the kernels lack the ability to convert their sugar into starch. Instead of becoming full and plump, the kernels remain wrinkled and sugary, an inherited trait common to other vegetables, notably garden peas.[22] This shrunkenness in sweet corn is a recessive genetic character, one that may have first been noticed and developed in the highlands of South America and that then spread northward in pre-Columbian times.[23]

The first ears of sweet corn — picked, husked, and plopped right into the pot to boil — are one of the real highlights of the home-garden year. But more gardeners should also try growing the other types of corn: to eat young as we eat sweet corn, to dry and grind for cornmeal or flour, or to hull and use for popping or in winter soups.

Modern hybrid sweet corns have been bred to be "sugary-enhanced" or "super sweet," and without a doubt these are the sweetest varieties available. But, like a lot of other folks, I value the other half of the sweet corn equation, too — the corn part. I enjoy sweetness, but I also like to know I'm eating real corn, not candy corn. Picked at just the right milk stage, many of the heirloom corns listed below (not just the sweet varieties) make excellent fresh eating, and the extra starch content makes them taste even richer and more satisfying. Try them and see if you agree.

How to Grow

Corn needs a warm soil (65–75°F) to germinate, so wait until after the last spring frost date to direct-seed. Add plenty of dried manure or a balanced organic fertilizer to the row or bed several weeks before planting corn. Sow seeds about 1 in. deep, 3–4 in. apart, in blocks of short rows spaced 30 in. apart. (Planting corn in blocks or hills helps ensure good pollination and well-filled ears.) Thin young plants to 12 in. apart in the row.

Most corn varieties have shallow roots, so you'll need to provide water during dry periods; mulching after the soil is warm and the plants are about 2 ft. high helps conserve soil moisture. To help support the stalks and prevent them from blowing over, hill soil up around the base of the plants with a hoe once or twice during the growing season. Fertilize when plants are about 3 ft. high by side-dressing with compost, dried manure, or a liquid fish or seaweed emulsion. Fertilize again once the first silks appear.

Gardeners in short-season areas who have trouble growing corn to the mature seed stage (typically between 100 and 120 days) can start corn seedlings inside in warm soil, then transplant outside after the last spring frost date. Once up, corn plants will grow well in cool soil. My friend Gretchen Poisson has had good luck transplanting flour corn in our New Hampshire climate and recommends doing it like this:

First, water the seedbed thoroughly before transplanting, until it is really muddy. Like other vegetables, corn transplants best during rainy weather rather than in hot, dry, or windy conditions, which can set the plants back severely. Second, take up each corn plant with its long feeder root as well as its shallow roots. Spread out the roots as much as possible in the planting hole, and space plants about 12 in. apart in the row. Keep the plants well watered until they become established.

Since corn is wind-pollinated, you'll need to isolate different varieties if you don't want them to cross-fertilize. There are several ways to accomplish this, including physical isolation (planting in separate plots at least 300 ft. apart), staggering plantings by a week or so, and hand-pollination. See the books on seed saving in "Further Reading," p. 320, for more information. It's especially important to isolate sweet corn from popcorn and other "ornamental" varieties to prevent unwanted crossing.

Harvest

The dates to maturity listed in seed catalogs for different varieties are good approximations, but corn's actual growing season varies according to seasonal weather conditions. Corn requires a certain number of "heat units" to mature fully, so in a warm summer the crop tends to develop more quickly than in cool weather. By the same token, corn usually matures faster in warm climates than in the cooler areas.

Pick sweet corn in the milk stage for boiling or roasting once the silks have dried and turned brown and the ears have filled out. Pull back the top of each husk before picking to make sure the ears are ready. Sweet corn that has become overmature and starchy can still be picked and used to make fritters, corn soufflé, or other cooked dishes.

For dry corn, harvest dent, flint, flour, and popcorn varieties when the green husks begin to turn dry and tan. Mature corn can withstand a few light frosts and should be left on the stalks as long as possible before harvest. If the autumn is rainy, though, let the corn dry on the stalk as long as possible, then harvest and finish drying inside. Shuck the ears and dry them on screens or racks under cover. Once the kernels are hard and dry, the ears are ready for shelling. Grind kernels in a hand mill to make cornmeal or corn flour.

Pests and Diseases
The best way to avoid fungal diseases (leaf blight or corn smut) and insect pests (corn borers or earworms) is to till in stalks and other crop wastes after harvest or remove them to the compost pile; also, practice crop rotation. To dispose of corn borers, make a slit in the stalk below the entrance hole and locate and remove the larva. If you've had problems with earworms, place a drop of mineral oil into the tip of each ear after the silks have withered and turned brown.

Raccoons are the most serious threat to corn, and they seem to have an unerring sense of when the corn is just entering its sweet and toothsome state. One effective deterrent is a good electric fence (see "Organic Control of Pests and Diseases," p. 14). Through Southern Exposure Seed Exchange, I recently learned of an even cheaper, exquisitely low-tech solution. It comes from animal ecologist Michael Conover of the Connecticut Agricultural Experiment Station: Take a roll of ¾-in.-wide strapping tape, the kind used for sealing packages. Circle the tape once around the ear, about 1 in. above the point at which it attaches to the stalk. Then wind the tape once around the stalk. Finally, circle the tape around the ear about 1½ in. below the tip of the ear. The tape prevents raccoons from pulling off the ears, and it also keeps birds off the corn.

■ RECOMMENDED VARIETIES

Sweet Corn, White

'Black Mexican' ('Black Aztec'; before 1860)
An old and celebrated heirloom variety; Lawrence Hollander of CRESS suggests that 'Black Mexican' may have been derived from an Iroquois sweet corn called "black puckers." Burr listed it in 1863 simply as 'Black Sweet'. In recent years a similar variety called 'Black Aztec' has become widely available, and Rob Johnston Jr., of Johnny's Selected Seeds considers the two varieties identical.

'Black Mexican' is almost legendary among old seedsmen. Hedrick, in his *Sweet Corn of New York* (1934), is effusive in his praise, saying "the epicurean of vegetable morsels may not rest in his search for the acme of all sweet corn until he has eaten 'Black Mexican' fresh from the field." At milk stage, the kernels are white, but they turn purple and bluish black at maturity. Ears are 7–8 in. long and have 8 rows of kernels (sometimes 10 or 12); stalks grow 5–6 ft. high; plants are hardy; good for fresh use or ground as blue cornmeal; 65–85 days.

'Catawba' (1909)
Developed by the Rev. J. E. Tinker of Rock Stream, New York, by crossing 'Black Mexican' with another white corn. The white kernels dry to a beautiful dark purple shaded with red; Rev. Tinker named the corn after the grape common to the New York wine country. The stalks are ornamental, too, with a reddish color on the stalks and leaves. Hedrick describes it as a good home garden variety in 1934. Not currently listed by seed companies, but Seed Savers Exchange maintains 'Catawba' in its collection and is planning to grow out a supply for sale to home gardeners.

'Country Gentleman' (1890)
Also known as 'Shoe Peg' because of its small, deep, narrow white kernels that are not set in rows on the cob; 6–8-in. tapered ears; stalks 6–8 ft. high; sweet and tender; good yields; late; 80–100 days.

'Hooker's Sweet Indian' (1930s)
First grown by Ira Hooker near Olympia, Washington. Short stalks, 4–5 ft. high, with 2–3 ears per stalk; ears are 4–6 in., thin, with good-tasting white kernels that dry to purple-black; productive and space-saving for small home gardens. Some growers report bicolored ears with both white and pale yellow kernels; 70–80 days.

'Howling Mob' (1905)
Developed by C. D. Keller of Toledo, Ohio; according to Keller, as soon as his wagon came to market, he was swarmed with buyers, hence the name. Midseason, with 10–12 rows of white kernels on 8-in. ears; plants to 6 ft.; 80 days.

'Luther Hill' (1902)
Developed by and named for Luther Hill of Andover Township, New Jersey; a parent of the famous hybrid 'Silver Queen'. Short stalks, 4–5 ft. high, are good for gardeners with limited space. Productive, usually 2 ears per stalk; suckers produce additional ears. Ears are 5–6 in. long with white kernels and good, sweet flavor; 75–85 days.

'Stowell's Evergreen' (1848)

Developed by Nathan Stowell of Burlington, New Jersey, this is one of the oldest named varieties of sweet corn in existence. In 1934 Hedrick called it "probably the most widely known and appreciated variety ever to be introduced." Large plants, 8–10 ft. in height, bear 1–2 large ears; ears are 8–9 in. long and usually have 16–18 rows of white kernels. "Evergreen" refers to the fact that this variety holds its fresh quality for a long time in the field, allowing for a long harvest. Needs a long growing season; 80–100 days.

Sweet Corn, Yellow

'Golden Bantam' (1902)   p. 52

Developed by J. G. Pickett near Greenfield, Massachusetts. Before 'Golden Bantam' came along, white-kerneled sweet corns were much more popular and numerous than yellow varieties, which most folks associated with livestock feed. But when E. L. Coy discovered 'Golden Bantam' in western Massachusetts, he sent along the seed to Burpee with a note that read "you now own the very sweetest and richest corn ever known." Hedrick reports this in his *Sweet Corn of New York* (1934) and also suggests that Pickett may have selected 'Golden Bantam' from a 19th-century yellow variety called 'Golden Sweet'.

Whatever its parentage, 'Golden Bantam' remains the standard for open-pollinated yellow sweet corn. Stalks are 5–6 ft. high and bear 2 or more ears per stalk; ears are 5–7 in. long and have 8 rows of golden yellow kernels; classic corn taste; high yielding; fairly early; 70–85 days. Improved strains of 'Golden Bantam' have been bred to be even earlier, or to set 10–14 rows of kernels.

'Golden Early Market' (1925)

Another good early yellow sweet corn, which arose as an accidental cross between 'Golden Bantam' and 'Early White Market'. Sturdy, 3–5-ft. stalks and 7–8-in. ears that have 10–12 rows of kernels; good flavor; productive; 57–72 days.

'Mandan Red Sweet' ('Nuetta'; 1912)

Introduced by Oscar H. Will & Co. in 1912, this is actually a pre-Columbian strain grown by the Mandan tribe of the northern Great Plains. The synonym, 'Nuetta', is the native name for the Mandans. Short 3–4-ft. stalks send out many tillers and produce 2–6 short ears that have 8–10 rows of beautiful, slightly wrinkled kernels ranging in color from orange-yellow to pale reddish brown at maturity. Ears are used for roasting rather than steaming; very unusual and well worth trying; 75–90 days.

Dent Corn

'Bloody Butcher' (1845)
A beautiful variety that has recently made a comeback as an ornamental corn. Very tall, 10–12 ft., sturdy stalks; productive, with at least 2 large ears per stalk, to 12 in.; cobs are either pink or red, a character common to many old corn varieties. Kernels are red and streaked with darker red, with an occasional white ear. Good flavor for fresh eating when young or for making red-flecked cornbread; excellent for autumn decorations. Drought-tolerant; needs a long season; complete drying under cover if fall weather is rainy; 100–120 days.

'Hickory King' (before 1900) p. 52
An old-time favorite southern variety; ears are roasted in the milk stage; kernels are made into hominy grits, flour, or cornmeal at maturity. Stalks are 8–12 ft. in height and bear 2 ears per plant; 8–9-in. ears have large, flat, white kernels. Tight husks guard against damage from beetles or earworms; plants are blight-resistant. Another strain of 'Hickory King' has yellow kernels; 85–100 days.

'Nothstine Dent' p. 53
An heirloom from northern Michigan, this variety makes a sweet, delicious cornmeal for use in baking and as a hot cereal. Stalks to 7 ft.; 7–8-in. ears have glossy yellow kernels with white caps; not high-yielding. Dries early in the field and is good for short-season areas; 95–100 days.

Flint Corn

'Garland Flint'
A New Hampshire family heirloom selected by George Garland. Stalks are 7–8 ft.; ears are 7–8 in. with 8 rows of bright yellow kernels; a few ears are colored a solid, deep red; 98–110 days.

'Longfellow Flint'
A tall flint corn, with 7–12-ft. stalks bearing 1 or 2 long, slender, 9–11-in. ears. Ears have 8 rows of beautiful golden-orange kernels that make a sweet cornmeal. High-yielding; matures late; 115–120 days.

'Rhode Island White Cap'
A white flint corn, not currently offered by seed companies,

that seems very similar to a variety called 'Narragansett', which was introduced around 1860. Stalks are 6–7 ft. in height; ears are 6–7 in. long with 8 rows of ivory-white kernels and an occasional red ear. Originally thought to have come from the Narragansett Indians; 100–120 days.

Flour Corn

'Anasazi'
A beautiful heirloom flour corn from the Anasazi peoples, who lived in the Four Corners area of the Southwest beginning around A.D. 100 (*anasazi* is Navaho for "ancient ones"). Stalks are 6–9 ft. high with multiple ears; ears are multicolored with rounded kernels; extremely variable and is probably the parent of many of the Southwest's corn races; very ornamental; 90–120 days.

'Mandan Bride'   p. 53
An early, multicolored corn from the Mandan tribe who lived in what is now North Dakota. Plants are 5–6 ft. high; ears are 7–8 in. long with 8–12 rows of kernels that are white, yellow, purple, red, and variegated. Kernels are filled with soft white starch, making them easy to grind for flour; one of the most ornamental types for autumn decorations. Ripens well in short-season areas, and is not well adapted for areas below 38° longitude; 90–95 days. Several other, single-colored strains of Mandan flour corn are also available.

'Taos Pueblo Blue Corn'
An ancient traditional blue flour corn grown in the high country of New Mexico; hardy, and grows well in other regions of the country. Plants grow to 8 ft. and bear large 10–12-in.-long ears that have 14–16 rows of dark blue-black kernels. Drought-resistant; excellent for making blue cornmeal; 100–125 days.

Gardeners who need an earlier blue corn should try 'Hopi Blue', another ancient variety that grows shorter ears than 'Taos' but is equally, if not more, drought-tolerant, with a long taproot. Other Hopi flour corn selections include varieties with yellow, white, pink, purple, red, and turquoise kernels. Seeds of southwestern corns can be planted a little deeper than other races and do not need frequent watering.

'Tuscarora' (before 1712)
A very old variety that Hedrick says was brought to New York State by the Tuscarora Indians when they emigrated from North Carolina in 1712. Fearing Burr described it in 1863 as being 5–6 ft. in height with very large ears, 12 in. or

more in length and up to 3 in. in diameter at the base. Ears have 8 rows of large, pure white kernels that are roundish, flattened, and filled with soft starch; cobs are red. Burr also mentions that 'Tuscarora' makes good fresh eating, particularly for people who don't like excessively sweet corn.

Currently absent from the seed trade, I've included 'Tuscarora' (like 'Catawba' and other varieties) in the hopes that gardeners and seed savers will begin to seek it out. Lawrence Hollander at CRESS, who works with native peoples in the Northeast, says that 'Tuscarora' represents the most widespread food corn of the Iroquois Nation today, although it is often mixed with another Iroquois flour corn.

Popcorn

'Pennsylvania Butter-Flavored' (before 1885)
Grown by German settlers in Pennsylvania, this popcorn has 8-ft. stalks that bear an average of 2 ears, 4–6 in. long; ears have 26–28 rows of small white kernels; flavor is superior to commercial popcorn; well worth trying; 100–105 days.

'Strawberry' ('Dwarf Strawberry') p. 54
The most widely available variety of popcorn; the 2–3-in. mahogany-red ears are mostly grown as an ornamental corn for autumn decorations, but the kernels also pop well. Plants are 4–5 ft. tall and bear 2–4 ears per stalk; 80–110 days.

'Tom Thumb Yellow' p. 54
A good popcorn for short-season areas, selected from a New Hampshire heirloom by the eminent plant breeder Elwyn Meader. Dwarf 3½-ft. plants bear 2–4 small ears, 3–4 in. long. Kernels are yellow and pop up very sweet and tender; 105 days.

Corn Salad (Mâche)

Valerianella locusta var. *olitoria*
A lovely little European native, corn salad gets its name from its habit of growing wild in grain fields (in Britain, the word *corn* refers to various kinds of grain, especially wheat). Also known as mâche, lamb's-lettuce, fetticus, and a host of other names, corn salad forms a low-growing rosette of tender, spoon-shaped leaves that have a mild, somewhat nutty taste. Under its currently popular name of mâche, corn salad has become a fixture of the gourmet salad garden, included in mesclun mixtures to balance the more assertive taste of other greens.

Italian corn salad *(Valerianella eriocarpa)* is very similar to regular corn salad, except that the plants are slightly taller and the leaves slightly longer, with a pale green color.

How to Grow

Corn salad is quite cold-hardy and grows best when daytime temperatures are below 75°F. Direct-seed a couple of weeks before the first frost date for a late fall or early spring crop; plant again in early spring for late spring greens. The plant grows best in rich loam but also does well in average garden soil.

Sow seeds rather thickly in wide rows or beds spaced 18 in. apart. Make small succession plantings to ensure a continuous harvest throughout the cooler months of the year. Thin young plants to 6 in. apart in the row or bed. Seeds take up to 2 weeks to germinate, but plants grow quickly after that.

In milder climates, corn salad will overwinter in the garden with mulch protection. Even in colder areas it makes an excellent salad crop for the winter cold frame.

Harvest

Pinch off the whole rosette of leaves once it has fully formed, usually in 45–60 days. Individual leaves or young thinnings can be harvested before that time. Fall-planted crops will produce in late fall and, if given winter protection, will continue to produce greens until the spring-sown crop is ready. Corn salad doesn't bolt readily, but even after it goes to seed, the leaves remain edible and tasty.

Because corn salad has such a mild flavor, it's best dressed with a simple, light vinaigrette. One of my favorite dressings uses raspberry vinegar and walnut oil.

Pests and Diseases

Animals like woodchucks, rabbits, and deer find corn salad as tasty as humans do. Protecting your crop with a good fence is the only reliable solution.

■ RECOMMENDED VARIETIES

'A Grosse Graine' ('Big-Seeded')
Described by both Burr in 1863 and Vilmorin-Andrieux in 1885. An excellent early variety for spring seeding; tolerates the heat of early summer better than other types. Both the seeds and leaves are larger than other varieties; 45–50 days.

'Coquille de Louviers' ('Coquille') p. 55
A fine, mild-flavored variety with dark green, spoon-shaped leaves. Plants are vigorous and frost-hardy. Good for fall har-

vest in short-season areas, or as a winter crop in milder regions. Recommended by Shepherd Ogden of the Cook's Garden as the prettiest of all corn salads; 45–60 days.

'D'Etampes' ('Verte d'Etampes')
Another old heirloom that has been cultivated for more than a century; listed by Vilmorin-Andrieux in 1885. Dark green leaves are thick, fleshy, and narrow, with prominent veins; plants are compact and very tolerant of cold; this is a good variety for overwintering in the garden or growing in a cold frame or cool greenhouse; 45–60 days.

'Verte de Cambrai' ('Green de Cambria')
I suspect this corn salad may be the same variety Thomas Jefferson grew in his vegetable garden at Monticello, listing it as 'Candia' in 1810. The dark green oval leaves resist yellowing and have a delicate texture and mild flavor; very cold-tolerant and resistant to downy mildew; another good type to sow in fall and overwinter; harvest leaves when 4–6 in. long; 50–60 days.

Collards. *See* Kale and Collards

Cowpeas. *See* Peas

Cucumber

Cucumis sativus
Cucumbers probably originated in India and have been cultivated for more than 3,000 years. The ancient Greeks, Romans, Chinese, and other peoples grew them, and they apparently came to the New World with the first European explorers. In 1535 Jacques Cartier mentioned seeing large cucumbers being grown at what is now Montreal, and in 1539 DeSoto found Indians in Florida growing cucumbers that were "better than those of Spain."[24]

Cucumbers vary greatly in shape and size, from tiny, prickly, and seedy fruits to long, smooth-skinned slicing varieties that contain few seeds. The typical skin color is either white or green at the eating stage, usually turning golden yellow or russet brown as the fruits ripen and mature seeds. The main distinction gardeners and growers make is between pickling and slicing types, though many varieties are versatile enough to be used for both.

How to Grow

Like their close relative, the muskmelon, cucumbers are very frost-tender and like warm weather. To get an earlier crop, start seeds indoors, sowing ½–¾ in. deep in small pots about 3–4 weeks before the last frost date. Don't start them any earlier, as the plants will get too big and rangy and make transplanting harder. Provide some gentle bottom heating during germination (with an electric pad or by placing on top of the refrigerator) and place young plants in a sunny location at room temperature (around 70°F). Harden off seedlings and transplant to the garden when soil temperatures are warm, 70°F or higher, setting out two pots about 12 in. apart inside a circular hill or mound.

An easier method is to wait until after the soil has warmed up and then direct-seed cucumbers in circular hills spaced 4 ft. apart in rows spaced 4–6 ft. apart (to allow the cucumber vines some room to spread). Plant 8–10 seeds per hill, ½ in. deep and about 2 in. apart in a symmetrical pattern; after seedlings emerge, thin hills to the 3 or 4 best plants. Or, to save space in the garden, grow cucumbers up a sturdy wire trellis, allowing 1–2 ft. between plants in a row. You can also control the size of vines and promote fruiting by pinching off the fuzzy growing tips of vines once they have grown to a length of 4 ft. or more.

Cucumbers need lots of water, both when the plants are young and again after blossoming, when the vines are beginning to set fruit. The first time to fertilize is before planting or transplanting in the hill; dig in a good amount of compost, dried manure, or a balanced organic fertilizer. The second important time to fertilize is while the vines are still upright, just before they spread out on the ground and begin to "run." Scratch some organic fertilizer into the soil around the plants at this time, being careful not to disturb their roots.

Harvest

Pick cucumbers at any size during the "green" eating stage; once the vines start setting fruit, keep harvesting frequently so that the cucumbers will keep producing. Plants will continue to set fruit until frost, or until days grow short. White-skinned cucumbers generally begin to turn yellow before green-skinned varieties; if picked soon enough, the yellow skin does not mean they are beyond the eating stage.

Pests and Diseases

Control striped and spotted cucumber beetles by dusting leaves with rotenone or pyrethrum, or by covering plants

with a floating row fabric. It's important to control these insects, since they can infect plants with bacterial wilt.

Cucumbers are subject to a host of other viral and fungal
diseases as well, including anthracnose, angular leaf spot, cucumber mosaic, scab, and downy and powdery mildews.
Control by growing varieties that have resistance to these diseases, by rotating crops, and by removing all vines and plant
wastes from the garden and composting them at the end of
the growing season.

■ RECOMMENDED VARIETIES

Pickling Cucumbers

'Boston Pickling' (before 1880)
A good, slightly tapered, small cucumber, 5–6 in. long, with
smooth, dark green skin; black spines; very productive if kept
picked; still popular and widely available; 50–60 days.

'Chicago Pickling' (1888)
As its name suggests, this variety originated near Chicago.
Medium green, blunt-ended fruits are 5–6 in. long; thin,
warty skin; black spines; disease-resistant and prolific; makes
great dill pickles; 55–60 days.

'Early Cluster' (1778)
One of the oldest cultivated cucumbers; a truly historic variety. Produces early, bearing fruit in clusters near the root of
the plant; good for trellising; fruits are plump, 5–6 in. long,
with blunt ends; light green skin is thin but tough; black
spines; seed mass is large and solid. Good for slicing; keeps
well after picking; grows well on a trellis; susceptible to mosaic virus, so provide good growing conditions; 50–55 days.

'Early Russian' (1850s)
Fruits are slender and short oval in shape, 3–5 in. long; skin
is medium green; black spines; flesh is very mild, never bitter;
vigorous plants produce all season if kept picked; good for
short-season areas; 50–60 days.

'Vert de Massy'
A French variety from the 1800s that produces the small
pickling cucumbers known as cornichons. Plants are vigorous
and produce lots of the slender, dark green fruits, which can
be picked when finger-sized or at 4 in. in length, when they
are good for pickling or slicing; black spines; slightly tangy
flavor; scab-resistant; 50–55 days.

Slicing Cucumbers

'Boothby's Blonde' p. 55

An heirloom variety from the Boothby family of Livermore, Maine. Fruits are short oval in shape, 6–8 in. long, with blunt ends; skin is warty and has a nice creamy yellow color; black spines; seed mass large and loose; delicious, sweet flavor; 60–65 days.

'China Long' (1862)

A long Oriental cucumber that is actually one of the "snake melons" (*Cucumis melo*, Flexuosus group). Vines are vigorous with large leaves and long tendrils; plants will produce straighter fruits if grown on a trellis; fruits are 12–14 in. long and plump; skin is medium to dark green speckled with pale yellow; white spines; flesh is crisp, firm, and mild-tasting; great for slicing, not for pickles. Produces over a long season; very dependable and mosaic-resistant; 65–75 days.

Hedrick lists under this name in his *Cucurbits of New York* (1937), but there appears to be some confusion between current listings for 'China Long' and another variety listed by Hedrick as 'Chinese Three Feet' (introduced 1933) that has longer fruits (18–24 in. or more), fewer seeds, and a slightly more bitter taste than 'China Long'. Check variety descriptions before purchasing seed.

'Japanese Climbing' (1892)

From Japan, this plant has vigorous vines with strong tendrils, making it one of the best varieties for trellising. Fruits are cylindrical, 7–9 in. long, with a slightly ridged surface; skin is light to medium green speckled with yellowish green; black spines; very tender and crisp, with a slightly tart flavor; excellent slicer; 58–65 days.

'Lemon' (1894) p. 56

A popular and unusual home garden variety, this cucumber has spherical, broad oval fruits that are 2–3 in. long; when the skin is translucent or very pale yellow, fruits can be sliced and eaten either peeled or unpeeled; fruits turn golden yellow at maturity and become bitter; numerous black spines and lots of seeds; flesh is very thick and white; plants are widely adapted and disease-resistant. Kids enjoy growing this variety, which is very similar to another cucumber called 'Crystal Apple' that comes from New Zealand; 60–70 days.

'Long Green Improved' (1842)

A selection from an even older variety named 'Long Green Turkey' that was grown in the 1700s. Still a dependable home garden variety; vigorous and productive. Fruits are plump, 10–12 in. long, with tapered ends; skin is medium green and bumpy; black spines; flesh is firm and thick with few seeds; good for slicing or pickling.

'Longfellow' (1927)
Developed as a cross between 'Emerald', a variety from the late 1800s, and another unknown variety. Fruits are cylindrical, 12–15 in. long, and moderately plump; skin is very dark green; white spines; holds color and crispness well after picking; 62–74 days.

'Straight 8' (1935)
Named as an All-America Selection for 1935, and still one of the most popular home garden varieties. Fruits are slender and cylindrical, 8–9 in. long; skin is dark green and smooth; white spines; plants are vigorous and mosaic-resistant; 52–75 days.

'Suyo Long' p. 56
Rosalind Creasy, who gardens in northern California, says this is one of her favorite cucumbers. Originally from northern China. The fruits are 10–18 in. long and best grown above ground on a trellis or other support. Skin is dark green with ridges; white spines and few seeds; crisp, tender flesh that is mild and sweet, not bitter; plants are heat-tolerant and disease-resistant; 60–70 days.

'West Indian Gherkin' (1793)
Actually a separate species, *Cucumis anguria,* this unique plant is the true "gherkin" for pickles or relishes. It arrived in the U.S. from Jamaica in 1793 and may have come originally from Africa. The vines are vigorous, with smooth leaves like those of a watermelon; fruits are short, plump, and oval, 2–3 in. long; the skin is pale glossy green, prickly and burrlike; numerous pale green spines and many small seeds; flesh is thin, elastic, and greenish in color; the taste, like everything else about this plant, is distinctive; worth trying if you've never had a real gherkin; 60–65 days.

'White Wonder' (before 1890) p. 57
Originally developed in western New York State, this is an attractive white cucumber. Fruits are plump and oval, 6–9 in. long, with rounded ends; skin is ivory white at the slicing stage and creamy yellow at maturity; black spines; flesh is thin, crisp, firm, and mild-tasting; plants are vigorous, productive, and tolerate heat; good for slicing or pickling; 57–60 days.

Eggplant

Solanum melongena

Native to India, the eggplant figures much more prominently in the cuisines of other cultures than it does in America, where we tend to overwhelm it — breading it, frying it, baking it, and drowning it in tomato sauce and cheese to make eggplant parmigiana. Home-grown eggplant deserves better at our hands. Instead of cooking it to death, try making ratatouille (summer vegetable stew), baba ghanouj (creamy eggplant dip), or caponata (cooked eggplant relish with celery, capers, and olives). Served cold, caponata is terrific spread on toasted slices of French bread; I also like it as a filling for summer omelets, served with a glass of good red wine.

Everyone knows the typical dark purple, oval or pear-shaped eggplant, but there are other interesting colors and shapes out there as well, just waiting to be discovered by home gardeners: skinny fruits for stir-fries; white, green, and orange fruits that really are the size and shape of an egg; and beautiful lavender and white bicolors. I learned a lot about eggplant in August of 1994 when I spent a day walking around the heirloom field trials at Penn State University's Larsen Agricultural Experiment Station with Professor Mike Orzolek. There were dozens of unusual varieties from all over the world, supplied by the USDA. Unfortunately, most of them have not yet become widely available in this country; suffice it to say that eggplant lovers definitely have something to look forward to.

Up until the early 1900s, American gardeners grew eggplant mainly as an ornamental plant, and it still looks right at home growing in a bed or border. Many eggplant varieties have attractive foliage and pretty purple or white flowers. Some even have a long, showy, green or purple calyx that almost covers the fruit and that can have very sharp spines. These prickly specimens may have more value as a garden accent than as a food plant.

How to Grow

Eggplant grows slowly and needs a long, hot season to set fruit, conditions that can be difficult to provide in cool, short-season areas.

For best results, start eggplant seed in flats or cells about 8 weeks before the last spring frost date, planting seeds ¼ in. deep. After the seedlings show 3 true leaves, pot up into individual 2–3-in. pots, transferring again to bigger pots when plants get larger.

Transplant to the garden about 2–3 weeks after the last spring frost date, after the soil has warmed up. Eggplant prefers a fertile, well-drained sandy loam, though it is fussier about temperature than soil type. Harden off seedlings by gradually reducing water and temperatures, to avoid transplant shock. Set out plants 18–24 in. apart in rows spaced 36 in. apart.

When night temperatures fall below 70°F, as is common in northern areas, eggplants will not set fruit. To provide plants with extra warmth, particularly early and late in the season, use a black plastic mulch to retain heat in the soil, or cover the plants with plastic cloches or a floating row fabric. Water regularly, though not daily, during dry weather. Hoe up soil around the stem when plants are 12–16 in. high.

Harvest
Eggplant will continue to set fruit during hot weather so long as plants are kept well picked. Ripe fruits have a glossy skin that yields to gentle pressure.

Pests and Diseases
Flea beetles are the worst enemies of eggplant; badly infested plants have leaves that are honeycombed with holes from the insects' feeding. To prevent damage, begin by hardening off seedlings on a table or other support that is at least 3 ft. above the ground. Control beetles on growing plants by dusting with rotenone or pyrethrum or by covering plants with a floating row fabric for 3–4 weeks after setting out.

Colorado potato beetles will also chew on eggplant leaves. Look for the insect's orange egg masses on the undersides of leaves and remove and crush them by hand.

Verticillium wilt poses the most serious disease problem with eggplant. This fungal condition can cause leaves to curl or wilt and turn yellow at the margins. It can usually be avoided by rotating crops, making sure not to grow any members of the nightshade family (eggplant, tomato, pepper, or potato) successively in the same spot. Remove any infected plants from the garden to avoid spreading the disease.

■ RECOMMENDED VARIETIES

'Black Beauty' (1902) p. 57
The most widely grown standard eggplant, with glossy dark purple skin; fruits are smooth, oval, 1–3 lb., 6–7 in. long and 5 in. in diameter, blunt at blossom end; good flavor and quality; plants are 24–30 in. high and bear 4–6 fruits; does well in warm seasons in the North; 72–85 days (from transplants).

'Listada de Gandia' p. 58
One of the loveliest of the Italian bicolored eggplants, the 5–6-in.-long fruits have vertical lavender and purple stripes;

very ornamental. Suzanne Ashworth, the Seed Savers Exchange curator for eggplant, reports that three different color strains exist, one with stripes that are more pink than purple. Rosalind Creasy calls it "the most successful open-pollinated variety."

Plants are 14–16 in. tall, with a 24–30-in. spread, and have large leaves; drought-tolerant, sets fruit well during hot weather; may be daylength-sensitive; not recommended for northern states, though it grew well in adverse conditions at Penn State trials; thin skin does not need to be peeled before cooking; harvest fruits promptly, since there is some tendency to bronzing; 75 days (from transplants).

'Pintong Long' p. 58
A long, skinny eggplant from Taiwan that's great for slicing and stir-fries; rosy purple fruits are 10–14 in. long, 1 in. wide, and weigh 2–3 oz.; plants are 12 in. tall and upright, providing good shade for the fruit; flowers are lavender with darker purple veins; leaves are oak-shaped with purple veining; productive, hardy, and disease-resistant; early to midseason harvest; 90 days (from seed).

'Rosa Bianca' p. 59
A beautiful Italian heirloom with rounded, 4–6-in., teardrop-shaped fruits colored rosy lavender and white; flesh is creamy, meaty, mild, and tender with no bitterness; 75 days (from transplants).

'Thai Green'
Green-skinned eggplants are quite common, though rarely grown in this country. This heirloom comes from Thailand and has slender, light green, 10–12-in.-long fruits; plants are 24–30 in. tall; flowers are lavender with spineless green calyxes; tender flesh with a nice mild flavor; fruit turns hard and yellow when seeds are mature; very productive and hardy; said to withstand light frosts; 80 days (from transplants).

'Turkish Orange' ('Turkish Italian') p. 59
A most unusual heirloom, originally from Turkey, that bears miniature, round, 2-oz., orange-red fruits that look like small tomatoes. In fact, it is a different species, *Solanum integrifolium*. Plants are tall, 36–48 in., and bear heavily; very susceptible to flea beetle damage, so cover with a floating row cover when young. Fruits are bite-sized and seedy, best for eating when still green; cut in half and cook in caponata or curries. Worth growing as an ornamental, since the fruits mature from all-green to green striped with orange to all-orange; yields early to midseason; 95 days (from seed).

'Violette di Firenze'

Another outstanding Italian eggplant with large, oblong to rounded fruits; exterior is ribbed with a lavender skin sometimes striped with white; does well in northern areas if given extra heat with black plastic or cloches; 100 days (from seed).

Endive (Escarole)

Chicorium endivia

Endive is thought to have originated either in India or around the eastern Mediterranean. Wherever it came from, though, it was used as a food plant by the ancient Egyptians, Greeks, and Romans, and remains popular as a salad and cooking green. Not to be confused with Belgian endive (witloof chicory), this closely related species also likes cool weather but is somewhat less frost-hardy than the other types of chicory (see p. 168).

Americans use the term *escarole* when referring to the broad-leaved type of endive, while varieties with curly leaves are simply known as endive, or by their French name of *chicorée frisée* (usually shortened to just *frisée*).

How to Grow

Endive likes the same cool weather conditions as lettuce. Start seeds in flats or small individual cells about 3–4 weeks before setting out, or direct-seed outside in early spring, as soon as the ground can be worked. Sow seeds ⅛ in. deep and about 1 in. apart in beds or rows spaced 18–24 in. apart. Thin young plants to 12 in. apart in the row or bed.

For a fall crop, start sowing in late June in the North, progressively later in warmer climates, and harvest plants before the first hard frost.

Blanching the heads makes them sweeter and less bitter. About 7–10 days before harvest tie up the heads by slipping a wide rubber band around the outer leaves. Some gardeners recommend simply covering the heads with a dark-colored plastic flowerpot or a piece of cardboard or tile. With some varieties, tying or covering isn't necessary, since they have tightly packed heads that blanch the inner hearts.

Harvest

Cut endive heads as soon as they reach their mature size to avoid problems with tip burn or bottom rot. Fall crops can stand a few light frosts, which will make them sweeter, but they should be harvested before the first killing frost.

For an extended harvest, tie up plants before a hard frost

and dig them up, roots and all, leaving as much soil on the roots as possible. Remove all dead and yellow leaves and re-plant the roots in a container of light, sandy soil or peat moss in a dark root cellar. Water lightly around the roots and har-vest as needed. An even simpler option is to transfer endive from the garden to a cold frame in mid to late fall.

Curly-leaved endives also make a nice addition to a mesclun (mixed greens) planting. Cut greens just above the ground when 4–6 in. high and allow to grow back for an-other harvest.

■ RECOMMENDED VARIETIES

'Broad-Leaved Batavian'
Described by Fearing Burr in 1863, this is the type most often identified as escarole. An improved variety of 'Batavian' was introduced in 1934 and named an All-America Selection. Large, broad, lettuce-like outer leaves enclose a round head measuring 12–16 in. in diameter. Deep, creamy white hearts are well-blanched and buttery; good in salads, soups, or sautéed; withstands light frost; 85–90 days.

'Green Curled Ruffec' p. 60
Another variety mentioned by Burr in 1863, this endive has deeply cut, dark green leaves that blanch well and have thick, white midribs; plant is thickly tufted and rosette is large, 16–18 in. in diameter; tolerates cold, wet weather; in milder climates can stand into winter with a light mulch protection; a good variety for fall harvest; 75–100 days.

'Grosse Bouclée'
An old variety of escarole with a very tight heart and savoyed leaves that are rounded and well blanched; easy to grow; bolt-resistant; 85–90 days.

'Tres Fine Marachiere' ('Frisée') p. 60
Like 'Broad-Leaved Batavian', this has become associated with a type of endive that includes several varieties. Minia-ture and quick-growing French endive, with frilly, finely cut leaves; 6 in. in diameter, so can be spaced closer in the row or bed; bolt-resistant. Mild, nutty flavor is great for salads; blanch before harvest; 60 days.

Fava Beans. *See* Beans

Florence Fennel (Finocchio)

Foeniculum vulgare var. *azoricum*

More popular in Europe than America, Florence fennel is an odd but very appealing vegetable with a mild, sweet, anise-like flavor. The fleshy white bases of the overlapping leaves form an above-ground bulb, called the "apple." The plant's short stalks are light green and look much like celery ribs; these stalks have a stronger flavor than the bulb and are sometimes added to soups and stews. The feathery top leaves resemble those of dill and make a good herb for seasoning fish, chicken, shellfish, and other delicate dishes.

Florence fennel belongs to the same species as the common or wild varieties of fennel; these latter types are grown mainly for their seeds, which are used as a seasoning and in liqueurs. Native to temperate zones of Europe and Asia, the plant was slow to gain much of an audience outside Italy. Bernard McMahon mentions it in his *American Gardener's Calendar* in 1806, but only in recent years has fennel really caught on as a gourmet vegetable and begun to appear in markets.

How to Grow

Direct-seed fennel from mid-spring to early summer, sowing about 10 seeds per foot in rows spaced 18 in. apart. Thin young plants to 6 in. apart in the row. Fennel will not transplant well unless you start seeds in individual cells or small pots, since disturbing the roots can cause premature bolting. In hot summer areas, grow fennel as a fall crop, direct-seeding in midsummer.

Fennel grows best in a fertile, well-drained, slightly acid soil; if your garden soil is light or sandy, dig in plenty of organic matter before planting. Keep plants well watered. Clip off any seed stalks that may form.

Harvest

When the bulbs have grown to the size of a egg, pull up soil around the base of the plants. This will help blanch the bulbs and give them a milder taste. Begin harvesting the larger bulbs 7–10 days later, while they are still tender and about the size of a tennis ball or a clenched fist.

■ RECOMMENDED VARIETIES

'Romy'   p. 61

An Italian heirloom with large, globe-shaped bulbs. The outer wrapper leaves of the bulbs are not as tough and fibrous as other varieties and can be used along with the tender inner leaves. Fine texture and delicate, sweet flavor; fast-growing and fairly early; 89 days (from seed).

Garlic

Allium sativum

Anyone who cooks, or simply enjoys good food, would be hard pressed to imagine a world without garlic. According to Pliny, the Egyptians ranked garlic next to the gods when swearing an oath,[25] and Roman laborers and soldiers consumed lots of raw garlic, which was thought to give them strength. (If nothing else, at least their breath was strong.) The ancients may in fact have been on to something, since recent scientific studies have suggested that allicin, a chemical compound found in garlic (especially raw garlic), may ward off colds and infections and act as a blood purifier.

As useful and ubiquitous as garlic is today, most American consumers still know of only a single type, the long-storing supermarket garlic with the tightly wrapped white head and layers of inner cloves. But garlic actually comes in several distinct types and in hundreds of named varieties. In the summer of 1994 I saw 192 different varieties of freshly harvested garlic being cured at the Seed Savers Exchange headquarters in Decorah, Iowa. Rest assured, there wasn't a vampire within 50 miles of that place.

Ron Engeland is one of the world's leading authorities on garlic, growing nearly 350 strains at Filaree Farm in Okanogan, Washington. Ron has developed a "family tree" for garlic that divides the hundreds of known varieties into five basic types. I have based the general and specific descriptions that follow on his system.

Garlic probably originated in south-central Asia, selected and developed by humans from an ancestral wild plant that may have been the species now called *Allium longicuspis*. Almost all cultivated forms of garlic have lost the ability to produce fertile flowers and true seed. To propagate, therefore, gardeners must buy or save individual cloves from the previous season's crop and replant them.

There are two basic classes of garlic: hardneck or "ophio" garlic *(Allium sativum* var. *ophioscorodon)* and softneck garlic *(A. sativum* var. *sativum)*. Hardnecks send up a stiff flower stalk (or "scape") that produces small aerial cloves called bulbils. Once this flower stalk is removed, the plant's underground bulb will grow, generally producing a head with a few large cloves in one outer layer. Softneck garlics don't normally send up flower stalks, and they usually produce bulbs with many smaller cloves arranged in overlapping layers. Softnecks store longer than hardnecks and are generally easier to grow, more productive, and more adaptable to a wide range of soils and climates. Hardnecks are more cold-hardy than softnecks and perform better in regions that have frigid winters.

Ron Engeland has further subdivided hardnecks and softnecks into five different horticultural types. Under hardnecks he lists rocambole, purple stripe, and porcelain; under softnecks he includes artichoke (or common) and silverskin (the kind most frequently sold in supermarkets). Each of these five types has a specific character that is based on the plant's form; the shape, size, and color of its bulbs and cloves; and other factors like storability. It's good to know something about these varietal groups before buying and planting your own garlic. See Recommended Varieties, below, for descriptions of specific heirloom varieties belonging to each of the five types.

The huge bulb sold in markets under the name "elephant garlic" belongs to a different species, *Allium scorodoprasum*, and is actually a bulbing kind of leek. The heads can grow very large (weighing up to 1 lb.) and they contain on average only 4 huge cloves that have a nice mild garlicky taste. Elephant garlic performs best in mild winter areas and should be planted deeper than regular garlic (4–6 in. below the surface). Remove the flower stalk to increase bulb size.

How to Grow

Plant garlic in the fall, at the same time you would put in other hardy bulbs like tulips. In the North, this would be in October, after the first fall frosts but 4–6 weeks before the ground freezes for the winter. In southern and milder climates, adjust the planting date accordingly, from November through early January. The goal of fall planting is to allow enough time for roots to get established before winter, but not enough time to encourage green top growth. Hardneck (ophio) garlic winters over better than softneck types; in regions with long, cold winters, softneck varieties can be spring-planted, but the harvested bulbs will be smaller.

Grow garlic in a well-drained, well-worked, moderately fertile soil with plenty of organic matter. Break up bulbs and plant individual cloves scar side down about 2 in. deep and 4–6 in. apart in the row or bed. Select the largest cloves for planting, since big cloves produce big bulbs. Mulch the bed heavily after planting to protect the ground from frost-heaving during the winter.

When plants emerge in the spring, begin watering them like other greens. To provide extra nitrogen, water with fish emulsion or manure tea.

Hardneck garlics will send up a coiled flower stalk in late spring or early summer. After about a week the stalk will start losing its coil. As the stalk begins to straighten up, snip it off to focus the plant's energy into growing a bigger bulb. Use the stalk's topsetting bulbils in cooking, or cure them and save them for planting ½ in. deep in fall or spring for a crop of garlic greens (great for salads or pesto).

Even more than other vegetables, garlic will adapt itself to a particular location and climate. After growing it for a few years and selecting the best bulbs for replanting, you should have a strain that is well adapted to your own soil and growing conditions. By the same token, it will take garlic at least a year to get completely used to its new home in your garden. This doesn't mean your first harvest will be a bust, only that you can usually expect much better in coming years.

Harvest
Garlic is ready for harvest in mid to late summer, when a little over half the leaves have yellowed and become dry and the necks start getting soft. Bulbs left in the ground too long can start sprouting and break their outer skins.

As harvest time approaches, cut back on water and don't keep the soil wet, or bulbs may mold or stain. Fork around plants to loosen the soil and then lift the bulbs. Bring inside immediately into an airy place that is out of direct sunlight.

Bunch 5–10 plants together and hang up for a few weeks to cure, or dry on screens. Softneck garlic takes longer to cure since the cloves are in overlapping layers. Trim the necks back to ½ in. above the bulbs; if bulbs have not cured sufficiently, the cut area will still be moist. Once fully cured, store bulbs in net bags. Garlic keeps best when stored at room temperature or slightly cooler (down to 55–60°F). The different horticultural varieties have different storage lives: rocamboles and purple stripes keep for 3–6 months; porcelains and artichokes store well for 6–9 months; and silverskins can keep for 12 months or longer. Silverskins are also considered the best type for braiding.

■ RECOMMENDED VARIETIES

HARDNECK (OPHIO) GARLIC (var. *ophioscorodon*)

Rocambole Type
'Carpathian' p. 61
From the Carpathian Mountains of southeast Poland. Large, uniform, off-white bulbs with thin copper veins and some purple blotches; 6–10 large brown cloves per bulb; few double cloves. Vigorous, deep green plants; large scape; bulbs mature about 7 days later than other rocamboles. Classic garlic flavor: hot, spicy, and strong.

'German Red' p. 62
Filaree Farm's strain comes from old gardeners of German descent in Idaho. Vigorous, deep green plants and large bulbs.

Cloves light brown with faint purple at base; 10–15 cloves per bulb; double cloves common. Flavor is strong, hot, and spicy.

'Spanish Roja'   p. 62

A Northwest heirloom, brought to the Portland area by Greek immigrants before 1900 and still sometimes known as 'Greek' or 'Greek Blue'. Bulb wrappers have light purplish streaks; clove color varies with soil and climate from lighter to darker brown with red-purple blush; 6–13 cloves per bulb; double cloves common in large bulbs. Can keep 4–6 months in storage if well grown. Often does poorly in mild winter climates. Easy to peel; classic garlic flavor.

Purple Stripe Type

'Chesnok Red'

Originally from Shvelisi in the Georgian Republic. Tall plants and large, attractively colored bulbs and cloves. Purple stripes are the only garlics to produce fertile flowers, which may suggest this is the one of the oldest cultivated types. Cloves are buff-colored overlaid with red-purple streaks and blush; 8–12 cloves per bulb; good aroma and flavor that stands up well in cooking. Harvest 3–7 days after rocambole types.

Porcelain Type

'Romanian Red'

Introduced to British Columbia from Romania many years ago. Bulb wrapper color varies: on poor soils it may be blotched with purple like rocamboles; on rich soil wrappers are paper white. Cloves are plump, 4–5 per bulb, and buff-brown with streaks and lines. Flavor is hot and pungent with a good, lingering bite. Stores very well.

SOFTNECK GARLIC (var. *sativum*)

Artichoke Type

'Inchelium Red'   p. 63

Discovered on the Colville Indian Reservation in northern Washington State and named after a town on the Columbia River. Very large, dense bulbs; 4–5 clove layers with 8–20 cloves per bulb. Mild but lingering flavor; taste can sharpen in storage.

'Lorz Italian'   p. 63

A Northwest heirloom variety, brought from Italy to Washington's Columbia River Basin before 1900. Very large, somewhat flattened round bulbs; 3–5 clove layers and 12–19 cloves per bulb; cloves are milky to yellowish white with a light pink blush. Plants stand summer heat well. Good flavor, in some years very hot.

Silverskin Type

'Nootka Rose' p. 64
Another Northwest heirloom, from the San Juan Islands off the coast of northern Washington. Medium to large bulbs. Clove color is mahogany heavily streaked with red and with dark, solid bright red tips; colors fade in rich soil. Cloves often have a long papery tail. Usually 5 clove layers and 15–24 small cloves per bulb. Good for braiding; strong flavor.

'Silverskin'
Large bulbs with white wrappers. Cloves are white to tan with pink blush at tip; bottom half of clove often brownish; cloves are tall and concave. Usually 5 clove layers and 15–20 cloves per bulb; few small cloves. Mild, sweet taste builds in hotness and lingers. Productive; good keeper.

Ground Cherry. *See* Tomatillo

Husk Tomato. *See* Tomatillo

Jerusalem Artichoke (Sunchoke)

Helianthus tuberosus   p. 64
One of the few garden vegetables native to North America, the Jerusalem artichoke has nothing whatsoever to do with either Jerusalem or the common globe artichoke *(Cynara scolymus)*. One theory suggests that the misnomer resulted from the mangling of its Italian name, *girasole articiocco*, meaning 'sunflower artichoke'. Today the plant also goes by the name "sunchoke," which, while less colorful, is perhaps more descriptive.

Jerusalem artichoke is a perennial kind of sunflower, but unlike other garden sunflowers, which are grown for their large seedheads, this plant is grown for its tuberous roots. The plants grow vigorously, 6–8 ft. in height, and sport 3–4-in. daisylike blossoms that have a pleasant chocolaty scent. The plants infrequently produce fertile seeds; propagation is accomplished by cutting and planting pieces of the tuberous roots, in much the same manner as potatoes.

The first mention of the Jerusalem artichoke by a European

author appears to be that of the French explorer Samuel de Champlain, who noticed the plant being cultivated by the Huron Indians in 1605.[26] In the four centuries since that time the Jerusalem artichoke has become known in various parts of the world, but it is still considered a decidedly minor vegetable. The indifference of gardeners may be due to the plant's aggressive tendencies (left to its own devices, it can become invasive and weedy) or to the knobby tubers common to some varieties, which can make them hard to peel.

Notwithstanding its difficult reputation, the Jerusalem artichoke can make a nice, no-fuss crop for home gardeners. The tuberous roots are crisp and tasty, a good fresh vegetable from fall through early spring. Instead of starch, the freshly dug roots contain a polysaccharide known as inulin, which means that they are excellent for diabetics. The roots are also low in calories, and their nutty taste is good either raw in salads or steamed, scalloped, or pickled. What's more, the plants do double duty by forming a tall, ornamental border or windbreak outside the regular vegetable garden.

Several varieties of Jerusalem artichoke produce relatively large, smooth tubers that make them easier to peel and prepare. As with potatoes, skin color is used to differentiate between varieties. In 1863, Burr listed the four basic skin colors that still exist today — white, yellow, red, and purple.

How to Grow

Plant Jerusalem artichokes in the fall, at the same time you would plant hardy bulbs in your region — after the first fall frosts but 4–6 weeks before the ground freezes. Suppliers usually ship tubers for fall planting, but if you can get spring planting stock or already have an established bed you can also replant overwintered chokes at any time beginning about 8 weeks before the last spring frost date.

Prepare a permanent bed outside the regular vegetable garden, since Jerusalem artichoke is a perennial and can become invasive. The best kind of soil is a light sandy or silty loam, but any well-worked soil will do. Loosen up the soil with a fork before planting and remove large stones, then dig in compost or other organic matter. A loose seedbed will help make the roots easier to lift next year at harvest time.

Cut or break the tubers so that each piece is about 1 in. in diameter and bears one or two "eyes." Don't let the cut pieces dry out before planting. Plant pieces 4–6 in. deep about 12–18 in. apart in the bed. Mulch heavily with leaves or straw after the ground freezes to prevent frost-heaving.

Harvest

Plants usually flower in mid to late summer, and roots become ready for digging from the end of summer through the fall. Use a garden fork to lift tubers and harvest only what you can eat at any one time, since Jerusalem artichokes tend to shrivel when stored inside. Harvested chokes keep well for 1–2 weeks in the refrigerator.

At the end of the first harvest season, mulch the bed heavily and continue harvesting roots as needed through the winter. Early the following spring (about 18 months after you first planted the tubers), you will want to dig up all the remaining tubers in the bed, saving the largest and smoothest roots for replanting and eating the rest. This is because unharvested roots will naturalize and tend to become smaller and of lesser value. By digging up and replanting only the best roots every year, you will improve your Jerusalem artichoke patch and keep it within bounds.

■ RECOMMENDED VARIETIES

'Dave's Shrine' ('Judy's Red', 'Wolcottonian Red')
Collected by Dave Briars of Craftsbury, Vermont. Long (3–4 in.), fat tubers have beautiful bronzy purple skins; ivory-colored flesh contains lots of dry matter, which gives this variety a "saltier," more meaty taste than other chokes. Not currently carried in the seed trade; available through the Seed Savers Exchange Members Network.

'Maine Giant'
An old variety from Maine (a state that has produced many good types of choke). Tubers are creamy white, knobby, and dense. A very productive variety formerly offered by Pinetree Garden Seeds and still available through the Seed Savers Exchange Members Network.

'Smooth Garnet' ('Garnet') p. 65
Very attractive ruby-colored skin; tubers have a smooth, rounded shape and few knobs; one of the better keepers.

Kale and Collards
Brassica oleracea, Acephala group
Kale and collards are leafy, nonheading greens that probably represent the earliest cultivated forms of the European wild cabbage. Botanically speaking, the two plants are essentially the same, though different varieties are still listed under one or the other common name. Many sources list collards as simply one type of kale, but to collards fans, at least, they are a breed apart.

Among the most cold-hardy of vegetables, both collards and kale taste sweeter and better after a frost, and if properly mulched can be harvested through much of the winter, even in the North. I once lived in an old converted hay barn in Williamstown, Massachusetts, and fondly remember looking out my bedroom window on cold December mornings. The garden would be absolutely bare and frozen, except for a row of 'Red Russian' kale peeking up through the first snows of the season.

In addition to its hardiness, kale also makes an outstanding ornamental plant. These days many gardeners grow the brightly colored hybrids sold under the name "flowering kale" or "flowering cabbage" (though it is not flowers but the central leaves that turn variegated colors after a frost). To my mind, other forms of kale are every bit as interesting as these ornamental kales, which are really useful only for garnishing. With a wide range of growing habits, leaf shapes, and colors to choose from, you should experiment with different heirloom varieties of kale to find your favorites.

Americans usually associate collards with southern cuisine, but gardeners in all regions can grow this cold- and heat-tolerant vegetable. Its large, cabbagelike leaves appear coarse, wavy, and somewhat crumpled. Both collards and kale are very nutritious, containing lots of calcium, potassium, and vitamins A and C.

How to Grow

Kale and collards grow best in cool weather and are most often planted as a fall and winter crop. Direct-seed in the garden about 12 weeks before the first fall frost date, sowing seeds about 1 in. apart and ¼ in. deep in rows spaced 24–30 in. apart. Thin plants to 12–15 in. apart in the row. You can also start kale in flats or cells and transplant seedlings to the garden at the 12–15-in. spacing.

Kale and collards, like other members of the cabbage family, appreciate good, fertile soil, but are far less demanding and will grow well in average garden soil.

Harvest

Begin cutting individual leaves about 60 days after sowing. Continue harvesting the larger lower leaves; older leaves left on the plants will get tough and stringy. Kale becomes sweeter after a hard frost; collards are more heat-tolerant than kale, and their flavor is good at any time. When harvesting collards, cut the inner leaves, leaving the crown and 6 outer leaves intact to keep the plant alive.

Collards and kale will winter over outside with some mulch protection in mild climates (Zone 7 and warmer). Even in much colder areas, mulching the bed will extend the harvest season into the early winter. In severe winter climates, cover plants with plastic cloches or tunnels for an extended harvest. Both kale and collards are biennials and will go to seed in the spring if wintered over in the garden.

Pests and Diseases
Kale and collards are less susceptible to insects and disease than other members of the cabbage family. Do not grow either plant in a spot where another brassica (broccoli, cauliflower, cabbage, Brussels sprouts, mustard, turnips, etc.) has grown in the previous season. If necessary, control cabbage worms with Bt (Dipel) or by placing a floating row cover over plants.

■ RECOMMENDED VARIETIES

Kale

'Dwarf Blue Curled Scotch' p. 65
Except for its distinctive leaf color, this variety is identical to 'Dwarf Green Curled Scotch', mentioned by Burr in 1863 and most other garden writers. Plants are compact, 12–15 in. high, and spread to 20–35 in.; extremely hardy and productive; will overwinter with minimal protection. Leaves are blue-green and finely curled and do not yellow even in severe cold; 55–65 days.

'Lacinato' p. 66
This unique Italian heirloom is one of the most ornamental kinds of kale, probably the same as the variety Vilmorin-Andrieux describes in 1885 as 'Cavolo Nero' or 'Tuscan Black Palm'. Plants grow to 2 ft. and bear very dark blue-green straplike leaves that look almost black at a distance; the 10-in.-long leaves curl back at their edges and are heavily blistered over their surface. Very tolerant of both heat and cold; flavor is sweet and mild, particularly after frosts; 62 days.

'Pentland Brig'
An English variety that is the result of a cross between the smooth-leaved 'Thousand-Headed' type of kale and curled-leaf types. Leaves are finely curled; where plants can overwinter, broccoli-like sprouts can also be harvested for eating; very hardy and productive; 55–75 days.

'Red Russian' ('Ragged Jack') p. 66
My favorite. This old variety was introduced to Canada by Russian traders. It has flat, smooth gray-green leaves with

wavy margins that resemble oak leaves; leaf stems and veins are reddish purple. In cold weather the leaves turn entirely reddish purple. Burr describes this variety as 'Buda Kale' in 1863, and Vilmorin-Andrieux briefly mentions 'Ragged Jack' in 1885. Leaves are very tender and tasty; use or refrigerate after picking, since leaves wilt faster than curled types. Plants grow 2–3 ft. in height; varieties sold as 'Ragged Jack' may be somewhat shorter; 50–55 days.

'Thousand-Headed' (before 1863)
According to Vilmorin-Andrieux, this type of kale originated in western France. Large, vigorous plants grow 3–4 ft. high and branches along the stem produce lots of large, smooth, tender, dark green leaves. Vilmorin says the variety is not as cold-hardy as other kales; other sources say it overwinters well in mild climates and can live for years; 120 days.

'Walking Stick' (*Brassica oleracea* var. *longata*)
Sometimes listed under cabbage, this unusual variety is, strictly speaking, neither a heading cabbage nor a kale. It has been grown in the Channel Islands for over 200 years. When spring-sown, the plant's strong stem will grow 5–7 ft. high in most soils and produce a kale- or cabbage-leaved head at the top. In the fall, cut, dry, and polish the stem to make an attractive walking stick. Definitely more of a novelty than a food crop. In 1885 Vilmorin-Andrieux lists this under the name 'Tree Cabbage' or 'Jersey Kale'.

Collards

'Georgia' (before 1880)
The old standard variety of collards, very popular in the southern U.S.; plants grow to 3 ft. and produce large, wavy, blue-green leaves in loose, open heads; leaves are tender, juicy, and mild-tasting. This variety tolerates heat and sandy or poor soils; like kale, the flavor of the greens improves after a light frost; 75–80 days.

'Green Glaze' (before 1860)
Upright plants grow 30–34 in. tall; leaves have a bright green sheen that has inspired another common name, 'Greasy Collards'. Tolerates both heat and frost and has good resistance to cabbage worms and loopers; slow to bolt; 73–79 days.

'Morris Heading'
An old favorite that produces loose, heavy heads on short stems; plants grow 18–24 in. tall; leaves are smooth and dark

green with light green veins; slow to bolt; excellent flavor; 70–75 days.

Kohlrabi

Brassica oleracea, Gongylodes group

With its swollen, globe-shaped stem that squats just above the ground and looks like a small green apple, kohlrabi certainly is an odd vegetable. In fact, the only indication of its membership in the cabbage family are the small leaves that stick straight up from the sides of the bulbous stem. Sometimes called "stem turnip," the kohlrabi has a crisp, sweet flavor that is great raw or lightly steamed or sautéed.

As garden vegetables go, kohlrabi has not been around very long. No clear mention of it exists before the 16th century, when it first appeared in Italy and from there spread to central Europe.[27] Several varieties of kohlrabi, both open-pollinated and hybrid, have been introduced in recent years, but the basic color types — with green, white, or purple skins — have remained essentially the same.

How to Grow

Like other brassicas, kohlrabi likes cool weather; since it is fast-growing and matures quickly, it makes a good spring or fall crop. It grows best in rich, fertile soil but will also perform well in average garden soil.

Direct-seed kohlrabi around the time of the last spring frost date; for a fall crop, sow about 8–10 weeks before the first fall frost date. Plant seeds ¼ in. deep and about 1 in. apart in beds or rows spaced 12–18 in. apart. Thin plants to 4–6 in. apart in the row or bed. You can also start seeds early in flats or cells and transplant to the garden at a 4–6-in. spacing. In areas with moderate summer weather, make succession plantings every 2 weeks from early spring to late summer to ensure a continuous harvest.

Kohlrabi doesn't need fertilization, but it does like a consistent supply of moisture. Keep watered and mulch lightly around plants to help conserve soil moisture.

Harvest

Most kohlrabis are best harvested young, when the bulbous stems have grown to about 2 in. in diameter. At this stage, the inner flesh is sweet, crisp, and tender; when the bulbs grow much larger they get woody and fibrous. To prepare for kitchen use, remove the side stems and leaves and peel the bulbs. The cabbagelike leaves are also edible.

Some larger, long-season varieties, called "winter kohlrabis," store well in a cool, humid root cellar or can overwinter outside in milder climates if protected from freezing with a heavy mulch.

Pests and Diseases
Kohlrabi is not as susceptible to insects and diseases as other members of the cabbage family. Control cabbage worms with Bt (Dipel) or by using a floating row cover.

■ RECOMMENDED VARIETIES

'Early Purple Vienna' (before 1860) p. 67
Mentioned by Burr in 1863, this purple-skinned variety makes an attractive addition to the garden. Plants have small tops and bulbous stems and are slightly larger, later, and more flavorful than 'Early White Vienna'; less susceptible to cracking than other types; 55–60 days.

'Early White Vienna' (before 1860) p. 67
A widely adapted, early dwarf variety; enlarged stems are pale green and slightly flattened globes; plants are 10–12 in. tall with small leaves borne on thin stalks; along with 'Early Purple Vienna', still the standard variety for home gardeners; 50–55 days.

'Gigante' ('Gigant Winter')
An heirloom variety from the former Czechoslovakia, reselected by famous New Hampshire plant breeder Elwyn Meader. This "winter kohlrabi" produces huge stems that swell to 10 in. in diameter and regularly exceed 10 lb. in weight. According to Nichols Garden Nursery, the world record is 62 lb. (leaves included). Unlike other kohlrabis, its flesh remains crisp, white, tender, and mild-tasting even at its maturity instead of turning woody. Harvest bulbs for eating at any size; leaves of large plants can be harvested and eaten like kale or collards. Central Europeans shred the bulbs to make a kind of sauerkraut.

Sow in early spring for a fall crop or set out transplants in fall in milder climates and mulch heavily to overwinter in the garden; stores well in a root cellar; 62 days from transplants, 130 days from spring-sown seed.

Leek

Allium ampeloprasum var. *porrum*
Leeks hold an ancient and honorable place in culinary history. The ancient Egyptians consumed them, and the Roman

emperor Nero ate leeks regularly to clear his voice before singing recitals — so regularly, in fact, that the Romans gave him the nickname Porrophagus, or Leek-Eater.[28] The leek is also the ancient badge of Welshmen, said to have been worn by warring Britons as a sign of recognition when they defeated a Saxon army in A.D. 540. Shakespeare even used the Welsh leek as a plot device in *Henry V*. Being part Welsh myself, I eat a lot of leeks, especially in the fall and winter, when they are perfect as a flavor base for soups or as a braised vegetable side dish.

One of the most cold-hardy vegetables, leeks stand up well to fall frosts and remain perfectly edible even after freezing solid and thawing. As such, they make a good candidate for growing in the northern winter, inside a cold frame, extended cloche, poly tunnel, or other season-extending device. In areas that have milder winters, leeks can overwinter in the garden under a thick layer of mulch. Like other hardy vegetables, the flavor of leeks actually improves after a frost.

How to Grow

Leeks require a long growing season. Sow indoors in flats 8–12 weeks before the last spring frost date, planting seeds thickly, about ¼ in. apart and ¼ deep. When seedlings are about 3 in. high, carefully replant them about 1–2 in. apart or into individual cells. When plants are about the diameter of a drinking straw (approximately 10 weeks after seeding), harden off for a week and then transplant to the garden, setting out 4–6 in. apart in beds or rows spaced 12–24 in. apart. Set into a narrow planting hole about 6 in. deep, backfilling very loosely with soil and leaving only a couple of inches of the leaves above the surface.

Not surprisingly, the largest leeks tend to grow on the most fertile soil, but leeks also like garden soil to be rather light and well-drained. Work compost or dried manure into the bed a few weeks before transplanting. About 6 weeks after transplanting, hoe up soil around the plant stalks, which forces the leaves higher and blanches more of the lower stem; repeat once or twice more as plants grow taller. Another way to blanch leeks is to mulch plants as they grow, which also helps suppress weeds and conserve soil moisture.

Harvest

Well-grown leeks will have a sturdy underground system of rootlets; because of this, pulling them for harvest is easier with the help of a hand fork, like the kind used to dig up dandelions. Gently loosen the leeks and pull them up. Harvest as needed, from early fall throughout the winter; mulch plants heavily after the first hard frost. Leeks store better in the ground where this is possible, but large leeks will also store well in a root cellar.

Leeks, like globe onions, are biennial plants that will go to seed in the spring if left in the garden or replanted. They send up a tall stalk and form a flower head called an umbel. Leeks will cross with other varieties of leeks, but not with other commonly grown members of the onion family. Their seed, if properly stored, will maintain a decent viability for 2–3 years.

■ RECOMMENDED VARIETIES

'Blue Solaise' ('Bleu de Solaise')   p. 68
An attractive old variety with blue-green leaves that turn violet in cold weather; large, medium-long plants are extremely hardy and great for late fall and winter harvest; good for short-season areas; 105 days.

'Giant Caretan' (1874)
A great old French variety described by Vilmorin-Andrieux in 1885 as possibly an improvement on 'Large Rouen'. Stems are medium tall, very thick and solid. Does best when grown in very fertile soil; requires an especially long season but is excellent for late fall harvest or for overwintering in the garden; 130 days.

'Giant Musselburgh' (1870)   p. 68
This variety also goes by the name 'American Flag' or 'Scotch Flag', though it has nothing to do with patriotic sentiment — the old term *flag* refers to plants that have swordlike foliage, like iris or leeks. Still one of the most popular types, it has broad green leaves and 9–15-in. stalks that are 2–3 in. thick, white, mild-tasting, and tender. Very hardy; overwinters well in most regions; does well in both southern and northern regions; 100–120 days.

'Lyon' ('Prizetaker'; 1886)
An English heirloom seldom grown in the U.S. but still available to home gardeners and described as one of the finest varieties in cultivation; plants are tall (to 36 in.) and thick with solid, pure white stalks; grows to a large size but retains its tenderness and mild flavor; needs a long season but is very cold-hardy; 135 days.

Lettuce

Lactuca sativa
Designer salad ingredients may come and go — from tortellini to oranges to steak tartare — but lettuce remains the fun-

dament and the leafy soul of salad bowls around the world. It has been this way since at least 550 B.C., when Herodotus reported that Persian kings served lettuce on their royal tables.[29] The first cultivated forms of lettuce probably originated in the eastern Mediterranean and may have been selected from *Lactuca serriola,* one of many wild species. Leaves of this early lettuce probably grew on tall stems, much like the seed stalk modern lettuce produces when it bolts. In fact, the genus name *Lactuca* refers to the plant's milky sap, to which both the Assyrians and the Egyptians ascribed aphrodisiacal properties.[30] The Romans enjoyed lettuce and according to Pliny grew at least nine different varieties in classical times. The Romans also popularized a type of head lettuce with erect leaves, which they had found growing on the Greek island of Cos. This lettuce became so popular in Rome that in later years it took the name "romaine" from the Eternal City, though we still call it "cos lettuce," too, in honor of its true birthplace.[31]

Not so many years ago, the only kinds of lettuce in the market were the basic green romaine and the watery, insipid crisphead type most people know as "iceberg" (although the original 'Iceberg', introduced in 1894, does not deserve comparison with these transcontinental duds). But gardeners and local growers know that there's a much wider range of lettuce varieties out there, with enough variety in color, texture, and shape to please the most jaded palates.

Basic lettuce types include looseleaf or cutting lettuce (*L. sativa* var. *crispa*), which forms a nonheading rosette of fringed or curled leaves; head lettuce (var. *capitata*), which includes both the crisphead (or cabbage) type and the tender, floppy-headed type known variously as butterhead, bibb, or Boston lettuce; and cos or romaine lettuce (var. *longifolia*), which has tall, cylindrical heads and long oval leaves.

How to Grow

Most varieties of lettuce prefer cool weather and fertile, well-drained garden soil. Reading variety descriptions is important, since different types of lettuce have varying degrees of tolerance to heat, cold, or other growing conditions.

Start seeds in small plugs or cells about 3–4 weeks before transplanting. Fertilize when watering with a solution of fish or seaweed emulsion. If you grow lettuce in a sunny window or cold frame, give the flats partial shade and water regularly to keep soil temperatures cool. When plants are 2–3 weeks old, carefully lift a few of them and check their roots. If the roots have grown to the edge of the plug and started to circle, it's time to transplant. If not, keep checking regularly.

Harden off plants by reducing water and temperatures for

2–3 days before transplanting. Set out seedlings as soon as the ground can be worked in the spring, spacing plants 8–12 in. apart in beds or rows spaced 12–18 in. apart.

You can also direct-seed lettuce, sowing seeds thinly, about 1 in. apart in rows, and lightly covering with ⅛–¼ in. of soil. Water the seedbed after planting if the ground is dry. Thin plants to 8–12 in. apart in the row or bed.

Whether you transplant or direct-seed, try to grow successions of different kinds of lettuce throughout the season, moving from varieties recommended for spring planting to heat-tolerant types like romaine in the summer, and finishing off the season with fall and winter varieties like 'Brune d'Hiver'. One common way to grow lettuce more successfully in hot summer weather is to site the plants in the partial shade of other crops, such as underneath a teepee of pole beans.

Provide a consistent supply of moisture for lettuce as it grows. Fertilize plants by watering with a fish or seaweed emulsion or a compost or manure tea. Don't mulch beds of lettuce, since this can provide a welcome cover for slugs.

Harvest
Cut individual leaves at any time for salad use. Harvest head lettuce before the central crown begins to elongate and the plant prepares to bolt. Gardeners who live in warm climates or those who are growing summer lettuce should select heat-tolerant, bolt-resistant varieties, based on both personal experience and catalog descriptions.

Pests and Diseases
The greatest threat to lettuce for home gardeners comes from nibbling animals like rabbits and woodchucks; erect physical barriers or an electric fence to deal with these interlopers. If slugs are a problem, dust around the plants with sharp diatomaceous earth or fine, dry wood ashes.

Overfertilizing lettuce can result in tip burn on the leaves, though the condition also sometimes indicates a calcium or potassium deficiency in the soil. Lettuce mosaic virus is a seed-borne disease that can cause yellowing or stunted growth in plants; mosaic virus can be spread by aphids, so control them with an insecticidal soap spray if they make an appearance.

■ RECOMMENDED VARIETIES

Looseleaf Lettuce
'Black-Seeded Simpson' (1850) p. 69
Still one of the most popular leaf lettuces, with light green,

crinkly leaves; early, easy to grow, and slow to bolt; heat- and drought-tolerant; excellent for spring and early summer crops; taste is crisp and juicy, never bitter; 40–55 days.

'Bronze Arrow'

An heirloom from California that stands well without bolting in hot weather; large leaves are shaped like an arrowhead, green with a reddish bronze tinge; hardy and adaptable; delicious flavor; 60 days.

'Deer Tongue' (1740s) p. 69

Also known as 'Matchless', this is one of my favorites. The tender green leaves are triangular in shape with a thick midrib, somewhat reminiscent of a deer's tongue; leaves grow in a nice rosette around a 7–9-in. loose, bibb-type head; very tolerant of both heat and cold; 55–65 days. 'Red Deer Tongue' has lovely red-tinged leaves.

'Grandpa Admire's' ('Grandpa's'; 1860s)

Named for George Admire, a Civil War veteran born in 1822. Large, thick leaves are tinged with bronzy red; forms a loose, bibb-type head; resists bolting and remains tender; fine flavor; 45–60 days.

'Oak Leaf' p. 70

A popular variety from at least the 1800s, though Sturtevant lists a reference to an oak-leaved type from 1686. Attractive, medium green, deeply lobed leaves grow upright in a tight rosette; tolerates hot weather and stands well in the garden without becoming bitter; 40–60 days. 'Red Oak Leaf' is very ornamental, with dark red leaves when grown in full sun. 'Royal Oak Leaf' is an improved variety.

Heading Lettuce

'Brune d'Hiver' (1855). A cold-hardy French heirloom with pale green leaves tinged with bronze, turning redder in cold weather; leaf shape is intermediate between bibb and romaine. Compact plants; overwinters with protection and can be fall-planted for spring harvest; 55–60 days (main season); 120 days (fall-planted for spring harvest).

'Hanson' (before 1855)
A very large crisphead type with frilled, yellowish green leaves and a solid, white heart; stands heat well; not recommended for forcing or wintering over; sweet, crisp, and tender; 65–80 days.

'Iceberg' (1894) p. 70
The true 'Iceberg' crisphead is a home garden variety, not the pale generic heads shipped to supermarkets. Compact, medium-large heads have a crisp heart and light green leaves with a waxy bronze fringe; mosaic-resistant and heat-tolerant; does well in the East and mountain areas; 50–85 days.

'Limestone Bibb' ('Bibb'; 1850) p. 71
The first American gourmet lettuce, originally from Kentucky; thick, soft, dark green leaves sometimes tinged with reddish brown; inner leaves blanch golden yellow; best planted in early spring; bolts in hot weather; nice, delicate flavor; 55–75 days.

'Merveille des Quatre Saisons' ('Four Seasons') p. 71
A beautiful French heirloom bibb lettuce; outer leaves are bright burgundy red; tight hearts are pale and creamy; heads are 6–10 in.; very dependable variety that holds flavor in hot weather but will bolt; 55–70 days.

'Mescher' ('Schweitzer's Mescher Bibb') p. 72
A family heirloom that dates back to the 1700s and was brought to the U.S. from Austria sometime after 1900. Small, tight, crisp heads of green leaves ringed with red; extremely cold-hardy; best grown in cool weather; 50 days.

'Speckled' ('Spreckled') p. 73
One of the most beautiful lettuces in the Seed Savers Exchange collection, this variety comes from Mennonite gardeners and has green leaves flecked with maroon. Bibb-type heads are small and firm with soft leaves; center blanches pale yellow; 90 days. A similar, more widely available speckled butterhead is 'Pirat' (p. 72), an improved variety of the old German type (55–65 days).

'Tennis Ball' (before 1804)
A bibb lettuce that Thomas Jefferson grew on his estate at Monticello; forms small to medium-size tight rosettes of light green leaves that pale to yellow-green at the base; very cold-hardy but bolts in hot weather; best for early spring planting; 55 days.

'Tom Thumb' (1830) p. 73
An English heirloom. Small, 5-in.-wide plants produce a miniature butterhead that is about the size of a tennis ball, just the right size for a single serving; leaves are medium green and crumpled; fine, sweet flavor; grows well in cold frames or containers; 48–55 days. The name of this variety is

sometimes used interchangeably with 'Tennis Ball', though Charles Johnson in 1906 lists them as distinct varieties.

Cos (Romaine) Lettuce

'Ballon' ('Balloon'; before 1885)
A large French romaine lettuce that forms a large heart; tender and well-formed leaves; heat-tolerant and cold-hardy; seldom runs to seed; 75 days.

'Paris White Cos' ('Romaine Blonde Marachiere'; before 1868)   p. 74
Medium-size heads are 8–10 in. tall; classic romaine type with light green, slightly savoyed outer leaves that have strong midribs; heart blanches white; great flavor, tender and crisp. Grows well in the North; likes rich soil and lots of water; 50–83 days.

'Rouge d'Hiver' ('Red Winter'; 1840s)   p. 74
Deep reddish brown outer leaves form a loose cylindrical head; inner leaves are green with bronzy red tips; large, upright plants are extremely cold-hardy and also tolerate heat; very ornamental and rather early; 60 days.

Lima Beans. *See* Beans

Mâche. *See* Corn Salad

Melon

Cucumis melo
The government of Turkmenistan recently issued a decree making the second Sunday of August a national holiday celebrating melons. Such a declaration may sound whimsical and even a bit goofy to us in the West, but for centuries melons have played a big part in Turkmen culture and traditions, and people over there take them pretty seriously.

Located in the southernmost part of the former Soviet Union, Turkmenistan lies just north of Iran on the eastern shore of the Caspian Sea. A semiarid land with long, hot summers, the Turkmen climate is ideal for melon-growing. In 1259 the Chinese traveler Tch'ang Te discovered melons, grapes, and pomegranates of excellent quality growing in the region. Around 1519 the Emperor Baber is said to have shed tears while cutting up a Turkmen melon in India after his conquest, its sweet flavor bringing his distant homeland to mind.[32] It's a noble fruit that can inspire such emotion.

As gardeners, we generally distinguish between green-fleshed and orange-fleshed varieties of melon, though the colors in fact can be far more subtle, ranging from an almost whitish yellow-green to salmon pink or deep orange. Botanically, melons are divided into several basic groups: the two most commonly grown types are muskmelons (*C. melo*, Reticulatus group), which have a netted skin when ripe, and casaba or honeydew melons (Inodorus group), which require a long season and have a smooth, yellowish green skin.

How to Grow

Melons like a sunny location and a well-drained sandy loam. In areas with a short growing season, it's best to start plants inside about 3 weeks before transplanting to the garden. Plant seeds directly into individual 2–3-in. peat pots, since melons don't like having their roots disturbed. Melon seeds need warm soil temperatures to germinate (around 75–85°F).

A common mistake is starting seeds too early. Melons should go out to the garden only after all danger of frost has passed and the weather is warm and settled. Starting seeds too early indoors means that your plants will start to sprawl and may become pot-bound — neither situation makes transplanting the tender seedlings any easier. When transplanting to the garden, set out plants 2–3 ft. apart in rows spaced 5–6 ft. apart.

In regions where spring weather is warm and settled, you can direct-seed melons in hills or mounds spaced 6 ft. apart, planting 6–8 seeds per hill and thinning to the best 2–3 plants in the hill. Allow 5–6 ft. between rows to give the melon vines room to spread. Melons are heavy feeders, so mix compost or a well-balanced organic fertilizer into the soil before planting or transplanting melons. Water young plants or transplants with a solution of fish or seaweed emulsion.

After transplanting, or when the direct-seeded plants emerge, you can provide additional heat by spreading a black paper or plastic mulch over the ground and covering plants with a floating row cover material. Remove the row cover when the plants begin to flower.

Keep melon plants well watered until the fruits grow to about the size of a baseball; after this time, don't water at all unless the weather is really dry and the leaves start to wilt in the midday heat. Cutting back on water in this way helps ripen fruits and makes the melons sweeter and more flavorful. Another simple way to encourage ripening and control the spread of plants is to pinch off the fuzzy tips of the vines. Also, examine the plants about a month or so before the end of growing season and remove any small fruits that will never have time to ripen; this concentrates the plant's energy on ripening the more mature fruits.

Harvest

Muskmelons are ripe when their skin becomes well netted and turns buff yellow, and when the fruit "slips," or separates from the vine easily with slight pressure from your thumb. Honeydew or casaba melons and the true (French) cantaloupes do not slip from the vine; they will have a yellowish skin when ripe, and the blossom end of the fruit will soften or crack and smell sweet. Harvest by cutting the stem.

■ RECOMMENDED VARIETIES

'Banana' (1883)

An unusual melon that has 14–18-in.-long, slender fruits that look like an overgrown banana; smooth, creamy yellow skin; flesh is salmon orange to orange in color, soft and juicy; flavor is strongly sweet (too sweet for some tastes); 80–100 days.

'Casaba, Golden Beauty' p. 75

U. P. Hedrick in his *Curcurbits of New York* (1937) says that the casaba melon is native to Asia Minor and named after the town of Kassabeh, near Smyrna. The type has been grown in the U.S. since around 1850 and is popular in California and the Southwest. 'Golden Beauty' is one of the older varieties of casaba, with a tough, wrinkled skin that matures to a golden yellow color; fruits are spheroid and average 7–8 lb.; flesh is thick, white, and aromatic with a spicy flavor; fruit keeps well for months after harvest. Needs a long season; well adapted to hot, dry regions of the country; 110–120 days.

'Collective Farmwoman' p. 75

This fine heirloom probably originated in the Ukraine and is a popular variety on the Crimean peninsula; once you grow it, you'll know why. Fruits are 6-in. globes that have buff yellow skin mottled with green when ripe; flesh is pale green and very sweet, firm, and juicy. An excellent variety for northern gardens and one of the real jewels in the Seed Savers Exchange Russian Seed Collection. Not yet available through seed companies, but SSE plans to offer it for sale; 80–85 days.

'Golden Champlain' (1923)

An early-maturing muskmelon developed by H. J. Walrath as a cross between 'Admiral Togo' and 'Lake Champlain'.

Medium-size fruits are globular with buff yellow skin mottled with green and coarse, open netting; flesh is golden yellow and moderately juicy and sweet; excellent for short-season areas; 75 days.

'Hale's Best' (before 1923) p. 76
A popular melon that I. D. Hale found being grown by a Japanese market grower near Brawley, California. Fruits are short oval and uniform in shape, weighing 2–3 lb.; skin is dark green mottled with yellow at maturity and heavily netted; flesh is thick, solid, and salmon-orange; aromatic and very good, sweet flavor. Plants produce heavily and are resistant to drought and mildew; 75–88 days.

'Hearts of Gold' (1917)
Developed by Roland Morrill of Benton Harbor, Michigan. Fruits are nearly globular, 3–4 lb., with dark green skin and heavy netting; flesh is deep orange, thick and firm; moderately juicy, tender, and sweet; very good flavor and aroma. Plants are vigorous, productive, and blight-resistant; 90 days.

'Honey Dew' (1915)
According to Hedrick, this popular melon may be the 'White Antibes' listed by the French seed house of Vilmorin-Andrieux in the 1880s. Fruits are broadly oval, nearly globular, 5–7 lb.; the smooth, hard skin turns from yellowish green to ivory yellow at maturity; flesh is pale green, very sweet, crisp, and juicy. A late variety that, like other honeydews or casabas, prefers a warm, dry climate; 95–115 days. Several other varieties derived from 'Honey Dew' are also available.

'Honey Rock' ('Sugar Rock')
Developed before 1920 by F. W. Richardson near Hicksville, Ohio; an All-America Selection in 1933. Fruits are globular and ribbed, 3–4 lb., with coarse, heavy netting; skin is gray-green turning a pale cream color at maturity; flesh is thick, sweet, firm, and salmon-orange. Vigorous plants produce 5–7 fruits and are resistant to fusarium wilt; good for northern areas; 82–87 days.

'Jenny Lind' (before 1846) p. 76
A nice little heirloom muskmelon, perhaps originally from Armenia, that has become popular again in recent years. Named for the singer Jenny Lind, who was billed as "the Swedish Nightingale." Fruits are small, 1–2 lb., and somewhat flattened, with a small turban or button on the blossom end; skin is dull brownish orange mottled with green; flesh is light green, soft, and juicy with a sweet flavor. Vines are fairly

short and spindly, but prolific and disease-resistant; early-maturing, good for northern areas; 70–85 days.

'Nutmeg' (1830s)
One of the oldest named melons; listed by Fearing Burr in 1863 as a long-cultivated variety; fruits are small, 2–3 lb., with a flattened oval shape; skin is dull yellowish brown mottled with green; medium netting; flesh is light green, soft, and juicy; very sweet, spicy, and aromatic; produces early and is good for northern areas; 80 days.

'Perfection' (1892)
Hedrick says 'Perfection' comes from Chenango County, New York; an early supplier claimed it was discovered growing as a chance seedling in a field near Boston. Fruits are nearly globular, 3–4 lb.; skin is deep orange mottled with green and heavily netted; flesh is salmon-orange, soft, juicy, very sweet, and aromatic. Matures early; 75 days.

'Rocky Ford' ('Eden Gem'; 1881) p. 77
Developed by J. W. Eastwood in Colorado, this melon is really the grandchild of 'Nutmeg', having been selected from Burpee's 'Netted Gem'. Fruits are globular, 2–3 lb., with dark green skin mottled with yellowish bronze and with heavy netting; flesh is green, fine-grained, firm, and juicy with a good, sweet flavor and aroma. Plants are productive and rust-resistant; 85–95 days.

'Vedrantais' ('Charentais')
Like 'Honey Dew' or 'Casaba', the variety name 'Charentais' actually describes a type of melon, in this case the "true" or French orange-fleshed cantaloupe. 'Vedrantais' is one open-pollinated variety now available, with the characteristic smooth, gray-green skin that turns creamy yellow at maturity. Another way to tell ripeness is to look at the long-stemmed leaf that attaches to the vine next to the fruit; when the fruit is ripe, this leaf is pale. Fruits average about 2 lb., and flesh is deep orange with a fine, sweet taste. Aromatic and juicy, the French serve this melon chilled, halved, and filled with port. Ripens early and is good for short-season areas; 75–80 days.

Mustard and Oriental Greens
Brassica juncea and *Brassica rapa*
Part of the large cabbage or mustard family (Brassicaceae), which also includes cabbage, kale, turnips, and many other

garden vegetables, mustard greens are native to eastern Asia and have been cultivated there for some 2,500 years. Ranging in taste from mild to peppery, hot, and pungent, mustard leaves make a piquant addition to salads when harvested young. Older, larger leaves are excellent for steaming or in stir-fries.

Leaf mustard *(Brassica juncea)* should not be confused with those mustards grown primarily for their small seeds, which are used either whole or ground to make the familiar condiment we spread on sandwiches and hot dogs; these seed types usually fall under one of two species: the brown, yellow, or white mustards *(B. hirta)* or black mustard *(B. nigra)*.

A few leafy vegetables that are closely related to mustard frequently appear in seed catalogs, either under the name "mustard" or, sometimes, "Oriental greens." Mizuna is one mild-flavored vegetable that fits this description; komatsuna (also known as "mustard spinach") is another. Both are members of the species *Brassica rapa,* as are the heading or semi-heading forms we know as bok choi, napa, or Chinese cabbage. Grown and used in much the same way as other mustards, they are included below.

How to Grow

Mustard grows best in cool weather and can be direct-seeded in early to mid-spring or in mid- to late summer for a fall crop. Sow seeds thinly, ¼–½ in. deep in rows spaced 18 in. apart. Thin young plants to 6 in. apart in the row; larger varieties like 'Mizuna' and 'Southern Giant Curled' should be thinned to 8 in. apart; Chinese cabbage should be thinned to 12 in. apart.

Spring-sown Chinese cabbage tends to bolt if nighttime temperatures dip below 50°F over several days; for this reason, it's best to wait until after the last spring frost date to plant or transplant. For transplanting, start seeds inside in cells about 4 weeks before the last spring frost date.

An even better idea is to direct-seed and thin Chinese cabbage in the summer as a fall crop. Flea beetles adore this vegetable, and spring-sown crops can have leaves that are absolutely riddled with holes. Although Chinese cabbage can be a difficult crop to grow organically in the spring, by late summer or fall the insect pests that bother it have generally run their course and pose less of a threat.

Harvest

Pick the side leaves of mustard plants first, being careful not to disturb the central crown. For salad use, use the hot-flavored mustards when the leaves are 4–6 in. in length; larger leaves are generally hotter and more pungent and should be

picked for steaming or stir-fries. Red- or purple-leaved mustard greens are particularly good as part of a spring or fall
mesclun (mixed salad) planting with other greens; harvest by
cutting leaves at least 1 in. above the ground to encourage a
later harvest.

Chinese cabbage heads harvested in the fall will keep for
several weeks in the root cellar if they are trimmed and
wrapped in newspaper.

Pests and Diseases
Place a floating row cover over the bed before plants emerge
or after transplanting, to protect mustard and Chinese cabbage from flea beetles. Dig in the sides of the row cover and
anchor them with metal clothes hangers or rocks. Using a
row cover and planting in the summer for a fall harvest are
the two best ways to avoid insect damage, though rotenone
and pyrethrum dust can be applied if necessary to control
infestations.

To prevent other problems, rotate crops regularly and do
not plant mustard or Chinese cabbage in a place where another member of the cabbage family has grown during the previous year.

■ RECOMMENDED VARIETIES

'Michihili' (*Brassica rapa*, Pekinensis group; 1870s) p. 77
This classic variety is widely available and accounts for much
of the Chinese cabbage grown for market in the U.S.; 14–24-
in.-tall cylindrical heads are 4–6 in. in diameter and look
something like a romaine lettuce; green outer leaves surround
a blanched white interior; good for stir-fries and pickling;
plant in mid- to late summer for a fall crop and to avoid insect damage; 70 days.

'Mizuna' ('Kyona'; *B. rapa*, Japonica group) p. 78
A Japanese green that produces a rosette of narrow, deeply
cut leaves on thin white stalks; plants grow 12–24 in. high
and will keep producing leaves over a long season if kept harvested; cold-hardy and also stands summer heat if kept well
watered; mild-tasting leaves are good for salads and stir-fries;
very ornamental; 40–65 days.

'Osaka Purple' p. 78
One of the prettiest mustards, with rounded, savoyed, dark
purple leaves veined with white; harvest leaves for salad use
at 4–6 in. or when they grow larger for steaming; excellent
as part of a mesclun salad planting. Flavor of the young
leaves is medium hot and pungent; 70–80 days.

'Red Giant' ('Giant Red') p. 79
Similar to 'Osaka Purple', but plants can grow even larger, with purple-red and green savoyed leaves and white midribs; very ornamental. Slow-bolting and winter-hardy; recommended for fall crops or even winter crops in mild climates. Harvest for salads or light cooking; moderate to strongly pungent flavor; 90 days.

'Southern Giant Curled' (1740s)
Vigorous, upright plants grow 18–24 in. tall and have large, bright green leaves with crumpled, frilled edges; flavor is mildly pungent; cold-tolerant; good for either spring or summer planting; an old favorite that's still widely available; 40–60 days.

'Tendergreen' (*B. rapa,* Chinensis group)
Also known as 'Komatsuna' or 'Mustard Spinach'; plants grow 10 in. high with a 16–22 in. spread; leaves are flat, smooth, oblong, and dark, glossy green with paler green midribs; fast-growing and slow-bolting; tolerates cold, heat, and drought; mildly pungent taste is somewhere between mustard and spinach; flower shoots are also edible. Long harvest period; plant after last spring frost date to prevent premature bolting; 21–50 days.

Okra

Abelmoschus esculentus
Although associated with southern cuisine, okra grows well in other regions of the country, too, and deserves wider cultivation as both an edible and an ornamental plant. Its straw-colored blossoms have violet-brown centers and resemble those of hollyhock, mallow, or hibiscus; in fact, until recently okra's botanical name was *Hibiscus esculentus*.

Okra probably originated in northeast Africa, and the plants have been found growing wild along the banks of the White Nile.[33] The actual name "okra," though, comes from West Africa, from the Ashanti word *nkruma*. The vegetable we know today as okra is the slender, cone-shaped seed capsule, which is picked and eaten when it is immature and tender. Many varieties have slightly ridged seedpods, and when cut horizontally the pieces look like little stars. When okra cooks down it acts as a thickener for soups or stews. In fact, the plant is also commonly called "gumbo" (from the Bantu word *ki-ngombo*), and no Creole cook worth her salt would make that dish without adding plenty of okra. Other good ways to use the small pods are to batter-fry or pickle them whole, or slice and stir-fry them along with other meats and vegetables.

How to Grow

To grow well, okra needs warm, humid weather and full sun, which is why it grows so well in the South. To grow an early crop, start seeds indoors, 4–6 weeks before the last spring frost date, in individual cells or pots, planting 3 seeds to a pot. (Do not start in flats, since okra doesn't like to have its roots disturbed.) Keep soil temperatures warm (80–90°F) until the plants emerge. Transplant seedlings to the garden after all danger of frost is past, setting out plants 12–18 in. apart in rows spaced 24–36 in. apart. Work some bonemeal into the planting holes when setting out seedlings. Mulch around the plants with black paper or plastic, or cover them with plastic cloches or a floating row fabric to provide additional heat early in the season.

In milder climates, where spring weather is warm and settled, direct-seed okra after the last spring frost date, sowing seeds ½–1 in. deep and 2–3 in. apart in a warm, well-drained soil in rows spaced 24 in. apart. When plants are 6 in. tall, thin to 12–18 in. apart in the row, depending on whether the variety is dwarf or tall-growing.

Harvest

Pick okra pods when they are young and tender and about 3–4 in. long; plants will keep producing if you keep them picked. Harvest any older pods and shell them for their unripe seeds, which can be cooked like peas.

Pests and Diseases

Okra is normally a trouble-free crop, but it occasionally can suffer from either fusarium wilt or downy mildew. Practicing good crop rotation should control downy mildew. If fusarium wilt causes plants to yellow and die, start future okra seedlings indoors in sterilized potting soil and transplant them to clean soil in the garden; do not rotate plantings of okra with other crops susceptible to fusarium wilt, such as peas or members of the nightshade family (tomatoes, eggplants, peppers, potatoes, etc.).

▪ RECOMMENDED VARIETIES

'Cow Horn' p. 79

Vigorous plants are 6–7 ft. tall and produce lots of green, 10–12 in., ribbed and spiny pods that are twisted like a cow's horn; pods remain tender even when long; good, old-fashioned okra flavor; 55–65 days.

'Louisiana Green Velvet' (1930s)   p. 80
Plants grow to 6 ft. or more; pods are light green, slender, spineless, and 6–7 in. long; produces heavily throughout season; pods retain color when processed; 57–65 days.

'Red Okra' ('Purple Okra')   p. 80
Bushy 3–4-ft. plants are tinged with red on leaves and stems; produces lots of 6–7 in. pods that turn from pink to bright red; heat- and drought-tolerant; pods are good when picked small and hold their color when processed; very ornamental; 55–65 days.

'Star of David'   p. 81
A variety that hails from Israel. Unbranching plants grow 6–8 ft. tall and have a purple color on the top of leaf petioles and major leaf veins; pods grow 5–9 in. long and have medium spines, but are best picked small for eating. Distinctive, strong okra flavor; produces well throughout season; 60–70 days.

ONIONS
Allium cepa and *Allium fistulosum*

There's an old legend that says that when Satan stepped out of the Garden of Eden after Adam and Eve fell from grace, garlic sprang up where he planted his left foot, and onions grew where his right foot fell.[34] If that were true, we would all owe the devil a great debt of gratitude. Onions have been cultivated throughout recorded history, and, although no obvious precursor to the common bulb or globe onion (*Allium cepa,* Cepa group) has ever been found growing in the wild, they probably originated in either western or central Asia.

The ancient Egyptians developed a mild-tasting onion that persons of all classes ate in quantity, and records exist of onions having been purchased as food for the laborers who built the Great Pyramids at Giza.[35] Long before European explorers arrived in America, most of the various shapes and colors of globe onions had become well established, and the cultivation of this important vegetable spread quickly with the arrival of settlers to the New World.

When we hear the word "onion," we automatically think of the common globe type with its papery outer skin that's colored yellow, brown, white, or deep reddish purple. Although the hollow leaf stalks of many onion varieties can be harvested young and used as "scallions" or green onions, one type of plant specifically grown for this purpose is the non-bulbing perennial, *Allium fistulosum*, commonly called bunching onion, ciboule, or Welsh onion. Although it was introduced to Britain as early as 1629, the Welsh onion has nothing to do with Wales; the plant is a native of Siberia and gets its name from the old German word *walsch,* meaning "foreign" or "alien."[36]

Still other types of onions are little known among American consumers but well loved by both home gardeners and epicures. The Egyptian onion (*A. cepa,* Proliferum group) — also known as topset, tree, or walking onion — forms small bulblets (also called bulbils) on the top of its stalk instead of a large underground bulb. Multiplier onions (*A. cepa,* Aggregatum group) form several underground bulbs from a single planted bulb and are better known as either shallots or potato onions.

Common (Globe) Onions

(*Allium cepa,* Cepa group)

How to Grow

Globe onions require a long season to grow bulbs from seed, and are often sold as small planting onions, or "sets." However, even in areas with relatively short growing seasons it is possible to grow onions from seed, and mature bulbs grown from seed tend to be of a higher quality and less disease-prone than those grown from sets.

Globe onions require a light, fertile, well-drained soil that is rich in organic matter. Prepare the seedbed if possible in the previous fall by tilling or working in plenty of organic matter, which will break down over the winter. Till and rake the seedbed again in the early spring as soon as the ground can be worked; at the same time, work in some bone meal and wood ashes, or a balanced organic fertilizer rich in phosphorus and potassium. Sow onion seeds ¼ in. deep, 2–3 seeds per inch, in rows spaced 12–18 in. apart; gently firm the soil over the seeds. Thin young plants to 3–4 in. apart in the row, depending on the variety's mature bulb size.

Many gardeners prefer to start onions indoors in mid-February to mid-March, about 4–6 weeks before transplanting them to the garden. In this case, sow seeds in flats ¼ in. deep, 4 seeds per inch, in narrow rows. When the seedlings are about 2 in. tall, water with a liquid fish or seaweed emulsion. Clip the tops back to 4–5 in. in height if necessary. Before setting out, harden off the onion seedlings for 5 days, bringing the flats in at night. Water the flats before transplanting and gently pull the clumps apart to separate and plant the seedlings, 4 in. apart in the row or bed.

Onions are shallow-rooted and require lots of water to form good-sized bulbs — about 1 in. per week. While the leaves are growing, water plants with a solution of liquid fish or seaweed emulsion to provide nitrogen and trace minerals. Weed religiously, because onion plants don't like competition; weed carefully, though, because you can easily damage the shallow root systems of onions. To help suppress weeds and conserve soil moisture, lay down an organic mulch around the plants.

Before ordering a particular onion variety from a seed supplier, try to ascertain whether it is a long-day or a short-day variety. This is important because onions differ in the length of day they need to form bulbs; in the summer, gardens in the North have a longer daylength, or *photoperiod,* than gardens in the South. Long-day onions form bulbs when the maximum length of day is greater than 15–16 hours; short-day varieties form bulbs when the maximum photoperiod is greater than 11–12 hours. Short-day varieties are usually recommended for gardens south of latitude 38° north; long-day varieties for regions north of that line.

Harvest

Globe onions are ready to harvest when most of the tops have begun to wither or fall over. Many gardeners bend over the tops of onions by hand at this time to hasten harvesting and form good outer skins for long-term storage; this technique works well with some varieties, but can adversely affect the keeping quality of other onions.

Pull up mature onion bulbs during the first period of settled, dry weather and let them cure under cover in partial shade for one or two days before bringing them under cover to complete drying on racks or screens. When the tops have dried completely, clip them back and store the onions in mesh bags in a cool, dry place. Use any onions with thick necks first, since they do not keep as well. Different varieties have different keeping qualities, so check plant descriptions before buying.

Globe onions are biennials and will form a seed stalk if stored over the winter and replanted in the spring, covering the top of the bulbs with ½ in. of soil. Save only the seeds you can use or share next season, since onion seed has a much lower germination rate after only 1 year of normal storage.

Pests and Diseases

Most fungal diseases and insect pests can be controlled through good crop rotation, not planting onions in the same spot over a 3- or 4-year period. Onions grown from sets seem more prone to some diseases, those raised from seed to others; separate any onion seedbeds from areas where you have planted sets.

If weevils or maggots attack the onions, pull up and destroy any affected plants and sprinkle wood ashes or diatomaceous earth around the remaining bulbs.

■ RECOMMENDED VARIETIES

Red- and Purple-Skinned Onions

'Red Torpedo' ('Italian Red Bottle') p. 81
As its name suggests, this beautiful onion has a bottle-shaped bulb that is 6–8 in. long, 3 in. in diameter, and averaging 1 lb. The outer skin is deep purple-red; soft, bright red flesh; spicy, tangy flavor; short-term storage, best for fresh use. An intermediate daylength type that will grow in the North but is recommended for southern areas; 95–120 days. This variety resembles the type described by Vilmorin-Andrieux as 'Ox Horn' or 'Spindle-Shaped' in the 1880s.

'Red Wethersfield' (ca. 1800)
Named for the town of Wethersfield, Connecticut, where it perhaps originated and where it was grown extensively for market in the 19th century. In 1863 Fearing Burr described it as one of the most prominent commercial varieties, and it is still widely grown today.

Bulbs are flattened globes with dark purple-red skin; firm, purplish white flesh; good, strong flavor; medium storage. A long-day variety best for northern gardens; 100–115 days.

'Southport Red Globe' (1873)
Large, deep globes with glossy purple-red skin; pinkish white, firm flesh; pungent flavor; medium storage. Long-day variety for northern areas; 100–120 days.

Yellow- and Brown-Skinned Onions

'Ailsa Craig Exhibition' p. 82
A huge, mild-flavored Spanish-type onion long favored by British gardeners and grown by them for garden shows (hence the name). Bulbs are large and round (to 3 lb. or more) with straw yellow skins; white, sweet flesh; medium storage. Grows well in northern regions like a long-day type, but may be intermediate or daylength-neutral; matures early and does not require a long, hot growing season to form big bulbs; 105–110 days.

'Australian Brown'
Listed by Charles Johnson in 1906 as a variety grown in the U.S. Medium-size flattened globes have dark reddish brown skin and firm, pale yellow flesh; very pungent flavor; medium to long storage. Presumably an intermediate or short-day variety; grows well in California; early; 100 days (spring-sown), 250 days (fall-sown and overwintered).

'Yellow Ebenezer' (1906)
Introduced to the U.S. from Japan. Medium-size bulbs are flattened globes about 3 in. in diameter, with thick, brownish skins; flesh yellowish white with a pungent flavor; medium storage. Early-maturing, long-day variety recommended for northern areas; 100 days.

'Yellow Globe Danvers' (before 1850)
An American variety, presumably first grown around Danvers, Massachusetts, and still a popular type. Vilmorin-Andrieux mentions that it was introduced to France around 1850. Medium-size, slightly flattened globes; necks very thin; skin coppery to golden brown; flesh white and fine-grained; good, strong flavor; long storage. Early-maturing, long-day variety for northern areas; not recommended for fall sowing; 100–110 days.

White-Skinned Onions

'Southport White Globe'
Listed by Charles Johnson in 1906 as being grown in the U.S. under this name and as 'Silver Ball' and 'White Rocca'; one of three similar 'Southport' or 'Rocca' onion varieties that have red, yellow, or white skins. 'White Globe' is still a popular market variety and widely available.

   Medium-size, deep globes with papery silver-white skins; very firm, white, fine-grained flesh; holds white skin color well if dried in partial shade; medium keeper. Lawrence Hollander of CRESS describes the flavor as nice and fairly mild, though more strong-tasting than other white onions. Young plants can be pulled up and used as scallions. Long-day variety recommended for northern areas; 65 days (for scallions), 110–120 days (for mature bulbs).

'White Portugal' ('Silverskin'; before 1800)
Medium-large flattened onion with a clear silver-white skin; firm, fine-grained white flesh; mild, sweet flavor; good slicer; medium storage. An early-maturing, short-day type that does well in southern regions but can also be grown in the North; 95 days.

Bunching (Welsh) Onions

(Allium fistulosum) p. 82

Bunching onions are perennial plants that are grown for their stalks and used like scallions. The plants divide and multiply at the base but do not form underground bulbs like common onions. Extremely hardy and evergreen in most regions, bunching onions can withstand temperatures as low as 0°F. They grow well in a sunny, sheltered location and make a good planting in a bed outside or to one side of the vegetable garden proper. In areas that have long, hot summers, bunching onions do better when planted in partial shade.

Plant either in early spring for a summer crop or in early autumn for a harvest of young shoots the following spring. Sow seeds ½ in. deep, 2–4 seeds per inch, in rows spaced 10 in. apart. Thin plants to 10 in. apart in the bed or row. Water and weed like other perennials or garden greens. Bunching onions can also be started or grown to maturity in containers; if transplanting to the garden, trim the roots to a length of ½ in. and cut back the tops.

These onions produce yellowish white flower heads; cut most of these back unless you plan to save seed from one or two plants for planting the following year. After plants are 3–4 years old, divide and replant clumps as necessary.

In regions with very cold winters, select the hardiest varieties of bunching onions and mulch beds before the ground freezes, or dig up some of the plants and transfer them to cold frames or containers for the winter, replanting them outdoors in the spring.

Harvest
Begin harvesting the stems of spring-sown bunching onions in summer; stalks from summer or fall plantings will be ready the following spring. Welsh onions have a flavor resembling chives, but stronger and more pungent. Once established, bunching onions will produce from early spring throughout the season. When harvesting, leave a few onions in each clump so the onions will divide and replenish themselves.

■ RECOMMENDED VARIETIES

'Evergreen White Bunching' ('He-Shi-Ko'; 1880s) p. 83
The most popular and widely grown perennial bunching onion; plants produce clusters of 4–9 slender, silvery white stalks, 12–14 in. long; white, pungent flesh. Nonbulbing and slow-bolting; very cold-hardy, overwinters well; resistant to thrips, smut, and pink root; plant in early spring or fall; 60–80 days (spring-sown), 120 days (fall-sown).

'Red Welsh Bunching'
Burr lists 'Red Welsh' in 1863 as the common form of Welsh onion. Plants produce clusters of 2–3 stalks that are 12–14 in. long with light green leaves; nonbulbing; extremely hardy; sow in either spring or fall; good in soups and salads; 65–70 days.

Egyptian (Topset) Onions

(Allium cepa, Proliferum group) p. 83
Egyptian onions (also known as topset, tree, or walking onions) form several smallish bulbs underground, with the chief difference between these onions and other multiplier types being the clusters of reddish, nut-sized bulblets (bulbils) that the plants form every summer at the top of each seed stalk.

How to Grow
Like bunching onions, Egyptian onions are quite cold-hardy and can be treated as a perennial, either planted to one side of the vegetable garden or in an ornamental bed or border.

Once Egyptian onions have become established, they will form their topsetting bulblets at the top of each seed stalk. Separate the clusters and replant the bulblets at any time from late summer through late fall. (These bulblets will keep for a while if you want to save them for planting later or give some away to gardening friends.)

Plant bulblets 4 in. apart in rows spaced 12 in. apart. Even if you don't get around to harvesting and replanting the bulblets, the onion stalks will simply bend toward the ground and take root anyway, increasing next year's planting all by themselves. You can also divide and replant clumps of Egyptian onions as needed.

Jan Blüm of Seeds Blüm in Boise, Idaho, describes an easy method of blanching Egyptian onions for later harvest: Plant the bulblets at the bottom of a trench about 9 in. deep; then, as the bulblets send up shoots, gradually fill in the trench with soil. This produces long, white, solid lower stems like the bottom part of a scallion.

Harvest
Lift clumps with a garden fork and separate the onions, taking some or all to use like scallions; replant any you don't take for kitchen use. Bulblets can be harvested and used in pickling other vegetables. The underground bulbs have a very strong flavor but can be used sparingly in hearty soups and stews.

■ RECOMMENDED VARIETIES

'Catawissa Onion'

A hardy, vigorous strain from Canada, listed by Vilmorin-Andrieux in 1885. The authors differentiate between 'Catawissa' and the common Egyptian onion by its height (to 30 in.) and the tendency of its topsetting bulblets to send out little green shoots even before they are detached or planted underground. Stalks produce 3–6 topset bulblets; 125 days (spring-planted), 250 days (fall-planted).

'McCullar's White Topset'

A rare heirloom variety from Missouri that produces clusters of 1-in. or larger white bulbs below ground level; harvest bulbs as well as the 20-in. green stalks; topsetting bulblets are greenish white. Cold-hardy and vigorous; very productive if clumps are periodically thinned or divided; 120 days (spring-planted), 250 days (fall-planted).

Multiplier (Shallots and Potato) Onions

(Allium cepa, Aggregatum group)

Like garlic, multiplier onions form a cluster of underground bulbs from each bulb planted. Also like garlic, it can take a few years to adapt these onions to your own garden, climate, soil, and growing conditions. Once established, though, shallots and potato onions will improve in size and quality, and their bulbs can be replanted year after year.

How to Grow

To start from seed, sow seeds in early to mid-spring, ½ in. deep and 1 in. apart in beds or rows spaced 12–18 in. apart. Harvest bulbs in summer and dry on racks and screens. Select and save the biggest and best-looking bulbs for replanting in the fall, using the rest for cooking.

Plant multiplier onion bulbs at the same time as other hardy bulbs like garlic or Jerusalem artichoke, before the first hard frosts. Plant the individual bulbs 6 in. apart in the bed or row, and just deep enough so that the tip lies even with the surface of the soil. Spread a few inches of mulch over the bulbs. The following spring, the plants will send up leaves; remove any seed stalks that happen to form, to focus the plants' energy into forming bulbs.

Multiplier onions don't require quite as much fussing or fertility as globe onions, but watering regularly and growing them on well-drained fertile soil does help produce larger bulbs. Planting small bulbs will generally produce a cluster of

1–2 larger bulbs; planting large individual bulbs can produce as many as 10–12 bulbs per plant.

Harvest
Harvest and dry bulbs as described in the growing information above. Store bulbs as you would globe onions, inside a mesh bag in a cool, dry location.

■ RECOMMENDED VARIETIES

'Odetta's White Shallot' (before 1900)
Family heirloom from Hartford, Kansas, introduced in 1985 by Southern Exposure Seed Exchange. Widely adapted; drought-tolerant. Forms nests of pearly white bulbs that average 1 in. in diameter; white flesh has a mild, delicate flavor. Thin, short green tops; plants can be pulled and used like scallions. Bulbs good for pickling; medium to long storage; 120 days (from spring-sown seed), 250 days (from fall-planted bulbs).

'Yellow Potato Onion' ('Hill Onion', 'Mother Onion', 'Pregnant Onion'; before 1886) p. 84
Forms clusters of 5 or more underground bulbs that are 3 in. in diameter; yellow skins and white flesh tinged with purple; flavor is strong but not hot. Plants are drought-tolerant and resistant to pink root; bulbs are winter-hardy. A widely adapted variety, but not recommended for Florida and southern Texas. Plants can be pulled and used as green bunching onions in the spring. Small- to medium-size bulbs keep for 8–12 months in good storage conditions; 120 days (from spring-sown seed), 250 days (from fall-planted bulbs).

Parsley

Petroselinum crispum
Arguably the most useful of all garden herbs, until recent years parsley has been underused as a seasoning in American cooking and overused as a garnish. While there's nothing wrong with a curly green sprig on the side of the plate, parsley deserves a more prominent role in our cuisine. The leaves are rich in iron and potassium as well as beta-carotene and vitamins A, C, and E; in fact, we'd probably be better off eating the parsley garnish than some of the omelets and alfredo sauces it adorns.

A native of the Mediterranean region, the two basic leaf types — plain and curled — have been known at least since

Roman times. Although both types can be used in the same way, most cooks today favor the plain, flat-leaved Italian parsley for its stronger flavor and use the curled-leaf form more for garnishing.

Root parsley (*P. crispum* var. *tuberosum*) is another old type that forms long, white, tapered roots. Grown like carrots or parsnips, the roots can be eaten raw or cooked as a savory fall vegetable.

How to Grow

Parsley seed germinates very slowly, with plants taking 3–4 weeks to emerge from the soil. To hasten germination, soak seed for a day or so before planting. Sow thinly, ¼ in. deep, in rows spaced 12–18 in. apart. For a continuous supply, sow once in early to mid-spring and again in midsummer.

Mature parsley plants are quite frost-hardy and can overwinter even in cold winter areas if given adequate mulch protection. In early spring, fertilize overwintered rows of parsley with compost or dried manure and cut back old stalks to encourage lots of new growth. You can also pot up parsley in the fall and bring it inside for winter use.

Parsley transplants well, and can be sown in either small flats or individual cells. If possible, place the planted (unwatered) flat in a large, sealed plastic freezer bag and set in the freezer for 1–3 days of chilling. This will help speed up germination. Remove the bag from the freezer but don't remove the flat from the bag until the plants have begun to germinate. Water and place under fluorescent lights or in a sunny window. Transplant seedlings about 4 in. apart in the row or bed.

Since parsley is a biennial, it will go to seed in the second year after sowing if you overwinter it. This, as well as its ornamental qualities, makes parsley a good candidate for a permanent bed or border in regions where it can overwinter and self-seed to produce new plants.

Root parsley needs a more fertile, well-worked soil than leaf varieties. Direct-seed like other parsleys, but thin young plants once or twice as you would carrots, to stand 6–8 in. apart in the row. Root parsley does not transplant well. Plan your planting so that roots will mature around the time of the first fall frosts.

Harvest

Cut leaves for fresh use at any time throughout the season. Parsley leaves also dry and freeze well for winter use.

Harvest root parsley in the fall or overwinter in the garden under several inches of mulch. Store in a root cellar like carrots, in a box of moistened sand or sawdust.

■ RECOMMENDED VARIETIES

'Gigante d'Italia' ('Giant Italian'; *P. crispum* var. *neapolitanum*) p. 84
An heirloom variety from northern Italy. Plants are bushy and grow 2–3 ft. high in good soil, producing lots of very large, shiny, deep green, flat leaves; sweet, rich parsley flavor is great for cooking or fresh seasoning; 75–80 days.

'Hamburg Root Parsley' (*P. crispum* var. *tuberosum*) p. 85
The standard old root parsley, known since at least the 16th century in Germany. Plant produces plain, deeply cut, dark green leaves that can be snipped and used like other parsleys. Roots are white and tapered, about 2 in. in diameter and 8–10 in. long; can be grown in any fertile, loose soil that grows good carrots or parsnips. Roots store well in a root cellar or overwintered with mulch protection; 85–95 days. A few improved varieties are also available, including 'Short Sugar', which has stumpy, 4-in.-long roots for gardens with more compacted or clayey soil.

'Moss Curled'
This variety is definitely similar, if not identical to the type Burr describes in 1863 as 'Dwarf Curled'. Plants are vigorous and compact, to 12 in. high, and bear very dark green, finely cut leaves that are so finely curled they resemble tufts of moss; flavor is more subtle than flat-leaved parsleys. Still popular and widely grown; very ornamental when planted in a bed or border; 75–85 days.

Parsnip

Pastinaca sativa

An old English proverb holds that, "Fine words butter no parsnips." The English hold this sweet-flavored root vegetable in high esteem; in fact, I once saw a picture of a whopping, 28-inch-long parsnip that had been grown in a section of clay piping at the Royal Botanic Gardens at Kew.

Parsnips are native to Europe, but they grow wild as an escape in many other parts of the world, including North America, where they were introduced by colonists in 1609.[37] Logically, the parsnip should have become popular and widely cultivated in southern gardens, since it has a long growing season. However, the sweet flavor of the white, tapered roots develops only after a hard frost, so parsnips have instead become a favorite among cold-climate gardeners. One of the hardiest vegetables, parsnips overwinter easily under a blanket of mulch and can freeze solid without losing any of their sweetness and flavor the following spring; in fact, some people feel that spring-dug parsnips are even sweeter and better-tasting than fall-harvested roots.

How to Grow
Parsnips grow best in an average garden soil that is loose and deeply worked. If your soil is heavy or shallow, try growing the crop in raised beds. Soil that is too rich causes parsnips to fork or develop hairy rootlets.

Direct-seed in early to mid-spring for fall harvest. Sow seeds ½ in. deep and 1 in. apart in rows spaced 18–24 in. apart. Seeds germinate slowly, in about 3 weeks. Keep the seedbed moist and weeded until plants emerge. Thin young plants to 4 in. apart in the row.

In areas with mild winters, plant parsnips in autumn for a spring harvest.

Harvest
Dig or fork up the long roots gently rather than trying to pull them out of the ground. Wait until after cold fall weather sets in to harvest, since parsnips develop their characteristic sweet flavor only after a hard frost. Plan to harvest some of the roots in the fall, leaving the rest of the crop in the ground over the winter underneath a blanket of straw or leaves to prevent frost-heaving.

Harvest overwintered parsnips early in the spring, before the plants begin to grow again. Trim and store any excess in the refrigerator, freezer, or root cellar.

Parsnips are biennials and will send up a large seed stalk in their second season. If you want to save them for seed, dig up overwintered roots in the spring and replant them 12 in. apart. Parsnip seed only remains viable for 1 year under normal storage conditions.

■ RECOMMENDED VARIETIES

'Hollow Crown' (1850) p. 85
Still the most widely grown commercial variety. Long, smooth, 10–15-in.-long white roots are uniformly tapered, 3 in. in diameter, and have few if any hairy side roots; flesh is white, sweet, tender, and fine-grained; extremely frost-hardy and a good winter keeper; 95–135 days. A few improved strains are also available.

'Offenham'
An early, heavy-yielding heirloom with broad, thick shoulders and half-long roots; widely adapted, but especially good for

growing on heavy or shallow soils. Flesh is sweet and tender, with a fine flavor; freezes well; 100 days.

'The Student' (1860)
Selected from seedlings of wild parsnip in the gardens of the Royal Agricultural Society at Cirencester, England. Thick, tapering roots grow 15–20 in. long, depending on the soil. Hollow crown; very regular roots are 3 in. in diameter. Fearing Burr described its flavor as "peculiarly sweet, mild, and pleasant" back in 1863 and considered it the best variety in cultivation. Vilmorin-Andrieux (1885) and Charles Johnson (1906) consider 'Student' synonymous with 'Hollow Crown', but the English heirloom called 'Sutton's Student' seems to be the separate and better-flavored local strain that we now call 'Student'.

PEAS
Pisum sativum
Peas rank alongside cereal grains as among the earliest of all cultivated plants. Evidence of peas has been found at a Stone Age lake village site in Switzerland, and it is likely that the wild form of today's garden pea (now unknown) originated in eastern Europe or western Asia.[38]

Considering their importance to prehistoric and ancient cultures, the habit of eating tender, fresh-shelled green peas as we do today seems a relatively recent innovation. Although people apparently cooked both dry shelled peas and whole, edible-podded types, green peas did not catch on in Europe until the 1600s. Even then, they were considered a frightfully decadent luxury. In a famous letter of 1696, Madame de Maintenon ridiculed the mania for fresh peas at the court of Louis XIV:

> The subject of Peas, continues to absorb all others; the anxiety to eat them, the pleasure of having eaten them, and the desire to eat them again, are the three great matters which have been discussed by our Princes for four days past. Some ladies, even after having supped at the Royal table, and well supped too, returning to their own homes, at the risk of suffering from indigestion, will again eat Peas before going to bed. It is both a fashion and a madness.[39]

While home gardeners today aren't quite so immoderate as these French ladies, there's a simple yet undeniable pleasure that accompanies the first fresh peas of the season. For instance, in northern New England bragging rights go to those gardeners who can produce a good crop of peas before the Fourth of July, to accompany the traditional poached salmon.

Peas are classified in a number of different ways: by height (tall, semidwarf, or dwarf vines); by flower color (creamy white for garden peas; pink, rose, lavender, or some combination for field peas); and by seed color and appearance (smooth or wrinkled skin). Yet most gardeners care first and foremost about the basic eating or usage types — shelling, sugar, snap, and soup. *Shelling peas* are harvested and shucked when the peas have filled out their pods. With *sugar peas* (often called *snow peas*), the pods themselves are eaten when they are young and tender, and while the peas inside are still tiny and undeveloped. *Snap peas* (Vilmorin-Andrieux calls them 'Butter Pea' in 1885) offer the best of both worlds; they are ready to pick when the thick, fleshy pods have swollen, and both peas and pod are sweet and edible. Shelling or field peas left on the vine to dry are often called *soup peas,* and they store well for use in soups or as seed stock for next year's crop.

Although peas self-pollinate like beans, they have been deliberately and extensively crossed and improved by centuries of plant breeders. Many fine heirloom varieties still exist, some named in honor of famous breeders like Thomas Laxton and Thomas A. Knight. Knight began hybridizing peas in 1787, and his work with wrinkled-seeded forms gave them a newfound popularity that they still enjoy today. "Wrinkledness" in peas is a simple inherited abnormality; the chief advantage wrinkled peas have over smooth-seeded varieties is their high productivity and especially sweet, tender flavor.[40]

How to Grow
Peas grow best in cool weather and can be planted as soon as the ground can be worked in the spring. For an earlier start in northern regions, some gardeners till the pea patch the previous fall and cover it with black plastic mulch, to preheat the soil in the spring and allow for earlier planting. Seeds may rot if planted in wet or cold soil (below 50°F). Gardeners in warmer regions should mulch peas after they are growing, to conserve soil moisture and keep the ground cooler.

Grow peas in well-drained garden soil that has a fairly neutral pH (between 6.0 and 6.8) and is rich is phosphorus and potassium. An application of bonemeal adds phosphorus to the soil; sprinkling a small amount of fine dry wood ashes in the row adjusts the pH of acid soil and provides a good source of potassium.

Moisten seeds slightly before planting and coat well with a bacterial inoculant powder, or sprinkle granular inoculant into the furrow when planting. Rhizobial bacteria contained in the inoculant form nodules on the roots of legumes such as peas and beans and convert nitrogen from the atmosphere into a form available to the plants. Treating your seed with an inoculant helps promote healthier, more productive plants. Sow seeds 1 in. deep and 3 in. apart (4 in. apart for tall climbing varieties). Tamp seeds down to firm the soil and water the seedbed if the ground seems dry.

For dwarf varieties plant double rows of seeds 6–8 in. apart, leaving 2 ft. of space on both sides of the double row to allow easy picking from either side. For tall climbing varieties, set up trellis supports down the center of double rows spaced 6–8 in. apart, allowing 3–4 ft. on either side of the double row. Truly dwarf varieties of peas (to 2 ft. in height) do not require trellising, but semidwarf types (2½ ft. or higher) often benefit from some kind of support, if only strings or wires stretched along either side of the double row.

Chicken wire makes a good trellis for climbing peas. Even better is the kind of biodegradable fiber mesh netting that is sold in rolls. At the end of season you can pull up the fiber mesh, with pea vines attached, and simply throw the whole thing on the compost pile. Whichever trellising system you use, set it up before planting peas to avoid disturbing the seedbed later on when plants are up and growing.

Peas can also be sown for a fall harvest, though in many regions spring-sown peas produce better crops. Select a disease-resistant variety if possible and plant seeds about 8 weeks before the first fall frost date. Since peas prefer cool weather, it's better to plant two different varieties of peas at the same time rather than to sow succession crops. Planting an early dwarf variety like 'Little Marvel' and a later-maturing climber like 'Alderman' will help to extend your harvest season.

Harvest
Pick peas for green shelling when the pods are large and well-filled. Pick sugar (snow) peas while the pods are still flat and tender and the peas are small and undeveloped. Pick snap peas when the thick, fleshy pods are filled out and the peas inside are full-sized. To remove strings from snap peas while picking, hold the vine in one hand and pull the pod upward and off the vine with the other. For soup peas or for seed-saving, allow pods to dry on the vine before harvesting and shelling.

Pests and Diseases
Several bacterial and fungal diseases can affect peas, notably fusarium wilt, root rot, and powdery mildew. To help prevent

disease, don't grow peas in the same spot year after year and select disease-resistant varieties if you experience problems.

To control pea aphids, spray leaves with an insecticidal soap spray. Rotate crops and remove all vines and plant debris from the garden at the end of each season.

■ RECOMMENDED VARIETIES

Shelling Peas *(P. sativum* var. *sativum)*

'Alaska' (1880)
An early semidwarf variety that was named not for the state but for a steamship that at the time of introduction held the transatlantic speed record. Plants are 26–36 in. tall; round, straight pods are 2–3 in. long and contain 5–8 small, smooth-seeded, light green peas; flavor is good, but not especially sweet; excellent for canning. Plants are productive, wilt-resistant, and grow well in cool soils; good for early fresh use or for dried split peas; 50–60 days.

'Alderman' ('Tall Telephone'; 1891)
The original seed stock of the 'Telephone' climbing pea, introduced in 1881, disappeared around 1930. 'Alderman' was selected by Thomas Laxton, probably from 'Duke of Albany'. Both 'Alderman' and 'Tall Telephone' come originally from 'Telegraph' and the two names have become synonymous.

Vigorous vines grow 5–6 ft. high and need trellising; straight, 5-in.-long pods contain 8–10 large, dark green peas; heat-tolerant and disease-resistant. Sweet flavor; also good for canning and flash freezing. Still one of the most popular climbing peas; 70–75 days.

'American Wonder' (1878)
This excellent variety is a cross between 'Champion of England' and 'Little Gem'. Plants are dark green and very dwarf, 12–14 in. high; high-yielding and drought-tolerant. Pods are straight and 3 in. long, containing 5–7 round, cream-colored peas; very sweet flavor; 60–65 days.

'Blue Pod Capucijners'
('Dutch Grey', 'Holland Capucijners'; *P. sativum* var. *arvense;* 1500s) p. 86
An old field pea developed by Capuchin monks, probably in Holland. This is one of my all-time favorite ornamental vegetable plants. Vines grow 4–5 ft. in height and need support; flowers are bicolored lavender and magenta-rose; pods and leaf axils are bluish purple. Pods are 3 in. long and contain 6–8 olive-brown seeds that are harvested dry and used in

soups; peas can also be picked and shelled fresh for canning or freezing, and young flat pods can be eaten like snow peas. Rarely seen, but well worth growing just for its beauty; 85–90 days.

'Champion of England' (1846)

One of the oldest wrinkled peas, introduced to the U.S. from England in 1849. The strain most grown today is dwarf or semidwarf, growing 3 ft. high or less, though the 1926 Henderson catalog describes a taller form, to 5 ft. Dark green leaves are slightly crinkled; both flowers and foliage are attractive. Peas are wrinkled and oblong, about 10 per pod; peas are tender and have a good, rich flavor. Prolific but produces rather late; currently unavailable through the seed trade but preserved by CRESS and through the Seed Savers Exchange Members Network; 75 days.

'Dwarf Telephone' (1888)

Hedrick describes this as a cross between 'Stratagem' and 'Telephone'. A late-maturing dwarf variety with plants growing 2 ft. high; pods are broad and straight with pointed ends, 4–5 in. long, and contain 8–9 light green peas; wilt-resistant; 70–78 days.

'Laxtonian' ('Blue Bantam', 'Hundredfold'; before 1907)

Dwarf vines, 18–20 in. high, with large, dark green leaves. Pods are curved with pointed ends, 4 in. long, and contain 7–8 peas. An early, dependable variety; 62–65 days.

'Lincoln' ('Homesteader'; before 1908)

Dwarf vines are 18–30 in. high and bear 3–4 in. pods that are tightly packed with 6–9 small, wrinkled, cream-colored peas; excellent flavor. Still widely available; performs well in the North; 65–70 days.

'Little Marvel' ('Improved American Wonder'; 1900)

An English variety that Hedrick reports is a cross between 'Daisy' and 'William Hurst'; introduced to the U.S. in 1908. Vigorous dwarf plants, 15–20 in. tall; pods have blunt ends and are tightly packed with 6–7 medium-size, dark green peas. High-yielding and wilt-resistant; extended picking season; 58–64 days.

'The Pilot' (before 1903)

Vines climb 4–5 ft. in height; pods are long, large, and deep green, with pointed ends; peas are dimpled and creamy white.

An English variety rarely grown in the U.S.; extremely hardy, extended picking season; good for spring or fall crop.

'Stratagem' (ca. 1879)
A late-season English variety introduced to the U.S. in 1883; when introduced it was praised as "the finest pea in the world" and it twice received the highest award from the Royal Horticultural Society. Vines are semidwarf, 28–30 in. tall; pods are deep green, 6 in. long, and contain 8–10 peas. Fine quality and flavor; high yields; good for the Northwest; 80 days.

'Thomas Laxton' ('Freezonian'; 1898)
Named after the famous pea breeder, this variety was introduced to the U.S. in 1900 and is still very popular. Hedrick lists it as a cross between 'Gradus' and 'Earliest of All'. Semidwarf vines, to 3 ft. in height, bear large crops of dark green, straight, blunt-ended, 3–5-in. pods that contain 7–9 large peas. Early to midseason, with an extended harvest season; very wilt-resistant; does well in maritime climates; 55–65 days.

Edible-Podded Peas *(P. sativum* var. *macrocarpon)*

'Dwarf Gray Sugar' (before 1773)
The earliest and dwarfest of the edible-podded "snow peas." Vines are bushy, 2–3 ft. in height, and prolific; lavender blossoms; flat pods are fleshy, curved, 2–3 in. long and light green, borne in pairs at the top of the plant. Wilt-resistant; one of the most widely grown sugar (snow) peas; 60–75 days.

'Golden Sweet' p. 86
A rare, edible-podded "wax snow pea" introduced to the U.S. from India. Vines grow 4–5 ft. high and need support; flowers are bicolored in shades of purple and very ornamental; pods are pale lemon yellow, 3 in. long, and borne in pairs. High-yielding and tolerates heat and drought; produces over long season; 70 days.

'Mammoth Melting Sugar' (before 1906) p. 87
Vines grow 4–5 ft. high and require support; thick, stringless pods are 4–5 in. long and can be used like snap beans. Plants are high-yielding and wilt-resistant; flowers are white. Pods are larger, sweeter, and more tender than those of 'Dwarf Gray Sugar' and remain edible even when they are older. Late-maturing; in some regions can be planted in mid- to late summer for a fall crop; 65–75 days.

Cowpeas

Vigna unguiculata

Cowpeas are also known as southern peas, crowder peas, or field peas (not to be confused with the other field pea, *Pisum sativum* var. *arvense*). Another common name for them is black-eyed peas, though this name really only applies to a few widely grown varieties of cowpea.

Aside from its common name, the cowpea has very little in common with the garden pea; its closest relative is the yard-long or asparagus bean (*Vigna unguiculata* var. *sesquipedalis*), whose skinny, 2–3-ft. pods are used like snap pole beans, especially by the Chinese, who call them *dow gauk*.

The cowpea is probably native to the East Indies. Widely grown in the southern U.S., cowpeas have never really caught on in other sections of the country. They grow best where summer nights remain warm but are worth trying in all but the coldest short-season areas of the country. Like other legumes, cowpeas fix nitrogen on their roots, and for this reason farmers often grow them as a green manure (to improve soil fertility) or as a forage crop for animals.

How to Grow

Cowpeas like a well-drained, somewhat acidic soil (pH 5.5 to 6.5), and they grow well even on relatively poor soil.

Direct-seed cowpeas after the last spring frost date, when the soil temperature is warm (70°F or higher). Plant seeds 4 in. apart in rows spaced 30 in. apart. Some bush varieties produce long runners; such plants should either be spaced 12–18 in. apart and allowed to run, or tied or woven on a trellis or support. The runners need help to climb because they lack the clinging tendrils of peas and pole beans.

Water cowpeas lightly and frequently while the plants are setting pods, especially during periods of hot, dry weather.

Harvest

Pick cowpea pods very young for use as snap beans. Their main use, though, is as a cooked green shell bean; harvest when the seeds have filled out the pods but before the pods turn yellow and the seeds become hard. Cowpeas also make good dry cooking beans, though they require a fairly long cooking time.

A friend once introduced me to a southern tradition of eating black-eyed peas on New Year's Day. This is supposed to ensure good luck throughout the year.

Pest and Diseases

Weevils sometimes infest cowpea seeds in storage. To kill the weevils, place thoroughly dry seeds that are ready for storage into the freezer for 24 hours, then remove and store in a cool, dry place.

■ RECOMMENDED VARIETIES

'Calico Crowder' ('Hereford Pea', 'Polecat Pea')
Bush plants have running vines that can grow up to 10 ft. in length; pods are 10–14 in. long and contain up to 16 medium-size seeds that are creamy white with maroon markings; seeds hold their color when cooked. Good, mild flavor; productive. Recommended for regions south of latitude 39° north; 70–80 days.

'Papago' p. 87
An old, rare Indian variety recommended by David Cavagnaro at Seed Savers Exchange. Adapted for planting during the summer rains in low, hot desert areas, yet can be grown successfully in the North. Seeds are pretty, mottled black and white; delicious flavor and fairly soft-seeded so requires less cooking time than other dry cowpeas. Drought-tolerant; productive; 70 days.

'Susanne' ('Susanne Cream') p. 88
An heirloom variety from Alabama. Vigorous plants produce first on bushy vines and later on runners that can be trained and grown on a trellis. Pods are 12 in. long and contain 14–16 medium-size, creamy white seeds; peas have a good flavor and make a dark pot liquor when cooked; 85–90 days.

'Whipporwill' p. 88
Plants are vigorous climbers; plant 12–18 in. apart in the row and train to a support. Pods are 10 in. long and set high on the plant; pods contain up to 16 peas, which are speckled buff and brown. Very productive and bears over a long period; 75–90 days.

'Zipper' ('Zipper Cream Crowder') p. 89
This variety's name refers to the ease with which the peas can be shelled from the pods. Bushy, compact plants produce lots of large pods; large white seeds have a good, mild flavor. Insect- and disease-resistant; 70–75 days.

Peppers
Capsicum annuum
Peppers are native to tropical America, where people have been growing and eating them for thousands of years. Ar-

chaeologists have found evidence of chilies at the very earliest levels at Tamaulipas and Tehuacan in Mexico, which date back to around 7000 B.C.[41] The Aztecs had at least seven different words for hot peppers, including *quauchilli, zenalchilli,* and *chiltepin,* from which we derive the generic term "chili."[42] Among the Incas of Peru, peppers even became a form of currency, a practice that was at once so convenient and so well established that as late as 1900 (A.D., that is), one could still go shopping in the plaza at Cuzco carrying only a handful of peppers.[43]

Columbus saw peppers growing in the West Indies and named them *pimiento* after the spice pepper (*pimienta*) that he had been seeking in the East Indies.[44] In his journal entry for January 15, 1493, Columbus wrote that the natives called the plant *aji* (pronounced ah-hee), a word that sounds something like the exclamation an explorer might have made upon biting into one of the hot fruits unawares. Columbus brought peppers back to Spain, and from there they spread rapidly throughout Africa, India, and the Far East before becoming popular in Europe and North America.

In their tropical and subtropical homeland, peppers are perennial plants that can grow quite large and shrubby. Most North American gardeners, though, grow peppers as annuals, since the plants are very sensitive to frost. By far the most important species to gardeners is *Capsicum annuum,* which includes a wide range of sweet and hot peppers (sweet bell, cayenne, jalapeno, and other well-known types), most of which grow well as annuals even in northern climates. The species *C. frutescens* includes the pepper used in making Tabasco brand hot sauce. Other lesser-known species such as *C. baccatum, C. chinense,* and *C. pubescens* are quite popular in South America, which is where they originated, but are only sparsely represented in North American seed catalogs at this time.

How to Grow
Sow seeds ¼ in. deep and 4 in. apart in flats or in individual cells, about 6–8 weeks before the last spring frost date. Peppers germinate slowly in cool soil, so provide flats with gentle bottom heating until the seedlings emerge. When seedlings are 2 in. tall and have their first true leaves, transplant them into 3-in. pots.

Harden off peppers after the last spring frost date and transplant to the garden when the soil is warm and the weather is settled. Set plants out 12–18 in. apart in rows spaced 2–3 ft. apart. Mix in a little bone meal and compost or dried manure into the planting hole. Growing peppers in an overly rich soil or fertilizing them heavily with nitrogen encourages lush plant growth but often results in a reduced fruit set.

Do not plant seedlings much deeper than they were growing in the pot. Place a paper collar around the stems of seedlings to guard against cutworm damage. Peppers like heat, so in areas with cool spring weather, provide additional warmth by mulching around young plants with black paper or plastic and/or covering them with plastic cloches or a slitted row cover material.

Fertilize peppers during growth by watering the foliage with a liquid fish or seaweed emulsion. When plants begin to blossom, dissolve a spoonful of Epsom salts in a plastic spray bottle and spritz some on the leaves. Epsom salts contain magnesium, which helps to encourage an early and abundant fruit set.

Harvest

Peppers are fully ripe when their skin turns from green to red, yellow, orange, or some other color. The fruits usually ripen gradually, one by one, over a long season. Once they change color, sweet peppers become sweeter-tasting and hot peppers get hotter; ripe peppers also contain lots of vitamins A and C. You can pick most varieties at any stage of color, however, and most gardeners end up picking at least some of them green at the end of the growing season when there's a threat of frost.

To avoid damaging plants when harvesting, cut the stems rather than twisting or pulling off the fruits. If you keep pepper plants well picked, they will continue setting fruit throughout the season.

Peppers also make good container plants and will overwinter indoors in a heated sunspace or greenhouse. Compact varieties with tiny, brightly colored fruits are particularly good when grown as ornamental houseplants.

Pests and Diseases

Like tomatoes, peppers sometimes suffer from blossom-end rot, which indicates a calcium deficiency in the soil. To prevent this, apply a high-calcium lime before the growing season starts, if indicated by a professional soil test. Also, provide plants with consistent moisture by watering lightly and regularly as needed; mulching around the plants also helps conserve soil moisture.

To prevent disease and insect problems, rotate pepper crops from year to year and don't plant them where other members of the nightshade family (tomatoes, potatoes, eggplant, etc.) have been growing. To protect against flea beetles, cover plants with a floating row fabric in the spring, or dust them with rotenone or pyrethrum. Control aphids by spraying leaves with water or an insecticidal soap solution.

■ RECOMMENDED VARIETIES

Hot Peppers

'Arledge Hot' ('Louisiana Hot')
One of the best Tabasco-type peppers (*C. frutescens*) available to home gardeners, this heirloom has been preserved by the Arledge family of Denton, Louisiana. Plants are productive and did extremely well for me in New Hampshire; fruits are 4 in. long, ripen from green to red, and are very hot; 75 days.
  Note: Tabasco peppers rate about an 8 on a hotness scale of 10, and it's a good idea to wear rubber gloves when handling fruits or cutting them for use in the kitchen; otherwise your fingers will burn and throb — not a pleasant sensation.

'Chiltepine' (*C. annuum* var. *aviculare*) p. 89
Also known as "bird pepper," this is the only hot pepper that grows wild within the borders of the U.S. As annuals, the plants are compact and bushy, to 1 ft. in height; but if grown in containers and brought inside for the winter they are perennial and can grow to 3 ft. The fruits are small, ovoid, ¼–½ in. long, and very hot. Several good strains are available, among them 'Texas', which comes from the Edwards Plateau west of Austin; 120–150 days (from seed).

'Chimayo' p. 90
Developed in the farming village of Chimayo, New Mexico, which lies between Santa Fe and Taos. These peppers are good for stringing into *ristras* for dried use. Plants are 24–30 in. tall and bear slightly curved, 4–5-in. fruits with thin walls; flavor is mild when fruits are green, medium-hot when red; 95 days.

'Czechoslovakian Black'
This heirloom pepper from the former Czechoslovakia is a very showy plant that grows tall, to 3 ft., and has green leaves that are veined with purple; flowers are lavender and white. Fruits ripen from green to purple-black to red and are medium-hot when fully ripe. A fine ornamental variety that is early and widely adapted; 58 days.

'De Arbol' ('Arbol'; 'Tree Chili')
Tall bushes bear lots of thin, slightly curved, spear-shaped red peppers about 2–3 in. long; fruits have thin skins and are very

hot and tasty; roasting enhances the flavor. Can be grown in colder regions of the country; Lawrence Hollander of CRESS recommends putting cages or hoops around the plants and covering them with a floating row fabric for added heating and frost protection. Ripens in the Northeast in late September or October; 90–120 days.

'De Comida' ('Zapotec di Comida')
From the Zapotec Indians of Oaxaca, Mexico. Medium-size plants produce decent yields of 4–6-in. glossy red peppers that are used in making traditional mole sauce; medium-hot and tasty; good for drying; 90–95 days.

'Grandpa's Home Pepper'   p. 90
Small plants grow to only 1 ft. in height but can produce 50 or more small, bright red, semihot peppers. This variety is from Siberia, where it is grown extensively as an indoor houseplant; set in a window it will produce all winter long, even in low-light conditions; 70 days.

'Karlo'   p. 91
A semihot, semisweet Romanian heirloom pepper. Short, compact plants produce an early crop of tapered, top-shaped peppers that ripen from yellow to red. Fruits are 3–4 in. wide at the shoulder and have medium-thick flesh; 50–55 days.

'Long Red Cayenne' ('Long Cayenne'; before 1827)   p. 91
Plants are 20–30 in. tall and leafy; fruits are 4–6 in. long, slender, and wrinkled, with glossy dark green skin ripening to crimson red. Hot taste; the standard variety for drying and grinding for cayenne pepper; 70–75 days. Several similar strains are available.

'Pico de Gallo'
The name of this flaming-hot pepper from Sonora, Mexico, means "rooster's beak," from the shape of the small, curved peppers. Plants have narrow leaves and produce lots of the slender, 3-in. peppers; 70–75 days. There is even a song performed by the folk group Trout Fishing in America that celebrates this little spitfire and the rocket-fuel salsa that you can make with it.

'Red Squash' ('Mushroom Pepper')   p. 92
An unusual hot pepper that really does look something like a red mushroom with a "cap" on the stem end of the fruit. Fearing Burr lists a 'Squash Pepper' in 1863 that may be the same as this variety. Plants grow 24–30 in. high and produce lots of peppers that are 2 in. long and 2 in. in diameter. Fruits

ripen from yellow-green to orange to red. A 'Yellow Squash' strain that ripens to yellow is also available. Good for pickling or cut open to dry; 100–110 days (from seed).

Sweet Peppers

'Aconcagua' ('Giant Aconcagua') p. 92
A large, long frying pepper that is named for Mt. Aconcagua in Argentina, where it originated. Plants are vigorous and 28–30 in. tall with lots of dark green leaves. Fruits are 7–11 in. long and ripen from light green to orange to red; good sweet taste even when green. Plants need to be staked and tied because of heavy fruit set. Produces well until frost; use fresh or roast and peel; 70–75 days.

'Bull Nose' ('Large Bell', 'Sweet Mountain'; 1759)
Introduced to the U.S. from India. An early-maturing heirloom with a unique taste; the ribs are pungent but the rest of the thick flesh is sweet. Plants are compact; fruits are 4 in. long and 3½ in. in diameter and ripen from green to scarlet. Peppers are uniform in size and shape and have 4 lobes; good for stuffing; 60 days.

'Cherry Sweet' ('Red Cherry'; before 1860) p. 93
Strong, bushy plants grow 20 in. tall and bear 1-in.-long, cherry-shaped fruits that ripen from dark green to deep crimson; good for pickling or canning; productive; 70–80 days.

'Corno di Toro' p. 93
An Italian frying pepper whose name means "bull's horn." As with other peppers, two strains exist, one that ripens to golden yellow ('Giallo') and one that ripens to deep red ('Rosso'). Plants are tall, to 3 ft., and bear 8-in.-long curved fruits; the flavor is peppery and neither sweet nor hot; 70–80 days.

'Golden Summit' p. 94
A variety that hails from Yugoslavia. Short plants produce good crops of attractive bell peppers that ripen from golden-green to bright gold-orange to deep red; peppers have thick, sweet, and juicy flesh. Plants bear early even if night temperatures are cool; 65 days.

'Merrimack Wonder' (1942) p. 94
A widely adapted variety that is early and especially good for short-season areas; blocky fruits measure 3½ by 3½ in. and have 4 lobes. Flesh is medium-thick and mild. Plants set fruit even in cool weather; 60 days.

'Nardello' ('Jimmy Nardello's Sweet Frying Pepper')
An outstanding Italian frying pepper introduced by Seed Savers Exchange and now commercially available. Plants are large and produce heavy crops of 6–9-in.-long, slender fruits; tie plants to stakes with cloth strips to support the heavy fruit set. Peppers ripen green to red; green fruits are pungent, red ones very sweet. Excellent for frying or in spaghetti sauce. One of my favorites; 80–90 days.

'Quadrato d'Asti Giallo Rosa' p. 95
A large sweet bell pepper from Italy. Two color strains, one ripening green to golden yellow, another ripening to red. Large fruits are 4 in. by 5 in. and have a very sweet, spicy taste; fruits have thick flesh and 3 or 4 lobes; very good for stuffing; 70–80 days.

'Sweet Banana' ('Hungarian Wax Sweet', 'Yellow Banana'; 1941) p. 95
This pepper is sold under many similar names and remains popular and widely grown. Plants are 16–24 in. tall and productive; fruits are 6 in. long, taper to a blunt point, and ripen pale green to yellow to orange to red; some fruits show purple markings in the green and yellow stages; flesh is thick with a sweet, mild taste. Reliable and heavy-yielding; 60–75 days.

'World Beater' ('Ruby Giant'; before 1912)
Developed from a cross between 'Chinese Giant' and 'Ruby King'. Tall plants have lots of leaves and produce heavy crops of large, blocky bell peppers that measure 5 in. by 3½ in. and ripen green to red; thick flesh is very sweet after peppers turn red; 70–75 days.

Potato

Solanum tuberosum
Native to the cool tropical highlands of western South America, potatoes were a staple food of the Incas. Of all the vegetables "discovered" by European explorers in the Americas, only maize, or corn, has figured more prominently in the diets of people around the world. Hardy, productive, and well suited to the temperate climate of northern Europe, the potato eventually became the food of the masses, especially in Ireland, where the population exploded from 3 million persons in 1750 to more than 8 million in 1841.[45] One person credited with introducing the potato to Ireland is Sir Walter Raleigh, who may have brought the tubers with him from America to his estate at Youghal in County Cork.[46]

Like most New World food crops, however, the potato went through a period of great suspicion in Europe. Its reputation as a tasty vegetable no doubt suffered when nobles ate potato leaves, which are poisonous, and became deathly ill. In Elizabethan times, people considered the potato (like so many other exotic foods) an aphrodisiac,[47] and nearly two centuries later, potatoes were still so novel among fashionable French nobles that Marie Antoinette adorned herself with potato blossoms.[48]

Yet it was among the Irish peasantry that the potato gained its most loyal following as a crop that was easy to grow and produced abundantly. Despite the potato's South American origins, many people today still refer to the vegetable as the "Irish potato," perhaps because early Irish settlers brought the crop with them to North America. The first record of potatoes in the northern colonies indicates that they arrived with a group of Irish Presbyterians who settled Londonderry, New Hampshire, in 1719.[49]

Unfortunately, the Irish became dependent on a single strain of potato, called 'The Lumper', and the island's crop was devastated in the mid-1840s by an American parasite, *Phytophthora infestans*, which causes the fungal disease called late blight. Blight rots potatoes, and the resulting Irish potato famine caused widespread hunger and disease, forcing many Irish to emigrate to the U.S. and other countries. As a result of this catastrophe, plant breeders began to examine the hundreds, if not thousands, of indigenous South American potato varieties, using them to breed blight resistance into new potatoes and greatly expanding the crop's genetic base.

Potatoes are usually propagated vegetatively, by saving a portion of the previous year's crop and replanting sprouting pieces of tuber next season. The potato plant does produce a small number of seed balls, but potato seed does not come true to type. The famous American plant breeder Luther Burbank used potato seeds in his breeding work, which resulted in the 'Russet Burbank' — the potato that made Idaho famous. Yet, for gardeners and growers, the only way to keep a strain pure is to plant pieces of tuber with sprouts or eyes attached.

In recent years, a whole rainbow of potato colors and shapes has become available to home gardeners, and there is no longer any reason to limit oneself to the few tried-and-true commercial varieties found in the supermarket. While market potatoes, in terms of taste, have it all over other agribusiness crops like tomatoes, the superior taste and variety of home-grown potatoes make them an excellent crop for backyard gardeners.

How to Grow

The best soil for growing potatoes is a light, sandy, well-drained loam that is slightly acidic (pH 6.0 to 6.8). If your garden's soil is heavy or clayey, prepare a bed for potatoes by digging deeply and working in lots of organic matter, which will help lighten heavy soil and also help retain water in sharply drained soil. If your soil is too alkaline (pH higher than 6.8), work a little powdered sulfur or gypsum (calcium sulfate) into the potato bed several weeks before planting.

Small seed potatoes, those about the size of an egg, can be planted whole. Cut larger seed potatoes with a clean, sharp knife into pieces that weigh 1–4 oz. and have at least 2 eyes. The sprouting potatoes will draw on the nutrients in the attached pieces of tuber during the first weeks of growth.

Plant pieces of tuber immediately, or allow them to dry in a shady place for a day or so before planting. Treat seed potatoes before planting if desired by placing a tablespoon of powdered sulfur in the bottom of a large paper bag, then adding the potato pieces and gently shaking to coat the pieces. This may help prevent scab or the risk of bacterial or fungal infection.

Potatoes that have already sprouted in storage are fine for planting and in fact encourage early growth; just be sure to handle the pieces gingerly when cutting and planting to avoid breaking or injuring the sprouts. Potatoes that have turned green in the presence of sunlight are also fine to use as seed potatoes.

Plant potatoes about 1–4 weeks before the last spring frost date. Potatoes tolerate cool soil but can rot in excessively cold or wet conditions. Dig or till a shallow trench about 3 in. wide and 6–8 in. deep. Set potato pieces in the furrow 9–10 in. apart in rows spaced 30–36 in. apart. Cover seed pieces with 2–3 in. of soil.

When the young plants are 6–8 in. high, hill them by pulling soil up around the stem from both sides of the row with a hoe. Leave the top 4 in. of the plant exposed. Hilling helps cover the tubers that will develop above the seed potato, protecting them from light (which makes them green and inedible). It also loosens and cultivates the soil. Pull up more soil around the plants 2–3 weeks after the first hilling.

Keep the soil around potatoes evenly moist but not wet from the time potato plants emerge until they flower. Mulching the hills with spoiled hay or clean straw at this time helps conserve soil moisture and suppress weeds. Cut back on water after potatoes have blossomed; as tubers form and mature, too much water can cause cracking or rotting. Fertilize plants after emergence and before flowering with a liquid fish or seaweed emulsion sprayed on the leaves of the plants. To avoid scab, don't use animal manures as a fertilizer for potatoes. Keep the potatoes well weeded during the early part of the season, being careful not to damage plants while cultivating them.

Another good way to grow potatoes, one that doesn't involve trenching and hilling soil, is under a covering of mulch. If you have access to a large supply of weed-free hay or mulch, this is definitely worth trying, since the potatoes you harvest at the end of the season will be clean, uniform, and easy to locate. Plant seed potatoes on the surface of the soil or at a shallow depth, at the spacings given above. Then shake mulch loosely over the bed until it is 6–10 in. deep. As plants emerge, hill them as described above, using more mulch instead of soil. If mice or other rodents become a problem, attach a windmill device to a metal pole stuck in the ground; the vibrations caused by this simple device help discourage these animal pests.

Harvest

Once the potatoes have blossomed (usually around 50–60 days after planting), you can begin to reach carefully into the hills to check for new potatoes. These tender morsels, lightly steamed and served with peas, are one of the real highlights of the gardening season. Harvest new potatoes carefully to avoid damaging the potato plant and any remaining tubers. Harvest the remaining potatoes for fresh use at any time you find some ready.

To harvest potatoes that will store well, it's necessary to wait until the plants die back. Frost will kill potato plants, or you can cut them down with a sickle at the end of the growing season. After the plant tops are dead, leave the tubers in the ground for 2 weeks. During this time the outer skins of the potatoes will toughen up, making the tubers better for storage and less susceptible to bruising or damage. Use a garden fork to lift plants gently, and look around for any potatoes of harvestable size. Try to harvest on a cool, dry day in the fall, and leave potatoes on the surface of the ground for a few hours to air-dry. Use any blemished, misshapen, or scabby potatoes first, and store the rest of the crop in a cool (40–45°F), dark place.

Pests and Diseases

Rotate potato crops so they do not grow in the same spot more than once every 3 years; do not rotate crops to follow other members of the nightshade family (eggplant, tomatoes, peppers, etc.).

The Colorado potato beetle is the most serious insect pest for potatoes. Cover potatoes with floating row fabric early in the season to exclude beetles. Also, look for yellow egg masses on the undersides of leaves and crush them. Treat beetle larvae with Bt, a biological control. Deal with larger larvae and adults by hand-picking them off plants, or treat plant leaves with the botanical insecticides rotenone or pyrethrum.

Scab can normally be avoided by selecting resistant varieties and by growing potatoes in good, well-drained, somewhat acidic soil. Various strains of virus can affect potatoes and if a potato variety has picked up several of these strains, the cumulative effect can be a gradual decline in the size and quality of the crop (a condition old-time gardeners call "running-out"). Unfortunately, many good heirloom varieties of potatoes have picked up these diseases. However, Seed Savers Exchange and other groups are now involved in tissue-culturing potatoes in the lab to create healthy, virus-free planting stock. Until this "cleanup" is complete, home gardeners should be sure to purchase certified seed potatoes from a reliable source.

■ RECOMMENDED VARIETIES

'All Blue' ('Blue Marker')   p. 96
Probably the best-known of the blue- or purple-skinned potatoes. Medium-size potatoes have dark blue skin and blue flesh with a thin white ring under the skin. Considered a novelty, but good for baking, steaming, or mashing; high mineral content. Good flavor; to preserve color, don't overcook. Reportedly more vigorous and disease-resistant than 'Purple Peruvian'. Midseason; over 80 days.

'Anna Cheeka's Ozette' ('Ozette'; late 1700s)
A rare, historic fingerling potato said to have been brought to North America by Spanish explorers who traded with the Makah-Ozette tribe. Potatoes are 2–8 in. long and slender with thin skins, yellow flesh, and lots of eyes. Very prolific and has a nice earthy taste. An especially good variety for growing in coastal areas of the Pacific Northwest. Late season; over 90 days.

'Beauty of Hebron' (ca. 1900)
A Maine heirloom, still around but rare. Small to medium potatoes are flattened; skins are buff-yellow and flesh is creamy and tasty; great in soups and stews. Early season; over 65 days.

'Bintje' (1911)
A Dutch heirloom that has become the most widely grown yellow-fleshed variety in the world. Vigorous plants produce

heavy yields of medium-size oblong tubers; yellow-brown skin and yellow flesh; shallow eyes. Flavorful and a good keeper. Late season; over 90 days.

'Cow Horn'

A New Hampshire heirloom fingerling type with curved, hornlike tubers; light purple skin; off-white, mealy, firm flesh; good yields. Good for boiling or baking; good keeper. Similar to another variety called 'Seneca Horn'. Late season; more than 90 days.

'Early Ohio' (1871)

An excellent potato with a reddish orange skin and white flesh; great flavor; good for frying or baking. Very popular in the early 1900s in the Midwest and deserves to be more widely grown. Early season; over 65 days.

'Early Rose' (1861)

A seedling from 'Garnet Chile'. Large yields of long tubers that have pink skins, white flesh, and deep-set eyes. Vigorous plants. Early to midseason; 65–80 days.

'Garnet Chile'

An heirloom that is the parent of many potato varieties, including 'Early Rose'. Potatoes are large and round or irregular in shape; skins are thin and rosy red; flesh is white; good keeper. Plants are vigorous and productive. Late season; over 90 days.

'Green Mountain' (1885)

A favorite old New England variety, but well adapted to a variety of soils and growing conditions; very dependable and productive. Large oblong potatoes have tan skins and white, mealy flesh. Late season; over 90 days.

'Lady Finger'

Brought to the U.S. by early German settlers. Slender fingerling potatoes are 4–5 in. long and 1 in. in diameter. Brown skins and yellow flesh; excellent flavor for steaming, boiling, or frying; especially good for potato salad. Mid to late season; 80–90 days.

'Russet Burbank' ('Netted Gem'; 1874)

The most widely grown potato in the U.S. and the potato that made Idaho famous; bred by the immortal Luther Burbank. Large oblong tubers have heavy russeted skins, shallow eyes, and white flesh. Great baking and frying type. Good keeper; scab-resistant. Mid to late season; 80–90 days.

'Russian Banana' p. 96

An excellent fingerling potato that probably originated in Russia and was introduced to British Columbia by early settlers. Medium-size potatoes are long and slightly curved, with buff-yellow skins and light yellow flesh. Waxy texture is great in summer potato salads; stores well. Plants resistant to scab and late blight. Late season; over 90 days.

Pumpkin. *See* Squash and Pumpkins

Radish

Raphanus sativus

Radishes remind me of utility infielders in baseball — they're flexible, fit in well wherever you stick them, and don't hang around for very long in the season. They're the first plants to germinate from seed in the spring and often provide the first fresh harvest of the garden, especially welcome after a long winter hiatus.

Radishes come from China, though they apparently had spread to the Mediterranean area at a very early date. They were widely cultivated by both the ancient Egyptians and the Greeks, who offered up radishes made of beaten gold to the god Apollo.[50]

The most familiar radish to American gardeners is the small, round-rooted type that grows quickly in the early spring and is harvested for use in salads or as a crudité. The long French radishes, often rosy red on top and creamy white at the tip, are another fast-growing form.

Long-season varieties include the white Oriental radish known as daikon, which matures in the fall and can grow more than a foot long without losing its crisp, mildly pungent flavor; it's good for stir-frying or pickling. Still other fall radishes develop a tough outer skin that makes them good candidates for winter storage. Finally, there is the "aerial radish," which is grown not for its roots but for its long, showy seedpods. These pods make a pleasantly hot addition to a salad or raw dipping platter if picked while they are young and tender.

How to Grow

Round and French radishes grow quickly, especially in cool weather; plant them from early through late spring and again from late summer through early fall. Make small plantings every week or two to ensure a continuous supply, because small radishes start to grow woody and lose quality within a week or so of reaching maturity. Sow seeds for small radishes ½ in. deep and ½ in. apart in a well-raked bed or wide-row planting. About 10 days after leaves emerge, thin plants to 2–3 in. apart in the row or bed. Water the radishes lightly and frequently to encourage good, fast root development.

Small, quick-growing radishes also make perfect companion plants for other crops, especially carrots, parsnips, and other root crops that take a long time to germinate. The radishes help to mark the planting row and will be up and out of the way long before these other long-season crops need the growing space.

Sow seeds of large, long-season daikon radishes 2 in. apart in loose, deeply worked soil — the same conditions in which you would grow long carrots or parsnips. Space rows 18 in. apart. Thin daikon radishes to 4–6 in. apart in the row. Daikon or other radishes intended for fall harvest should be planted after midsummer so they will miss most of the summer heat and will mature around the time of the first fall frosts.

Harvest

Harvest round radishes when they are the size of large marbles or olives. Radishes should be planted in small, frequent successions for a continuous harvest, because they can become pithy and harsh-tasting if they stay in the ground too long. If harvested promptly and refrigerated in plastic bags or containers, they will retain their crispness for several weeks.

Pull daikon and winter storage types of radishes for harvest before the first hard frosts in the fall. Like carrots, the roots will store for several weeks in the refrigerator or a cool root cellar.

Pick the seedpods of aerial radishes when they are young and tender. Older pods become tough and fibrous but can be harvested whole and dried to save for next year's seeds. Wait until winter to thresh the seeds out of the pods — it's an easy but time-consuming job to pick out and clean the seeds.

Pests and Diseases

Flea beetles like to eat holes in radish leaves, but unless you have a serious infestation they're not worth worrying about. The leaves aren't the part we harvest for eating, and in most cases the roots are up and out of the ground before the bugs do much serious damage. If you're growing for market or for show, cover the radishes with a floating row fabric and dig in the edges to keep out the beetles.

Cabbage root maggots are another story altogether; they can wipe out an entire radish crop in short order. Again, a floating row cover provides an effective physical barrier. Some

gardeners also try to raise the pH of their soil by watering
the seedbed with a dilute lime-water solution or by sprinkling
a small quantity of fine, dry wood ashes into the seedbed and
around the growing plants. Immediately remove any infested
radishes from the garden, and be sure to rotate radish crops
away from that location.

■ RECOMMENDED VARIETIES

'China Rose' (ca. 1850)
Reportedly introduced to Europe from China by Jesuit mis-
sionaries. A Chinese winter radish with smooth, rose-colored
skin; radish roots are 6–8 in. long and 2 in. in diameter; plant
tops are tall; good keeper; for spring or fall sowing; 27–55
days.

'French Breakfast' (1879) p. 97
A widely grown variety whose name also represents other varieties of this type. Radish roots are oblong and blunt-tipped,
2 in. long and less than 1 in. across; color is scarlet with a
white tip and very pretty. Flesh is white and crisp with an excellent, mildly pungent flavor; 20–30 days. The traditional
French variety called 'D'Avignon' is a longer, slender type
(3–4 in.) that is very fine.

'French Golden'
An uncommon variety not currently offered commercially but
preserved by the Seed Savers Exchange Members Network.
Roots are large, thick, and elongated with rough, brownish
gold skin and white, medium-hot flesh. Tolerates heat and is
resistant to pests and disease; 35–42 days.

'Long Black Spanish' (before 1828) p. 97
An old winter storage radish with cylindrical roots that are
7–10 in. long and 2 in. in diameter at the shoulder. Skin is
rough and black; flesh is pure white; crisp texture and pungent flavor. Strong tops; good keeper; store in moist sand in
the root cellar; 55–60 days.

'Munchener Bier'
('Munich Bier', 'Beer Garden', 'Birra di Monaco')
An old European radish that gives you a double harvest.
First it produces lots of tender, 2–3-in. aerial seedpods,
which are good in salads or stir-fries. The large white tapering roots have a mild, pungent flavor; they are traditionally
sliced thin, salted, and served with a good dark beer; a favorite around Munich, Germany. Plants grow to 24 in. high;
65–70 days.

'Rat's Tail' ('Mongri', 'Snake Radish'; before 1860)
From the island of Java, this radish is classified as *Raphanus caudatus*. Burr lists this type in 1863 under the name 'Madras Radish', though some sources consider 'Madras' a separate, milder-tasting variety. Not much grown today, but an unusual "aerial radish" that is well worth trying. This radish produces no edible root but bears a large crop of slender, 8–12-in. seedpods that are an attractive dark purple; flavor is hot, spicy, and pungent. Very tolerant of summer heat. Keep well picked since older pods get fibrous and tough. Pods are good raw in salads or pickled. A good variety for gardeners who have had trouble with root maggots; 45–50 days.

'Round Black Spanish' (before 1824)
This winter storage variety is similar in all respects to 'Long Black Spanish' except for the shape of its roots. It was introduced in the U.S. before 1824 but may date as far back as the 15th century in Europe.
   Sown in July or August, this radish forms large, turnip-shaped globular roots that are 3–4 in. in diameter; skin is rough and deep black and flesh is white, crisp, and pungent; does not become pithy when large. Like 'Long Black Spanish' an excellent winter keeper; store in moist sand in the root cellar. Still very popular and widely grown; 53 80 days.

'Tokinashi' ('All Seasons')
Raphanus bipinnatus. A good Japanese daikon variety with white roots that grow 12–15 in. long and weigh 1–2 lb. Flesh is white, fine-textured, crisp, and mildly pungent; good for pickling or stir-frying. Plant in spring or from midsummer to early fall; harvest young roots at 30 days if desired. Slow-bolting; sometimes damaged by wireworms; 70–85 days.

'Violet de Gournay' ('Gournay Violet'; before 1885)
Listed by Vilmorin-Andrieux in the 1880s, this winter storage radish has slender, cylindrical roots that are 8–10 in. long and taper toward the tip. Beautiful purple skin and white flesh that has a very sweet, mild flavor; 65–70 days.

'White Icicle' ('Lady Finger'; before 1896) p. 98
A very good but rarely grown heirloom with white, carrot-shaped roots that are 4–5 in. long; heat-tolerant. Flavor is mild and best when harvested small but remains mild even when roots grow larger; 30 days.

'Wood's Frame' (ca. 1870)
An excellent but rare variety that is not currently offered by the seed trade but is available through the Seed Savers Ex-

change Member's Network. Half-long, stump-rooted red roots; crisp, sweet flavor; 60 days.

Rhubarb

Rheum rhabarbarum

It has been said of the wild strawberry that God could have made, but never did make, a more perfect fruit. That sentiment echoes my own feelings about rhubarb. From spring through early summer this hardy perennial plant produces fleshy red and green leaf stalks that make some of the best preserves, sauces, crisps, and compotes around. And the chopped and sweetened stalks are so superior as a pie filling that the other common name for rhubarb is "pie plant." Especially for those gardeners who live in the North, rhubarb is a welcome spring tonic, perfect for raising the spirits and summoning up the blood after a long, dreary winter.

In fact, rhubarb's health benefits have been recognized since ancient times. More than 2,000 years ago, the Chinese were grinding up its dried roots to make a bright yellow powder, which they valued as a potent and effective medicine. The plant's reputation spread as far as Europe, where rhubarb pills were widely prescribed for rickets, scabs, itching, leprosy, scurf, and freckles.[51] Even Shakespeare's Macbeth, besieged by his enemies, cries out, "What rhubarb, senna, or what purgative drug/Would scour these English hence?"

Different species of rhubarb cross-pollinate readily, so the taxonomy of the genus is far from clear; however, it appears that the culinary form of rhubarb we know today originated in Siberia and southwest Asia. Rhubarb's name probably comes from *Rha*, an ancient name for the Volga River, and *barbarum*, which refers (in a typically superior Roman way) to the uncouth folks who inhabited that region.

Although we think of rhubarb as a fixture of the home garden, it didn't catch on as a food plant until modern times. Around 1809 an English nurseryman named Joseph Myatt brought five bundles of rhubarb along with him to market in London. The sour, astringent taste of rhubarb took a while to catch on, but by the 1840s Myatt's son William had planted 20 acres in the crop and was shipping three wagonloads at a time to Covent Garden for sale.[52]

Once established in a spot of its own, rhubarb plants will produce abundantly each year, enough for plenty of pies or for making the ultimate "tonic," homemade rhubarb wine. The plants die back in the fall and return each spring, living for up to 20 years or even longer. Few crops give so much and ask so little in return.

How to Grow

Most gardeners buy root crowns of rhubarb for planting, since the plant does not always come true to type from seed. Like asparagus, rhubarb takes a while to become established before it's ready for harvest; planting root stock means that the rhubarb is one year ahead of plants started from seed in the same season. Having said this, it isn't too difficult to start rhubarb plants from seed, though many suppliers sell and ship root stock within national borders.

Before planting roots, choose a permanent location outside or adjacent to the annual vegetable garden — preferably one that has full sun. Space planting holes 3–4 ft. apart. Rhubarb loves a rich, well-drained loam, so dig a deep planting hole and work in plenty of compost or dried manure. Plant roots so that the top of the crown sits about 2–3 in. below the surface of the soil. Fill in the hole and cover the roots, then gently but firmly compress the soil with your foot or the back of a spade. Top-dress with more dried manure during the first year of growth, and cut off any seed stalks that the plants may produce.

In the second year of growth, you can harvest a few stalks from the plants, but leave plenty of stalks attached to feed the growing roots. Top-dress with manure during the summer or early fall, after the plants have stopped producing. From the third year onward, harvest as many stalks as needed from the plants. Continue to cut off any flower stalks the plants may produce, unless you intend to save seeds for planting.

To start rhubarb from seed, sow seeds in the spring, ¼ in. deep in a well-drained seedbed (a cold frame is excellent for starting plants). Thin plants to 4 in. apart in the row or bed after they emerge. Fertilize by top-dressing plants with compost or dried manure during this first growing season; mulch around plants lightly at the end of the season to protect them from winter frost-heaving. The following spring, select the best-looking individuals for replanting and pull up and discard the rest. Dig up the roots and plant them in a permanent location as described above.

To divide the roots of older plants, dig up the root crown of the parent plant early in the spring. With a sharp, clean knife, cut off several root sections and then replant the old crown. Plant the other root sections as described above. Root division creates clones of the parent plant and is the only sure way to get new rhubarb plants that are genetically the same as the original variety.

Harvest

Cut off leaf stalks near the base of the plant with a sharp knife. Some people harvest stalks by simply twisting them off, but this can damage the plants if you're not careful. Harvest stalks sparingly in the second year of growth, but regularly in the third and following years. A single rhubarb plant can produce 2–6 pounds of stalks per year, and 4–6 plants should produce more than enough for even a rhubarb-loving family.

After cutting the stalks, trim off and compost all rhubarb leaves, which are toxic to humans. My friend Susan Peery has another use for the large, cordate leaves: she grinds them up in a blender with some water and a dash of cayenne pepper, then strains the mixture and sprays it on the leaves of other plants to control aphids.

■ RECOMMENDED VARIETIES

'Glaskin's Perpetual'
Rarely grown in the U.S., but a good variety for starting from seed. Delicious stalks are low in oxalic acid. The supplier claims that some stalks can be harvested in the first year of sowing, but this requires planting seeds early in the spring, transplanting seedlings to 24 in. apart, and growing plants in fertile, well-watered soil. In all but long-season areas, it's probably better to skip the first-year harvest and treat this variety like other rhubarb, harvesting lightly in the second year and regularly in the third year. Available as seeds.

'German Wine'
A widely grown variety in the Kent-Puyallup Valley of Washington, the state that produces about 60 percent of the commercial U.S. rhubarb crop. Large, red-stalked plants are hardy and vigorous. A good variety for the prairies and the North. Available as seeds or roots.

'Paragon'
An old rhubarb variety from England, introduced by Charles Kershaw. Easy to grow from seed; sow in May or June when soil is warm; harvest lightly in the second year of growth. Available as seeds.

'Victoria' ('Myatt's Victoria'; before 1863) p. 98
This is the standard rhubarb variety and still one of the most popular. Introduced back in the 1800s by Myatt, the Father of Rhubarb. Broad crimson stalks are thick and tender with green flesh. Reliably hardy; very productive. Available as seeds or roots.

Runner Beans. *See* Beans

Rutabaga

Brassica napus, Napobrassica group

Also known as Swede turnip, the rutabaga combines thick, turniplike roots with smooth, bluish green leaves that resemble those of cabbage. Not surprisingly, some authors have suggested that the rutabaga may have developed as a hybrid cross (either natural or artificial) between turnips (*Brassica rapa*) and some form of the European wild cabbage (*B. oleracea*). Since rutabagas are extremely hardy plants and grow well in northern Europe and Russia, such a cross might have occurred there sometime during the Middle Ages.[53]

Two basic types exist, one with yellow flesh, the other with white flesh. While the yellow-fleshed rutabagas are not as tender, fine-grained, or delicately flavored as turnips, the white ones taste almost as sweet and mild. Like other hardy fall crops, rutabagas taste better and sweeter if harvested after the first fall frosts. They taste terrific boiled and mashed, puréed with other root vegetables, or cooked in stews or vegetable soups.

How to Grow

Rutabagas like a loose, well-worked soil that is almost neutral or slightly acidic (pH 6.0–6.8). Like other root vegetables, they don't need a nitrogen-rich soil but appreciate a good supply of phosphorus and potash. Adding bone meal and a sprinkling of wood ashes to the bed before planting helps provide these nutrients.

In northern and moderate climates, sow rutabaga seed in the summer, about 3 months before the first expected frost date in the fall. Plant seeds ½ in. deep and 1 in. apart in rows spaced 18–24 in. apart. Thin young plants to 6–8 in. apart in the row. If midsummer weather in your region is hot and dry, you can also start rutabagas in flats or cells and transplant as seedlings later in the summer, setting them out 6–8 in. apart in the row or bed.

Gardeners who live in mild winter climates can treat rutabagas as a winter crop, direct-seeding or transplanting them in the early fall when the weather begins to cool.

Harvest

To improve their flavor and sweetness, allow rutabagas to stand in the garden through at least two good hard frosts before harvesting. Cut off the leafy top about 1 in. above the root crown, then store like carrots in a cool location, either in ventilated plastic bags (simply punch one or two holes in the bag) or in boxes of moistened sand. In mild winter regions, rutabagas will overwinter successfully in the garden under a protective layer of mulch.

Rutabagas sold in supermarkets usually have a protective coating of wax; home gardeners can dip the roots in melted paraffin, too, but this is usually unnecessary if storage conditions remain cool and humid.

Pests and Diseases
Rotate crops of rutabagas and do not plant to follow other members of the cabbage family (turnips, kale, kohlrabi, etc.). When you harvest the roots, remove any crop wastes (plant leaves, etc.) from the garden to discourage pests and diseases from overwintering.

To control cabbage root maggots use a floating row cover, digging in the edges of the fabric. Another option is to sprinkle a small quantity of wood ashes around the plants. This provides potassium, which the rutabagas need, and raises the soil's pH, which root maggots don't seem to like.

■ RECOMMENDED VARIETIES

'Bristol White'
A good white-fleshed rutabaga that is currently unlisted in the seed trade but available through the Seed Savers Exchange Members Network. Large roots are very attractive, colored creamy white below ground and rose-red above; white flesh is sweeter and milder than yellow-fleshed varieties; 90 days.

'Laurentian'
('American Purple Top Improved'; before 1920) p. 99
An improved version of the standard 'American Purple Top' variety; developed in Canada. Globular roots are 4–6 in. in diameter, creamy yellow below ground and deep reddish purple above; flesh is pale yellow, firm, and mild-tasting. Roots uniform and almost neckless; stores well; 90–120 days. Several different strains are available.

'Macomber' ('Sweet German')
Burr lists 'Sweet German' as an excellent white rutabaga in 1863. Large roots are almost neckless, 5–6 in. in diameter, and weigh 4–5 lb.; white skin is greenish purple above ground; flesh is white, sweet, and does not get woody or pithy when roots get big. Stores well; early-maturing; 80–92 days.

'Pike'
An heirloom variety from Maine that is similar to 'Laurentian' but has somewhat larger roots and tops. Tops protect roots from heavy frost; can be left in the ground later in the season. Yellow skins and purple tops; flavorful yellow flesh; stores well; 100 days.

Salsify and Scorzonera

Tragopogon porrifolius and *Scorzonera hispanica*

American gardeners have always considered salsify a minor crop, yet its unique taste and trouble-free nature have gained it a small but devoted following. A long-season root vegetable, it looks something like a skinny parsnip, with creamy white skin and white flesh. Salsify, though, doesn't taste sweet like parsnips; it has instead a rich, unique flavor that some people have compared to oysters (hence its other common name — oyster plant). Frankly, while I enjoy the taste of both salsify and oysters, I would never confuse the two.

Scorzonera, also known as black salsify, belongs to a different genus from salsify and has black skin and white flesh. The name scorzonera derives from the Spanish *corteza negra,* or "black bark." It's a perennial root and bears yellow flowers, whereas salsify has purple blossoms and is a biennial, like carrots, parsnips, and other common root crops. Other than that, the two roots are almost identical in terms of their culture and culinary uses. Both salsify and scorzonera originated in southern Europe.

Salsify doesn't appear in supermarkets very often, probably because it doesn't store as long as carrots or parsnips under normal refrigeration. The best way to keep salsify and scorzonera is in the ground, where both hardy plants will overwinter with mulch protection. Like parsnips, salsify and scorzonera taste better after a hard frost and remain tasty when harvested the following spring.

How to Grow

Both salsify and scorzonera need light, well-drained soil. If your soil is heavy or clayey, dig it to a depth of 18 in. and lighten it by adding plenty of finished compost, screened peat moss, or other fine organic matter. Pick out any large stones when preparing the bed.

Plant seeds in the spring, ½–1 in. deep and 1 in. apart in rows spaced 18–24 in. apart. Thin seedlings to 3–4 in. apart in the row or bed. Since the leaves are slender and grasslike, it's a good idea to interplant radish seeds to mark the row and avoid accidental hand-weeding.

Both salsify and scorzonera need a long growing season, 120 days or more, but they are extremely frost-hardy and good for even short-season northern areas. In mild winter regions like Florida, salsify can be planted in October for harvest the following March.

Harvest

Harvest salsify and scorzonera after a hard frost in the fall or early winter. Dig up only the roots you need, since both vegetables store well in the ground and will overwinter in all regions under a protective layer of mulch. Roots also store well when harvested in the fall and packed in boxes of moistened sand in a root cellar, like carrots.

In the spring, harvest the remaining salsify roots from the garden or thin plants to 12 in. apart and allow them to go to seed. Salsify plants will grow 2–3 ft. high and bear purple flowers. Both the young spring leaves and unopened flower buds of salsify and scorzonera are edible.

A short-lived perennial, scorzonera can either be harvested like salsify or allowed to grow larger roots in its second year of growth. In this case, plant it in a bed or row of its own outside the main vegetable garden, and cut off the flower stalks as they emerge in the spring. Harvest all roots in the spring of the third year, or let a few plants produce their yellow flowers and go to seed. Collect ripe seeds in the late summer or early fall and reestablish the bed next year. Both salsify and scorzonera seed lose their viability quickly, after only 1–2 years under normal storage conditions.

■ RECOMMENDED VARIETIES

Salsify

'Mammoth Sandwich Island' (1860s) p. 99
The standard and most widely available variety, with slender, creamy white roots that taper to a point. Roots are 8–9 in. long and measure about 1½ in. across at the shoulder; hardy and overwinters well in the ground or in a cool, moist root cellar. Harvest after hard frost, which improves the texture and flavor of the roots; 120–150 days.

Scorzonera

'Geante Noire de Russie'
An extra-long variety from Belgium that is highly prized by European cooks. Black-skinned white roots are long, thin, and cylindrical, with few side roots. Peel the roots and cook them like salsify. Roots will get larger if overwintered under mulch protection and allowed to grow for a second year; over 120 days.

Shallots. *See* Multiplier Onions

Soybeans. *See* Beans

Spinach

Spinacia oleracea

Spinach is a hardy annual that originated in central and southwest Asia and was first cultivated in what is now Iran. The plants go to seed quickly in hot weather but grow very well in the short, cool days of spring and fall. There are two main horticultural types: prickly-seeded and round-seeded (*S. oleracea* var. *inermis*). Most modern varieties are derived from the round-seeded type. A few prickly-seeded strains still exist, however, and are well worth growing for their delicious, arrow-shaped leaves that remain tasty even when the plants begin to bolt. Most gardeners and seed suppliers classify a spinach variety by the appearance of its leaves, which can be smooth, savoyed (crinkled), or somewhere in between.

Spinach produces mainly dioecious plants, which means that most individual plants tend to have either male or female characteristics, but not both. Like corn, the plants are wind-pollinated, and the fine pollen grains can travel up to a mile or more in a good breeze. If you plan to save seed from an open-pollinated spinach, raise only one variety at a time in your garden and pull out any odd plants that may crop up next season.

Hybrids account for approximately 85 percent of the spinach seed sold in the U.S. today.[53] Commercial growers prefer hybrids because of their high yields and disease resistance. Many good open-pollinated varieties still exist, however, and these are highly recommended for home gardeners and small-market growers.

How to Grow

Spinach grows best in cool weather in a rich soil that is fairly neutral (pH 6.5–7.5). Apply agricultural lime and colloidal rock phosphate to the garden in the fall or early spring to sweeten an overly acidic soil and free up plant nutrients.

Sow the first crop of spinach as early in the spring as the ground can be worked. Plant seeds ½ in. deep and 1 in. apart in rows spaced 12–18 in. apart. Thin young plants to 4–6 in. apart in the row or bed. Spinach germinates well in cool soil; to speed up germination and improve the early growth of plants, soak seeds overnight before planting. Spinach can also be started indoors in flats or cells and transplanted carefully, 4–6 in. apart in the row or bed.

Temperatures above 60°F during the first 6 weeks of growth may cause plants to bolt prematurely. In warmer climates, plant crops in partial shade, keep the soil cool by mulching, and water well. Fertilize spinach by side-dressing plants with composted dried manure.

Plant small succession crops of spinach every 2 weeks through mid-spring. Spinach does not grow well in the heat of summer, so during this time plant a similar heat-tolerant green such as New Zealand spinach *(Tetragonia expansa)*, which is an heirloom in and of itself, introduced to North America in 1772.

Resume planting true spinach when the days begin to shorten and the weather turns cooler — late summer in the North, early to mid-autumn in warmer regions. Fall plantings of spinach have a longer harvest period than spring plantings, since temperatures are dropping and days are getting shorter. Fall-planted spinach is hardy enough to overwinter in milder areas under a light straw mulch. In the North, spinach makes a good cold frame crop for harvest in winter and early spring.

Harvest

Harvest the outer leaves of spinach first, when they are about 6 in. long. Keep picking individual leaves as needed for salad use or cooking until the plants mature or look like they're ready to bolt, at which point you should pull up the whole plant.

My friend and neighbor Lea Poisson plants a lot of spinach and dries much of his crop in a solar food dehydrator. The dried and ground leaves make a spinach powder that adds flavor, color, and nutrition to a wide variety of foods.

Pests and Diseases

White lines that appear on spinach leaves indicate that the larvae of leaf miner flies are feeding and tunneling under the surface. Remove and destroy infested plants. To prevent adults from laying eggs on the leaves, cover plants with a floating row fabric, digging in the edges of the material.

Good growing conditions and crop rotation help avoid most diseases like blight, mosaic, and downy mildew. If these or other diseases pose a serious threat, look for resistant varieties of spinach, of which there are many.

■ RECOMMENDED VARIETIES

'Bloomsdale Long Standing' (1925) p. 100

By far the most popular and widely available nonhybrid spinach; bred from a single monoecious plant. Glossy, dark green savoyed leaves are heavily blistered and crumpled; plants are vigorous and upright; stands well in hot weather and is slow to bolt. Tender, fleshy leaves have a rich flavor; 40–60 days. Various strains of 'Bloomsdale' are available.

'Giant Nobel' ('Long-Standing Gaudry'; 1926)
Plants are large and spreading; space 6 in. apart in row or bed. Huge green leaves are smooth and thick, with rounded tips. Productive, slow-bolting, and good for late spring harvest; 40–55 days.

'King of Denmark' (1919)
Very hardy variety with large, smooth, dark green leaves that are rounded and somewhat blistered; fine flavor and texture. Long-standing and continues in good condition more than 2 weeks after other varieties have bolted; productive and holds well after cutting; 45–55 days.

'Norfolk' (1880s)
A Canadian heirloom from Quebec. Savoyed, well-wrinkled leaves; plants are extremely cold-hardy, reportedly to –30°F. Good for early spring or fall planting; 45–55 days.

'Virginia Savoy' ('Old Dominion'; 1921)
Developed at the Virginia Agricultural Experiment Station; a popular and disease-resistant variety. Dark green, medium-size leaves are thick and savoyed. Vigorous plants are resistant to blight, yellows, and mosaic; not resistant to downy mildew. Best for fall harvest; bolts quickly when spring-planted; very cold-hardy; 40–60 days.

'Viroflay' (1866)
Vilmorin-Andrieux listed this spinach in 1885 as 'Monstrueux de Viroflay'. An important variety that has been used in breeding modern hybrids. Smooth, dark green leaves are large, about 10 in. long, and about 8 in. wide at the base; low in acid. Plants are large and spreading; space about 8–10 in. apart in the row and fertilize heavily with composted manure for best results; 50 days.

Squash and Pumpkins
Cucurbita spp.
Along with beans and corn, squash figures prominently as one of the great staple crops of ancient America. Remains of wild or cultivated squashes that date back to around 9000 B.C. have been found in Mexico, and similar archaeological evidence from nearly 5,000 years ago has turned up in areas as far removed as South America and New Mexico.[54] According to Hedrick, seeds belonging to nearly all of the various *Cucurbita* species have been found in pre-Columbian graves, and squash flowers apparently held a sacred place in

the religious rites of various Indian tribes, suggesting that this vegetable has been cultivated since very ancient times.[55]

Yet the squash and pumpkin varieties we know today have come a long way from their prehistoric forebears. Plant researcher Edgar Anderson remarks that, while cultivated squashes are generally large and flavorful, wild species are "uniformly small and repulsively bitter." His theory of domestication suggests that ancient peoples may have first collected squash fruits to make into rattles for ceremonies and dances, then started using them like gourds, for dishes and storage vessels. Only after squashes had been grown for a very long time, Anderson argues, did ancient farmers begin to identify and cultivate new and improved varieties as food crops — first for their oily, protein-rich seeds, and last for their flesh.[56]

The terms "squash" and "pumpkin" are used rather indiscriminately in referring to different species and forms that gardeners usually call winter squash and summer squash. There are four main cultivated species of *Cucurbita*:

- *C. maxima* originated in South America and is probably native to Bolivia and Argentina. Plants have long, bristly vines and large leaves. Maximas tolerate cool temperatures and are well adapted to areas as far north as southern Canada. This species includes familiar types of winter squash such as 'Buttercup', 'Blue Hubbard', and 'Turk's Turban', as well as the "true" or "French" pumpkins.

- *C. mixta* until recently was lumped in with *C. moschata*. This species includes many of the traditional winter squashes known as cushaws, which have been grown since early times from Guatemala to the southwestern U.S. Mixtas are drought-tolerant, and their flesh is generally paler, stringier, and less sweet than other types of squash.

- *C. moschata* hails from the tropical lowlands of Central and South America and, not surprisingly, grows best in areas with warm night temperatures and high humidity. Plants have large leaves, sprawling vines, and smooth, five-sided stems. The species includes the winter crookneck squashes, of which 'Butternut' is the most popular and widely grown modern variety.

- *C. pepo* squashes grow on either bushy or vining plants. The species includes all of the popular types of summer squash, which are eaten in their tender, immature state (scallop or pattypan, summer crookneck, zucchini, etc.). Stems are five-sided and spiny. The species also includes many of the pumpkins used for jack-o'-lanterns and pies, as well as 'Acorn' winter squash.

Finding out which species a particular squash or pumpkin belongs to can sometimes prove useful, especially if you are interested in saving seeds and avoiding unwanted cross-pollination. Two varieties belonging to the same species will cross with one another, while two varieties from different species generally will not. Aside from this practical consideration, the species distinctions are far less important to home gardeners than the vital statistics of an individual variety: how long a season it needs to mature; what kind of climate and growing conditions it prefers; how much space it takes up in the garden; and, most important, how good it looks and tastes.

How to Grow

Direct-seed in the garden after the last spring frost date; squash seeds do not germinate well in ground that is wet or cool (below 70°F). Squash thrives in a rich, well-drained soil, so work in plenty of good compost or composted dried manure before sowing seeds.

Plant seeds of bush varieties ½–1 in. deep and 6 in. apart in rows spaced 4 ft. apart, thinning young plants to 1 ft. apart. I always plant bush summer squash in circular hills spaced 4 ft. apart in the row, planting 6–8 seeds per hill and later thinning to the best 3 plants. Direct-seed vining varieties in the same manner, but give them more room, spacing row plants 1½ ft. apart, hills 5–6 ft. apart, and rows 6–8 ft. apart.

You can also get a jump on the season by starting squash seeds 3–4 weeks before the last spring frost date. Plant 2 seeds in individual 3–4-in. pots or large 6-cell packs. Thin to the best plant in each pot, clipping off extra seedlings with scissors so as not to disturb the roots of the remaining plant. Harden off seedlings and transplant to the garden when the weather is warm and settled, spacing 2 ft. apart in the row and being careful not to disturb the plants' roots.

Once the weather turns hot, mulch around the base of plants to conserve soil moisture. To supply extra warmth and keep insects away from young plants, cover with a floating row fabric. Side-dress plants with a balanced organic fertilizer or water with a liquid fish or seaweed emulsion.

Harvest

Cut fruits of summer squash while they are still young, tender, and immature. Very small scallop (pattypan) squash are attractive and tasty morsels if left unpeeled and steamed lightly or batter-fried as tempura. Zucchini and summer straightnecks and crooknecks usually taste best when they are 4–8 in. long. Keep summer squash plants well picked to encourage continuous production; harvest any overmature squash, like "brickbat" zucchini, to stuff and bake or to grate and use in quick breads and vegetable fritters.

Harvest winter squash before the first fall frosts. As fruits ripen, their skins become duller-looking and the rind cannot be dented with a fingernail. Cut off the fruits, leaving at least 1 in. of the dried stem attached. Allow the harvested squashes to cure in the sun for 7–10 days, covering them at night if frost is expected. Store in a cool, well-ventilated location (45–60°F) for the winter. To prevent rot, dunk the squash in a weak bleach-water solution before storing (use 10 parts water to 1 part bleach).

Pests and Diseases
Avoid damage from cucumber beetles and squash bugs by covering young plants with a floating row fabric; control bugs on larger plants by dusting leaves with pyrethrum or sabadilla powder. Look for squash bug egg masses on the undersides of leaves and crush them.

Squash vine borers are the other major insect pest affecting this crop. Look for their holes on the lower stems of the plant in early summer. If you find any, slit open the stem in the vicinity of the hole and remove and destroy the borer. Mound soil over the slitted portion of stem. Applying rotenone around the base of plants also helps control vine borers. Squashes belonging to the species *C. mixta* and *C. moschata* are more resistant to insect damage than other non-hybrid varieties.

Diseases like bacterial wilt and mosaic virus can usually be avoided by rotating crops and controlling insects such as aphids that spread disease. Control aphids with an insecticidal soap spray. Fungal diseases such as downy and powdery mildew are usually caused by cool, damp weather and hot, dry weather, respectively. Use floating row covers to provide plants with additional heat or water and mulch in hot, dry weather. Remove infested plants and compost all squash vines and crop wastes at the end of the season.

■ **RECOMMENDED VARIETIES**

Cucurbita maxima

'Blue Banana' (ca. 1893) p. 100
A cylindrical winter squash with grayish green skin; can grow 18–30 in. long, 6–8 in. in diameter, and weigh 25–30 lb.; shell is medium-hard. Flesh is orange-yellow, fine-textured, tender, dry, and stringless. Dependable even in poor seasons; some resistance to squash bugs; 105–120 days.

'Boston Marrow' (before 1831) p. 101
To my mind, one of the prettiest maximas. Earlier this century 'Boston Marrow' was the standard early winter squash.

This variety, like many others, probably was grown by American Indians, and it is associated with the Iroquois. Hedrick also suggests it may be the same as a variety from Chile that was described in the late 1700s. Burr lists it in 1863 under the name 'Autumnal Marrow'.

Fruits are 12–16 in. long, 9–12 in. in diameter, and weigh 10–20 lb.; shape resembles a more rounded 'Hubbard'. Skin is bright reddish orange and lovely; shell is medium-soft. Flesh is yellow-orange, thick, fine-grained, tender, and fairly moist. A beautiful and historic old squash; 95–100 days.

'Buttercup' (1925) p. 101
Developed by the North Dakota Agricultural Experiment Station from a chance cross between 'Quality' and 'Essex Hybrid'. Fruits of this original strain are very small and flattened or drumlike, weighing 3–5 lb. Skin is dull green, thick and hard. Flesh is thick, dry, and golden yellow; sweet flavor; excellent keeper; 90–110 days. Many newer strains, including a bush variety, are also available.

'Hubbard' ('Green Hubbard', 'True Hubbard'; 1798) p. 102
The original variety of this popular squash type, which first came to Marblehead, Massachusetts, in 1798, perhaps from the West Indies or South America. J. H. Gregory introduced the variety to the seed trade in the 1840s and named it for Elizabeth Hubbard of Marblehead.

Fruits are dark bronze-green, 12–15 in. long, 9–10 in. across, and weigh 10–15 lb. Outer shell is hard; inner flesh is thick, fine-grained, dry, golden yellow, and mealy, with an excellent flavor; keeps well through the winter. A classic; 100–115 days. Other heirloom hubbard strains include 'Chicago Warted Hubbard' (1894), 'Golden Hubbard' (1898), 'Kitchenette' or 'Baby Blue Hubbard' (1921), and the popular 'Blue Hubbard' (1909).

'North Georgia Candy Roaster' p. 102
An excellent but rare variety that comes highly recommended by David Cavagnaro of Seed Savers Exchange. Plants are big with rampant vines and produce as many as a dozen squash. Cylindrical fruits resemble 'Banana' in shape but are even longer, 30–36 in., and skinny (about 4 in. in diameter). Outer skin is pink and inner flesh is orange. One of the sweetest and tastiest squashes for baking; 100–110 days.

'Queensland Blue' (before 1932)
A variety that hails from Australia. Fruits are small to medium-size, 8–15 lb., with a convoluted shape. Skin is an attractive blue-green color; flesh is orange, fine-textured, and

moist with a good, nutty flavor; good keeper; 110 days. David Cavagnaro of Seed Savers Exchange calls this variety "one of my favorites."

'Red Kuri' ('Orange Hokkaido')   p. 103

Hedrick does not list this variety in his *Cucurbits of New York* (1937), so its reputation as an heirloom is dubious. No matter; this squash from Japan deserves inclusion both for its beauty and superior quality. Teardrop-shaped fruits are bright scarlet-orange and small, weighing 4–7 lb. Flesh is smooth-textured and excellent for pies and purées, and for mashing; 90–95 days.

'Rouge Vif d'Étampes' (Étampes; 1883)   p. 103

Introduced by Burpee in 1883 but popular since the early 1800s in France, where it was widely grown. This is the "true" or "French" pumpkin, the one that Cinderella's fairy godmother turned into a coach in the well-known fairy tale. One of the most ornamental pumpkins.

Large fruits are flattened on top and bottom with beautiful reddish orange, deeply ribbed skin; pumpkins stand about 6 in. high and 18 in. across. Shell is thin and medium-soft; flesh is deep yellow, coarse-textured, and fibrous; flavor is insipid. Much better for fall decoration than for cooking; 105–130 days.

'Turk's Turban'   p. 104

Turban squashes are flattened and drumlike and have a protuberance on their blossom ends called an "acorn" (not to be confused with the common 'Acorn' variety belonging to *C. pepo*). This may be the variety Hedrick lists as 'French Turban', which was grown in France before 1818 and listed by J. B. Russell as 'Acorn' in 1827.

Whatever its origin, this unique squash makes a striking fall decoration, either in the field or in the house. Small flattened fruits are 8–12 in. across and weigh about 5 lb.; skin is orange when mature and the "acorn" is tricolored, striped with green, red, and white; stores fairly well; eating quality is only fair; 90–120 days. Very ornamental; I spotted this old favorite from a mile away while visiting the squash fields at Johnny's Selected Seeds in Albion, Maine.

Cucurbita mixta

'Green-Striped Cushaw' (1820s)   p. 104

The most widely available variety of *C. mixta* squash, probably from the West Indies. Fruits are very attractive, colored creamy white with green mottled stripes; pear-shaped with a crookneck; 16–20 in. long with a bowl that measures 8–10 in. across; weight averages 10–12 lb. Outer skin is hard, smooth, and thin; flesh is thick, pale yellow, and medium-coarse; sweet, distinctive cushaw flavor. Recommended for warm regions; in the Northeast and other areas it produces huge vines but fairly few fruit. Resistant to squash vine borer; 110 days.

'White Jonathan Cushaw' (1891)
This variety has beautiful, smooth white skin and a slight crookneck shape; medium-large fruits weigh around 15–20 lb. Flesh is cream-colored; somewhat prone to rot in the North; 90–100 days.

Cucurbita moschata

'Butternut' (1944) p. 105
Barely old enough to be considered an heirloom, but 'Butternut' is one of the most popular varieties and definitely here to stay. Bottle-shaped fruits are light tan, 3–5 lb., with straight, thick, solid necks; golden orange flesh is thick, dry, fine-grained, and sweet. Thin hard skin; good keeper; 75–110 days. Many improved strains are available; the most famous is 'Waltham Butternut'.

'Cheese Pumpkin' (1824) p. 105
One of the oldest cultivated moschatas in the U.S.; the name refers to the fruit's shape, which resembles an old-fashioned flattened cheesebox. In *Cucurbits of New York* (1937), Hedrick writes, "the cheese pumpkins are, as a group, quite different from other squash and pumpkins, and have remained remarkably stable."
   Fruits are flattened with wide ribs and shallow furrows, 12–18 in. in diameter; blossoms are orange-colored and very large, to 8 in. across. Skin is creamy tan; flesh is deep orange, thick, and very coarse-textured, but with a sweet flavor; not a good keeper; 110 days.

'Kikuza Early White' (1927)
A rare winter squash from southern China, though Hedrick lists Japan as country of origin in 1937. Plants are prolific and heat-tolerant. Ribbed fruits are tan, 3–5 lb.; flesh is pale yellow-orange, firm, fine-textured, and sweet; 100–125 days.

'Neck Pumpkin'
A forerunner of 'Butternut' that has 18–24-in.-long crookneck fruits; flesh is orange-colored, thick, dry, solid, and sweet; excellent for pies; 120 days.

'Seminole Pumpkin' (1916)

This tropical pumpkin was introduced in 1916 but has been grown in Florida by Seminole Indians for centuries; found growing wild in the Everglades by early explorers. Fruits are buff-colored and 6–8 in. long; shell is hard. Flesh is deep orange and very sweet; excellent for pie filling or in other pumpkin recipes. Vigorous, productive plants are well adapted to growing in the South; they tolerate drought and moisture and are resistant to insects and disease; 90 days.

'Tromboncino' ('Rampicante Zucchetta')

A unique variety from Italy that is eaten immature as a summer squash and in fact is often listed under *C. pepo*. Fruits grow long and thin and are best harvested when they are 8–18 in. long; flavor is fine and sweet. The blossom end of the fruit curves into a bell shape, making the squash look like a trombone or question mark. Vigorous vines are best grown on a trellis; otherwise fruits are susceptible to field rot. If left to mature on the vine, the fruit ripens into an unusual and decorative gourd; 60 days.

'Upper Ground Sweet Potato'

A butternut-type heirloom from Kentucky. Produces well under hot, dry conditions. Vines are long and vigorous. Fruits are small, 5–10 lb., tan-colored, and bell-shaped, with either no necks or short, straight necks. Flesh is orange-yellow with a good, sweet flavor similar to 'Butternut'. Excellent keeper; 100 days.

Cucurbita pepo

'Acorn, Table Queen' (1913)

One of the most popular types of winter squash. Vigorous vining plants produce medium-size fruits, 1–2 lb., that are dark green and deeply ribbed; thin, hard shell. Flesh is golden yellow, dry, sweet, and tasty; one of the best baking squashes when halved and seasoned with butter and maple syrup. Good keeper; 80–90 days. Many similar strains are available, some with bush growing habits, others with skin colored green-black, golden, or creamy white.

'Benning's Green Tint Scallop' (1914)

Hedrick lists this variety as 'Farr's Benning White Bush' in 1937 and says it was developed by Charles N. Farr. Slightly flattened, pale green, uniform fruits have scalloped edges and measure 3–4 in. across. Flesh is pale green and fine-textured; delicious when picked small. Hedrick calls this "one of the most beautiful strains of the whole group of Patty Pans," and

I agree. Plants are heavier-yielding than older bush scallop varieties; 50–60 days.

'Black Zucchini' (1931)

Bush plants are more vigorous than other zucchinis and are everbearing. Fruits are dark green-black, long and straight, with slight ridges; best picked when 6–8 in. long but remain good even when twice that length. Flesh is greenish white, crisp, and fine-textured; 45–65 days.

'Cocozelle' (1934)   p. 106

A classic strain of zucchini squash; bush plants produce lots of long, cylindrical fruits that are dark green striped with lighter green. Flesh is very firm and greenish white; fruits are tender and good when harvested from a very small stage to 10–12 in. in length; 55–65 days.

'Connecticut Field' (before 1700)   p. 106

One of the oldest field pumpkins in existence; almost certainly grown by North American Indians before European settlement. Fruits are large (15–25 lb.) and globe-shaped, slightly flattened at both ends; skins are bright yellow-orange with slight ribbing. Flesh is yellow, thick, coarse, and stringy. Poor quality for cooking, but one of the best varieties for carving jack-o'-lanterns; 100–120 days.

'Delicata' (1894)   p. 107

Another very familiar type of winter squash for baking. Vines are short but productive. Fruits are small, straight, and cylindrical, 7–9 in. long and 3 in. in diameter. Skin is ivory-cream streaked with dark green along the ribs. Flesh is deep orange, tender, and dry, with a rich, sweet flavor. Good keeper; 95–100 days.

'Early Yellow Summer Crookneck' (ca. 1700)   p. 107

Crooknecks, like scallop types, are very old forms of summer squash; Thorburn lists 'Summer Crookneck' as early as 1828, and the type is still very popular with home gardeners, though market growers prefer the straightneck types.

Plants are semiopen bushes and of smooth-skinned, light yellow fruits that turn orange and warted when past the eating stage. Fruits grow 8–10 in. long, but should be picked younger if possible. Flesh is creamy white, sweet, and mild; good for steaming or sautéing; 42–60 days.

'Ronde de Nice'   p. 108

For gardeners sick of the same old zucchini, this 19th-century French heirloom is a nice change of pace. Fruits are spherical and light green; delicious flavor. Harvest when 1 in. across for steaming, at 4 in. for stuffing. Delicate skin bruises easily but is good for home gardeners. Bushy plants are vigorous, fast-growing, and prolific; 45–65 days.

'Small Sugar' ('New England Pie'; before 1860)
Described by Burr in 1863 and still popular as the classic pumpkin for pies or canning. Plants are trailing. Fruits are small (5–8 lb.), round, orange globes, slightly flattened at both ends and lightly ribbed. Flesh is thick, yellow-orange, fine-grained, stringless, and sweet; 80–110 days.

'Vegetable Spaghetti' ('Spaghetti Squash'; 1890s)
The popular, hard-shelled variety that can be baked or boiled before having the stringy cooked flesh scraped out for use. Vines are vigorous, sprawling, and productive; fruits are cylindrical, 8–12 in. long, and cream-colored, turning buff-tan at maturity; stores up to 6 months; 70–115 days.

'White Bush Scallop' (before 1722)
One of the earliest-known squashes grown by the American Indians; possibly known in Europe before 1600 and called a "symnel" or "cymling." Bush plants are compact and productive. Fruits have scalloped edges and are smooth, pale greenish white, and flattened; they measure 3 in. deep and 5–7 in. across and weigh 2–3 lb. Flesh is white and fine-grained, with a good flavor; 45–55 days.

'Winter Luxury' ('Luxury Pie Pumpkin'; 1893)
Vines are rampant and vigorous; pumpkins are globular, 7–8 lb., with heavily netted orange skin. Flesh is pale orange, juicy, tender, and slightly sweet; good flavor for pies and canning; good keeper; 100 days.

'Yellow Bush Scallop' (before 1860)
Vigorous bush plants bear large, scalloped yellow fruits, 7 in. across. Flavor is distinctive from greenish white scallop types; this variety is very similar to the one called 'Golden Custard' introduced by Henderson in 1889. Resistant to squash bugs; 50–55 days.

Sunflower

Helianthus annuus
Virtually all of the important food crops that are native to the Western Hemisphere (corn, squash, potatoes, beans, etc.) originally came from tropical and subtropical climates. Not

so the sunflower. It's a North American original, domesticated almost entirely within the boundaries of what is now the United States. The common sunflower, *Helianthus annuus,* is the state flower of Kansas (the Sunflower State), and its branching plants with their small yellow rays grow wild and weedy from southern Canada to northern Mexico.[57]

Gardeners in the U.S. usually grow the huge, single-headed type of sunflower for its tasty seeds, either to harvest for themselves or to feed the birds. Many smaller-flowered forms make wonderful ornamentals, either planted in the vegetable garden or in separate beds or borders. The beautiful varieties of flowers include colors ranging from straw yellow to intense burgundy red, and everything in between. Flower forms are almost equally varied and include blossoms with multiple disk petals (commonly called "lion's mane") as well as puffy, fully double blooms that scarcely resemble a sunflower at all.

American Indians have valued sunflowers since prehistoric times for their many practical uses, especially as a food and dye plant. Several traditional strains still exist today, a few of which are mentioned below. Ironically, though, the sunflower is much more important as a crop plant in other parts of the world. My friend Anneke Wegscheider has seen fields upon fields of sunflowers in Germany through the windows of a train, all with their heads pointed in the same direction, toward the summer sun. And in the 1970s farmers in the former Soviet Union were planting some 12 million acres in sunflowers, two-thirds of the world's crop. The Russians and their neighbors use sunflowers to make about 90 percent of their vegetable oil, and they snack on the seeds in the same way many Americans eat peanuts.[58]

How to Grow
Sunflowers like hot weather and grow best in full sun in a light, well-drained, fertile soil. Plant seeds after the last spring frost date, when soil temperatures are warm (60–80°F). Sow seeds 1 in. deep and 4–6 in. apart in the row or bed. Thin plants to 12 in. apart when they are 4–6 in. high; large-headed varieties should be planted about 9–12 in. apart and young plants thinned to 18–24 in. apart.

Large, single-headed varieties of sunflowers may require some kind of staking or support as they grow, especially if planted in an unsheltered location. One solution to this problem is to grow sunflowers along a fence or trellis, to which the plants can be tied if necessary.

Harvest
Large sunflower heads can have between 1,000 and 4,000 tiny disk flowers, which are perfect (contain both male and

female parts) and produce the achenes, or seed-filled hulls, that fill out the mature head. To harvest seeds, wait until the outer "ray flower" petals have dropped off and the head has turned completely brown and filled out with seeds.

Cut off the head along with a short length of the plant stem and hang it to dry in an airy place inside. Remove seeds from the heads when they feel dry and firm to the touch. One way to do this is to scrape the heads over a 1-in. wire mesh screen into a pail or wheelbarrow. Hull a few seeds to check for dryness. Seeds are dry enough to store when they snap, rather than bend, when pressed between your thumb and forefinger. If the seeds need more drying, spread them out on trays in a warm area out of direct sunlight. Save some of the large, plump seeds from the outside of the disk for planting next year.

Pests and Diseases

Sunflower maggots can sometimes burrow into the stalks of large sunflowers and damage the plants. If you notice holes in the plant stalk, cut around it and remove and destroy the borer. Remove infested plants and burn or compost them. Control the adult flies with rotenone or pyrethrum.

Sunflowers are susceptible to various diseases, including rust and powdery mildew. Treating leaves with sulfur dust controls both of these conditions.

■ RECOMMENDED VARIETIES

'Arikara' p. 108
A traditional variety grown by the Arikara Indians in the northern Dakotas. Plants are 6–8 ft. tall and variable, some with single heads, others with multiple heads. Seed hulls are either black or mottled. A rare variety, not currently offered in the seed trade but still being preserved among gardeners.

'Havasupai Striped'
Another traditional variety grown at the bottom of the Grand Canyon by the Havasupai Indians. Plants are 6–8 ft. tall and produce a single 6-in. head with many smaller 2–3-in. side heads. Produces a good crop of seeds, whose hulls are black and white speckled or striped with brown or black. According to Lawrence Hollander at CRESS, this variety grows well in the Northeast; 80–100 days.

'Italian White' (*H. debilis* var. *cucumerifolius*) p. 109
An heirloom ornamental that's terrific for cutting. Plants are 6 ft. tall and branching; prolific, 4–5-in., cactus-type flowers cover the whole plant and have dark chocolate brown cen-

ters surrounded by a thin yellow ring; outer ray petals are creamy yellow with pointed tips. Leaves are smaller than *H. annuus* varieties and stems are smoother and more relaxed; 80–100 days.

'Mammoth Russian' p. 109
The familiar single-headed sunflower that towers over gardens everywhere. Plants grow anywhere from 7–12 ft. or even higher; heads measure 10–15 in. across; seeds are large with thin, striped hulls; rich in protein and oil. Productive, hardy, and disease-resistant; 90–110 days.

'Maximilian' (*H. maximiliani*)
A perennial sunflower native to the Plains states and named for Maximilian of Wied, a Prussian prince who collected it on his travels to America in the early 1830s. Plants are branching and grow 5–7 ft. tall, with attractive grayish leaves. Abundant flowers are golden yellow, 3 in. or more across, and appear in late summer or autumn. Widely adapted to a variety of soil types; a different kind of sunflower for perennial borders.

'Tarahumara White'
A rare traditional variety that probably originated with Canadian Mennonites. Plants are 7–8 ft. tall and bear 9–10-in. single seedheads that have golden disk and ray flowers. Seed hulls are pure white. Productive and drought-tolerant; a beautiful and unusual variety; 100 days.

Sweet Potato

Ipomoea batatas p. 110
The sweet potato is related to morning-glories and is native to the tropical lowlands of Central and South America. Like other American food plants, it became known in Europe by the early 1500s. Less well known, perhaps, is the fact that sweet potatoes had spread to Polynesia and New Zealand well before the arrival of the first Europeans.[59] By the 1600s sweet potatoes had arrived in New Guinea, probably via Chinese and Malay traders, and their successful culture on that island sparked a population explosion similar to the one the common white potato caused in Ireland.[60]

The sweet potato, however, is not related to the common potato. The confusion comes from the word *batata*, which is what the Taino Indians of the Bahamas and Greater Antilles called the sweet potato. Early European explorers gave the same name to the Andean tuber they found growing in South

America, and the two different plants have been yoked together ever since.[61]

Another common misnomer is calling a sweet potato a "yam." Real yams are tropical Old World plants that belong to the genus *Dioscorea* and are seldom grown in the U.S. except as exotic greenhouse specimens. This confusion arose from an advertising campaign started more than 50 years ago by Louisiana sweet potato growers, who decided that the assonant name "Louisiana yams" would add a certain *je ne sais quoi* to their product.[62] Americans are still trying to get things sorted out.

How to Grow

Although sweet potatoes grow best in warm, long-season areas (Zone 7 and higher), it is possible to grow them to a harvestable size farther north, so long as you provide them with additional heat. Generally, if you have a garden space that's large enough for winter squash, you will have enough room for sweet potatoes, which send their sprawling vines over a similarly large area.

Sweet potatoes are started from rooted sprouts, or "slips." Buy rooted slips from a mail-order supplier, or start your own in early spring. Stand up a sweet potato in a glass that's half-filled with water, then place it in a warm, sunny place to sprout. When the sprouts have grown 6–9 in. long, pick them off and put them in water until they form small roots. At this point, the slips are ready for transplanting to the garden.

Sweet potatoes like warm, loose, well-drained soil that is not overly rich. Make a long, raised planting ridge about 6 in. high in the middle of each sweet potato row, either hilling up soil by hand from between rows or using a rototiller with a hilling attachment. This keeps the soil warm and well drained for the sweet potatoes.

Plant the slips about 15 in. apart in ridged rows spaced 30–48 in. apart, depending on whether you are growing a bush or vining variety of sweet potato. Water the transplants well. Gardeners in the North need to give plants all the extra heat they can; one good method is to cover the planting ridge with black plastic, cutting slits or small holes in the sheeting every 15 in. to plant a slip. Covering the young slips with plastic cloches or a floating row fabric also helps provide extra heat in the northern spring.

Once the plant's vines begin to run, lift them off the ground and move them around every couple of weeks, to prevent the vines from rooting. Sweet potatoes like a consistent supply of water early in the season, so water regularly whenever necessary. Begin cutting back on water in late summer; too much water late in the season can cause the developing sweet potatoes to grow long instead of compact or cause the roots to crack.

Harvest

Sweet potatoes are usually ready for harvest from 100 to 130 days after transplanting the slips. Harvest when night temperatures dip below 50°F in the South, or when the first frosts have nipped the vines in the North. Remove any plastic mulch, if you've used it, and carefully pry up plants with a garden fork. Harvest any sweet potato roots that are large enough to keep and take them inside under cover to cure. Cure roots for 8–10 days in a very warm space (85–95°F) that is out of direct sunlight. Transfer to a cool room temperature area (60–65°F) for long-term storage, spacing roots apart on shallow, slotted racks or individually wrapping them in newspaper. In general, sweet potatoes don't keep as well as common potatoes.

Pests and Diseases

Use Bt (Dipel) to control armyworm caterpillars. Black rot and stem rot can usually be avoided by practicing good crop rotation. Remove all crop residues from the garden at the end of the season.

■ RECOMMENDED VARIETIES

'Nancy Hall'

A favorite old variety with creamy yellow skin and deep yellow flesh that is sweet and juicy. Plants are productive and have lush foliage. Excellent for baking; good keeping qualities; 110 days.

'Porto Rico Bush'

Developed by the Georgia Agricultural Experiment Station. Semi-upright plants have 12–30-in. vines. Roots have copper skin and deep orange flesh. Sweet and moist; excellent for baking; 110–150 days.

'Red Wine Velvet'

A beautiful sweet potato with beet red skin and yellow-orange flesh. Plants are vining and have vigorous runners; stems and leaves are green-purple. Moist flesh; excellent taste. Not currently offered in the seed trade but preserved through the Seed Savers Exchange Members Network; 110–120 days.

'White Yam' ('Southern Queen', 'Choker', 'Poplar Root')

One of the oldest varieties grown in the U.S. Vining plants produce roots with white skin and dry, white flesh; 120 days.

Swiss Chard

Beta vulgaris, Cicla group

Swiss chard is a hardy biennial vegetable that also goes by the name of spinach beet or silver-leaf beet. As these alternate names suggest, chard doesn't form a significant underground root like its close sibling, the common beet. It is grown instead for its tall rosette of leaves, which have fleshy, succulent leafstalks, or petioles.

Native to southern Europe, chard is apparently much older than the large-rooted forms of beets and may have developed from the wild beet more than 2,000 years ago.[63] Aristotle mentions a red-stalked chard around 350 B.C., and white, yellow, and dark green forms have apparently been known since ancient times.[64]

Over the course of its history, Swiss chard has found favor among gardeners as both a vegetable and an ornamental plant. In fact, chard makes a nice edging crop for a bed or border, since it tolerates most soils and grows well even in partial shade. Especially in northern areas, a single planting of chard will provide fresh greens throughout the growing season for salads and light cooking.

How to Grow

Direct-seed Swiss chard in early through late spring. For a fall or early winter crop, plant chard from late summer in the North through mid-fall in the South. Chard withstands both summer heat and light frosts once the plants are mature, but it grows best in cool conditions. A fall-sown crop planted in a cold frame, sunspace, or solar greenhouse ensures a good winter harvest. In mild winter climates, mature Swiss chard plants can overwinter in the garden under mulch protection.

Plant seeds ½ in. deep and about 2 in. apart in rows spaced 18–24 in. apart. Thin young plants to stand 8–12 in. apart in the row or bed.

Harvest

Break off individual outer leaves near the base of the plant, allowing leaves at the center of the plant to develop. To harvest whole plants, cut off all stalks 2 in. above the base of the plant; leave the plants in the ground, and they will produce a second crop of smaller leaves.

■ RECOMMENDED VARIETIES

'Argentata'

This Italian heirloom has broad, silvery white midribs and broad, deep green, savoyed leaves. Plants are vigorous and tall, 2–3 ft. in height. Flavor is mild, clean, and sweet; Wendy

Krupnick of Shepherd's Garden Seeds lists this as one of her favorites. Use as a substitute for spinach in omelettes and pasta dishes; 55 days.

'Fordhook Giant' (1750)
One of the most widely grown varieties of chard. Plants grow 24–28 in. tall and are extremely vigorous. Broad, dark green, heavily crumpled leaves and thick white midribs. Bears all season and stands several light frosts. Good flavor; excellent for greens; 50–60 days.

'Lucullus' (1914)
Named after the Roman general and epicure, Lucius Licinius Lucullus. Vigorous plants grow 24–30 in. high and tolerate hot weather. Light green leaves are large, thick, and heavily crumpled; midribs are large, white, and rounded. Productive; fine flavor; 50–60 days.

'Perpetual Spinach' ('Spinach Beet'; 1869)
My friend Jo Ann Gardner is a great fan of this fine old European strain, which is not widely grown in the U.S. Smooth, dark green leaves are smaller than most chard varieties, as are the small green midribs; plants resemble spinach. Tolerates drought and frosts; resists bolting. Produces leaves over a long harvest season; 50–55 days.

'Rainbow Chard' ('Five Color Silver Beet') p. 110
Probably the most ornamental strain of Swiss chard, this variety used to be offered by the English seed house of Thompson & Morgan but has fallen out of the commercial trade. That's a real pity, because it deserves to be much more widely grown.

Chard colors tend to be variable, as this strain proves. The plants I've seen had midribs colored orange, pink, crimson, silver-white, and yellow. Vigorous and handsome; still being preserved in the Seed Savers Exchange Collection and may be available again soon.

'Rhubarb Chard' ('Ruby Chard'; 1857) p. 111
One of the most popular chards for its vivid color; deep crimson stalks and leaf veins and dark green, heavily crumpled leaves. Stalks are thick, tender, and juicy; taste is milder and different from other chards. Lots of variation; very pretty. A great ornamental plant for either the vegetable or flower garden; 50–60 days.

Tepary Beans. *See* Beans

Tomatillo

Physalis ixocarpa

Tomatillos, also known as ground cherries or husk tomatoes, come originally from Central and South America. The tomatillo is closely related to the vigorous perennial plant called Chinese lantern *(P. alkekengi)*, a fact that becomes obvious as soon as the tomatillo begins to set fruit. The golf-ball-sized green or green-purple fruits are completely enclosed within a papery husk, or calyx, that looks very much like the brilliant scarlet-orange Chinese lanterns so popular in dried flower arrangements.

Left to their own devices, the tomatillo and all its relatives will self-sow readily from dropped fruit. Plant researcher Edgar Anderson once observed that, in western Mexico, the husk tomato grows semiwild as a tolerated weed in fields of maize. He adds that larger-fruited tomatillos were commonly grown in central Mexico,[65] and these improved types are doubtless either the same or fairly recent parents of our present garden varieties.

I first started growing tomatillos out of curiosity a few years ago, and since then I've become an ardent fan. Every year I seem to start more seedlings to give away to gardening friends. (It is next to impossible to find flats of tomatillos for sale in New Hampshire.) In the wretched summer of 1992, one of the coldest and wettest on record, my tomatoes barely produced ripe fruit before frost, but the tomatillos grew incredibly lush and set fruit continuously from midsummer through early fall.

The flavor of a tomatillo is complex and difficult to pin down. At first bite, the fruit tastes sweet, almost like a green apple. The aftertaste is astringent and slightly sour, but not unpleasantly so. Tomatillos make a tremendous green salsa, lightly roasted to bring out their flavor, then chopped up with chilies, salt, lime juice, and fresh cilantro. I eat lots of tomatillo salsa during the summer and freeze some to cook down in winter with ground roasted nuts and seeds to make a piquant mole sauce for grilled fish.

How to Grow

Start tomatillo plants indoors at the same time you would start tomatoes, about 6 weeks before the last spring frost date. Plant seeds ¼ in. deep in flats or cells; keep soil temperatures warm by bottom-heating until plants germinate. After plants have grown their first true leaves, transplant to individual 3–4-in. pots.

Harden off seedlings for 5–7 days before transplanting to the garden. Space plants 2–3 ft. apart. Use the 2-ft. spacing if you don't grow the tomatillos on a support; use the 3-ft. spacing if you cage plants. Tomatillos have smooth stems that spread outward and don't really climb like tomatoes. I recommend caging the plants, if only to give the stems some minimal support and direction.

Tomatillos prefer average garden soil that isn't overly rich. Water regularly in dry weather, and mulch to conserve moisture after the soil heats up. Plants usually don't need fertilizing but will benefit from an occasional watering with liquid fish or seaweed emulsion.

Harvest

Tomatillos set their husks or calyxes before forming fruit. The fruit is ready to pick when they have entirely filled out the husks and have turned from green to pale yellow-green in color. Gently feel the husks to check on fullness; some fruits will grow large enough to split the husks at the bottom and will be easy to spot. Another sign of ripeness is when the husks turn dry and straw-colored.

Pick fruit, husks and all, and dehusk inside the house. Tomatillo fruits are tacky or sticky when removed from the husk; this stickiness washes off easily under running water.

Tomatillos will provide a continuous harvest from the time they set fruit until the first fall frost. At the end of the season, remove and compost the plants and any fruits that have fallen to the ground.

Pests and Diseases

Tomatillos are attractive to some of the same insect pests as tomatoes. Colorado potato beetles will chew on the leaves, but rarely do major damage; in serious cases dust with rotenone. The tomato hornworm also sometimes attacks plants. If you see chewed leaves and stems in mid- to late summer, examine plants carefully, and cut off or pick off any green hornworms. Remove them from the garden and squish them underfoot.

■ RECOMMENDED VARIETIES

'Purple de Milpa'   p. 111

A superior and tasty variety that bears somewhat larger fruit than its relative, the Zuni or wild tomatillo *(P. philadelphica)*, which grows semiwild in the slash-and-burn cornfields, or *milpas,* of Mexico. 'De Milpa' plants grow 3–4 ft. high and are very ornamental, with green stems and husks veined with dark purple. Fruits are usually bicolored, green and purple; often the purple shows on the part of the fruit that is exposed through the split husk. Size of fruit is 1–2 in. across; flavor is sweeter than that of green tomatillos. Dry this variety by pulling back the husks and stringing the fruits together in wreaths, like garlic; hung up indoors to dry, purple tomatillos can keep for a few months. This traditional variety makes outstanding salsa; 80–90 days.

'Toma Verde' ('Tomatillo Verde')
This is the common green tomatillo most often grown by home gardeners. Two separate strains of green tomatillos exist, one producing rather squat and compact plants, another forming more erect and branching plants. Vigorous plants grow 2–3 ft. or higher and have about a 3–4-ft. spread. The tomatillo fruits are well enclosed inside their green husks and are relatively large, to 2½ in. in diameter. An excellent and easy-to-grow variety; 60–80 days.

Tomato
Lycopersicon lycopersicum
With the possible exception of beans, no vegetable has received more attention from heirloom aficionados and home seed savers than the tomato. And no vegetable is prized more highly by gardeners of all persuasions: tomatoes annually rank as America's number one home garden crop. The main reason for the garden tomato's popularity is not hard to guess. A quick trip to the supermarket reveals pale, hard, tasteless tomatoes that have been picked green, gassed into semiripeness, entombed in cellophane, and shipped across the continent. Bioengineered tomatoes (designed to be picked ripe and to remain fresh for a long time) have recently garnered a lot of media attention. Yet even the "manufacturer" of this new, genetically manipulated vegetable admits it won't hold a candle to the taste of vine-ripened, homegrown tomatoes.

The tomato comes from the tropics, with various species native to western South America and Mexico. Many wild or semiwild tomatoes bear small, intensely flavored fruits, such as the grapelike clusters of the species known as currant tomato *(L. pimpinellifolium)*. Some of the oldest types of cultivated tomatoes include those with prominent ribs (similar to the present 'Zapotec Ribbed') and small pear-shaped fruits (represented by 'Red Pear' and 'Yellow Pear'). Larger-fruited tomatoes probably originated on the eastern slopes of the Andes, in Peru or Ecuador.[66]

In its native habitat, the tomato grows as a perennial, but in temperate climates it is grown, like most vegetables, as an annual. Like other strange foods from the New World, it took time for the tomato to gain acceptance in European circles.

Not surprisingly, perhaps, the Italians were among the first to recognize the culinary value of the tomato, and large-fruited forms arrived in Italy at an early date, probably direct from their Peruvian homeland.[67]

Even in North America the tomato only gained favor slowly. Its popularity increased dramatically around the mid-1800s, though as late as 1863 Fearing Burr lists only 17 different varieties being grown in the U.S., most representing very general types. Since that time, however, plant breeders have been busily developing new tomato varieties for home and commercial growers. One estimate indicates that, between the mid-1800s and today, as many as 1,000 named varieties of tomatoes may have come and (mostly) gone from the seed trade.[68]

Fortunately, the tomato's popularity as a vegetable has helped preserve many fine varieties over the years, and more newly rediscovered heirlooms are appearing in commercial seed catalogs every year. Home gardeners still have hundreds of excellent nonhybrid varieties to choose from, and the superior taste and diversity of these classic tomatoes make them the perfect way to start your adventure into the world of heirloom vegetables.

How to Grow

Start tomato seeds in flats or cells, 6–8 weeks before the last spring frost date. Sow seeds thinly, $\frac{1}{4}$–$\frac{1}{2}$ in. deep. Provide bottom heating to keep the soil warm (75–85°F) until plants germinate, in 10–14 days. Once seedlings have produced 2–3 true leaves, transplant into individual 3–4-in. pots. Set plants slightly deeper than they were growing in the flat; this deeper planting allows new roots to form along the lower, buried section of stem. Water sparingly and fertilize with a liquid fish or seaweed emulsion.

Transplant to the garden after all danger of frost has passed and the weather have become warm and settled. Setting out plants early is no advantage if the weather remains cold. Before transplanting, harden off plants by setting them outdoors in a sheltered, partly shaded location for several days, bringing the pots inside at night. Slowly increase the plants' exposure to direct sunlight during this time to avoid sunburnt leaves.

Transplant seedlings of determinate varieties of tomatoes 12–24 in. apart; *determinate* plants stop growing at a certain height and do not require staking, caging, or other support. Plant indeterminate tomatoes 24–36 in. apart; *indeterminate* plants continue climbing throughout the season and need some support on which to grow. Plant seedlings deeper in the ground than they were growing in the pot, again so that new roots will form along the underground portion of the stem.

Place collars of stiff paper around the stems of young plants to prevent cutworm damage.

The wimpy metal tomato cages sold in most garden centers are a disgrace — under the weight of a vigorous plant they flop over, and the hoops seem to fall off at the slightest provocation. A better, and longer-lasting, solution is to make your own cages out of heavy-duty concrete-reinforcing wire. I make mine about 2 ft. in diameter to give the tomato plants plenty of room. Settle the cages around the plants right after planting, and drive two stakes into the ground on opposite sides inside the cage to secure it against winds and the future weight of the tomato vines and fruit. It's best to do this immediately so that you won't disturb the plant or its roots later on. These sturdy homemade cages will last for many years if brought under cover for the winter.

Other options for supporting indeterminate tomatoes include training the vine to grow up a tall, sturdy stake and growing the vines against a heavy-duty wire trellis. If using the staking method, plant tomatoes closer together — 14–20 in. apart — and attach the main stem of the plant to the stake, tying the stem loosely in a figure 8 loop with strips of soft fabric (cut-up strips of old shirts work well). Keep tying the stem to the stake as it grows higher. When the vine reaches the top of the stake, pinch off the terminal growing tip to stop the plant's vertical growth.

Even though determinate varieties of tomatoes don't need to grow on a support, they benefit from having soil hilled up around the stems when plants are 1–2 ft. high.

Tomatoes appreciate a soil that is well supplied with phosphorus and potassium, but not too rich in nitrogen. Feed plants during the season by watering with a liquid fish or seaweed emulsion. Most important, tomatoes need a steady, consistent supply of water to grow well. A few weeks after transplanting tomatoes, and after the soil heats up, spread an organic mulch around the base of plants to help conserve soil moisture and suppress weeds. To encourage ripening, cut back on watering once the plants have begun to mature fruit.

Harvest
Picking tomatoes as soon as they are ripe or almost ripe helps to ripen remaining fruits. Tomatoes that have started to change color will continue ripening inside the house on a tray or sunny windowsill. Always water plants after harvesting rather than beforehand.

Tomatoes will continue flowering and producing fruit either until frost or until the days become shorter late in the season. Gardeners in the Northeast almost always experience one or two frosts in early autumn, which are followed by perhaps 3–4 weeks of sunny, pleasant, frost-free weather. Thus, in short-season areas it makes sense to cover tomato plants or cages with old sheets or other materials, to protect them at night from the first light frosts and extend the harvest season.

Later in the fall, when frosty nights become a regular occurrence, it's not worth covering and uncovering plants every day. Harvest all fruits that have any hint of color at this time and bring them inside to ripen; one method for ripening almost-green tomatoes involves wrapping them individually in sheets of newspaper and storing them in the root cellar, where they will ripen slowly. Also, many people like green tomatoes, either breaded and fried or as the main ingredient in preserves or mincemeat.

Pests and Diseases

Tomatoes are susceptible to a number of diseases, many of which can be prevented or minimized through good cultural practices. Some varieties of tomatoes are particularly susceptible to blight, a condition in which leaves develop brown spots ringed with yellow; the leaves will eventually wither and fall off the plant. To help prevent blight, mulch underneath tomato plants once the soil has warmed up. Also, remove all crop debris from the garden in the fall and rotate tomato crops. Do not rotate tomatoes with other members of the nightshade family (eggplant, peppers, potatoes, or tomatillos). Control fusarium wilt and verticillium wilt by selecting resistant varieties and rotating crops.

Blossom-end rot is another common problem with heirloom tomatoes. This condition results in fruit rotting and turning black on the blossom end. It indicates either a calcium deficiency in the soil or a stressed plant that has not received consistent moisture. To control rot, give plants even watering in dry, hot weather and mulch the soil underneath plants to conserve soil moisture. Also, have a professional soil test done — it will indicate whether you need to apply calcium to your garden, and in what form.

Insect pests that bother tomatoes include flea beetles and Colorado potato beetles. Control flea beetles by dusting plant leaves with rotenone. Examine the undersides of tomato leaves and crush any orange eggs of the potato beetle you find there. In cases of severe infestation, control adult potato beetles with rotenone or pyrethrum.

The large green tomato hornworm can cause significant damage by feeding on tomato leaves. Examine plants frequently and carefully to locate hornworms. Their green color camouflages them very well, and it is often easiest to find them by looking for chewed leaves. Pick the hornworms off the plant by hand or with tweezers. Do not destroy any horn-worms that have little white egg cases on their backs. These eggs have been deposited by a brachonid wasp. Once the eggs hatch, the baby wasps will feed on the hornworms, thus controlling your pest problem naturally.

■ RECOMMENDED VARIETIES

Red Tomatoes

'Abraham Lincoln' (1923)
A classic red beefsteak-type slicing tomato. Vigorous, indeterminate vines; potato-leaved foliage. Plants are prolific; fruits are dark red and large, 1–2 lb., and free from cracks. Flesh is sweet and juicy with few seeds. The original 'Lincoln' strain has been reintroduced in recent years, and it matures a few days later than other varieties sold under this name; 87 days.

'Amish Paste'
This old Wisconsin heirloom ranks as one of the most delicious and best-tasting paste tomatoes. Indeterminate vines. Fruits are oxheart-shaped, 6–8 oz., with solid, meaty flesh and few seeds. Excellent for eating right off the vine or for making sauce; 80–85 days.

'Burbank' (1915)
Developed by the famous plant breeder Luther Burbank. Stocky, determinate plants grow 18–36 in. high; disease-resistant, hardy, and productive. Fruits are medium-size, 3–4 in., and borne in clusters. Good old-fashioned tomato flavor; 70–80 days.

'Chadwick's Cherry' p. 112
A fine cherry tomato, introduced to the U.S. by English master gardener Alan Chadwick. Plants are indeterminate and vigorous; very productive. Fruits grow to 1½ in. across, somewhat larger than other cherry tomatoes, and contain few seeds. Flavor is sweet but well balanced; one of the best-tasting varieties; 85–90 days. Wendy Krupnick of Shepherd's Garden Seeds describes 'Camp Joy Cherry' as a synonym for this variety.

'Costoluto Genovese' p. 112
This heirloom tomato from the Italian Riviera has an unusual appearance and a rich, hearty flavor. Vigorous, indeterminate vines love summer heat, but will continue producing even after the weather turns cool. Fruits are scalloped or ribbed on the outside and deeply lobed with hollow cavities inside.

Plants are drought-tolerant and prolific. Best for hot summer climates; 80 days.

'Cuostralee'

An heirloom beefsteak tomato recently introduced to the U.S. from France. Indeterminate plants produce large, slightly flattened, 1–2-lb. fruits with ribbed shoulders. Flesh is meaty with an excellent flavor and few seeds; 80–85 days.

'Dad's Mug'

Blocky deep pink-red fruits have thick walls and meaty flesh; nearly solid center with few seeds. Very good flavor; excellent for stuffing, slicing, or as a paste tomato; fruit stands and keeps well. Indeterminate plants are prolific bearers; 85–95 days. From the collection of the late Ben Quisenberry.

'Gardener's Delight' ('Sugar Lump')   p. 113

A large European cherry tomato that may not strictly qualify as an heirloom, but is clearly one of the best nonhybrid varieties of its kind. Indeterminate plants produce bright red, crack-resistant fruits in clusters of 6–12. Plants are very prolific and bear until frost. Fruits have a nice balance of sweetness and acidity; 65 days.

'Marmande'

The classic French slicing tomato. Plants are semideterminate, bushy, and vigorous. Fruits are scarlet-red and medium-size, 6–8 oz.; sometimes irregularly shaped with ribbed shoulders. Firm, meaty flesh; delicious flavor. Resistant to fusarium and verticillium wilts; 70–75 days.

'Old Brooks'

An heirloom beefsteak that's particularly well suited to home canning because of its high acidity. Indeterminate vines produce lots of medium-large, 6–12-oz. fruits; plants are resistant to blossom-end rot and early and late blight. Also good sliced for tomato sandwiches, on homemade white bread with just a dab of mayonnaise; 70–80 days.

'Red Pear'

A lesser-grown version of the gourmet variety 'Yellow Pear'. Burr mentions both varieties in 1863, but the pear (or fig) type is really much older. Indeterminate plants produce clusters of bright red pear-shaped fruits, about 2 in. long. Tomatoes are good whole or halved in salads, or for canning. Flavor is good and less subtle than 'Yellow Pear'. To control cracking, mulch around the base of plants and provide consistent moisture; 70–80 days.

'Riesentraube' (before 1847)

In German, *riesentraube* means "giant bunch of grapes," which is a great name for this old variety. The plants are indeterminate, but vines are compact and highly branched, with lots of foliage. Up to 350 blossoms are contained in every compact floral spray, and each cluster can produce 20–40 fruits. The tomatoes are the size of large cherry tomatoes and have a rounded pear shape that ends in a point on the blossom end. Flavor is superb, fruity and full; fruits hold well on the vine without splitting, and flavor improves as tomatoes become fully ripe. One plant can yield hundreds of fruits. A rare and remarkable tomato that deserves to be more widely grown; 75–80 days.

'Super Italian Paste' p. 113

This paste tomato from Italy grows extra-large oval fruits, 6 in. long and 4 in. in diameter; fruits are deep orange-red, with sweet, meaty, nearly seedless flesh. Indeterminate plants bear heavily. Begins bearing midseason but is best for warmer regions, since fruit ripens over a long season; 65–75 days.

Pink-Purple Tomatoes

'Anna Russian' p. 114

An excellent old-fashioned tomato, apparently from Russian immigrants. Vigorous, indeterminate plants have rather sparse, feathery foliage. Yields are not high, but fruits are early, medium-large, and high in quality; pink-skinned and usually heart-shaped with green shoulders and a nipple at the blossom end. Flesh is meaty and has a superb flavor; 65 days.

'Brandywine' (1885) p. 114

'Brandywine' has become almost legendary in recent years, as more and more gardeners grow it and discover how good a tomato it really is. This variety is an Amish heirloom that comes from the collection of the late Ben Quisenberry, who maintained hundreds of tomatoes from 1910 to the 1960s; Seed Savers Exchange inherited his collection and carries on his work. Lawrence Hollander of CRESS calls 'Brandywine' "the best — simply the best." Many others, myself included, agree with him.

Large, indeterminate plants have potato-leaved foliage and bear 1–2-lb. fruits with deep pink skin; the inner flesh is red, meaty, and highly flavored. Fruits are somewhat prone to radial cracking, but for home gardeners this outstanding tomato is hard to beat; 80 days.

Other strains of the regular pink 'Brandywine' are also available, including 'Red Brandywine', which Rosalind

Creasy recommends as superior, and 'Yellow Brandywine', an excellent orange-skinned variety.

'Brimmer Pink' (ca. 1905)
A great slicer, with large, meaty fruits that can grow to 2½ lb. or more. Indeterminate. Thick skins are a deep pink-purple; fruits are nearly all meat, with few seeds and no core. Flavor is mild and subacid. This variety was introduced in Virginia and is not recommended for northern climates, where it requires a long season to mature; 80–85 days.

'Cherokee Purple' (before 1890) p. 115
An unusual tomato from Tennessee, said to have come originally from the Cherokee Indians. Vines are indeterminate but relatively short. Fruits are smooth round globes, 10–12 oz., with dusky brownish purple skin and dark green shoulders. Flesh is brick red and full-flavored. Somewhat prone to concentric cracking around the shoulders; 70–75 days.

In 1994, at the Penn State heirloom trials, I came upon a similar, even lesser-known variety named 'Indische Fleisch', which I hope will be appearing soon in regional seed catalogs.

'Eva Purple Ball'
A hard-to-find heirloom, but definitely one worth growing; comes from the Black Forest region of Germany. Indeterminate plants are vigorous, producing lots of leaves and heavy yields of medium-size pink-purple fruits. Tomatoes are beautiful, smooth and uniform globes of 4–8 oz. that have a tendency to drop from the plant when fully ripe. Flavor is sweet and delicious; a real winner; 65–80 days.

'King Umberto' ('Umberto Pear')
Named for a king of Italy, this is one of the oldest named varieties of tomato still in existence. Not currently available through the seed trade, but maintained by the Seed Savers Exchange Members Network. Vilmorin-Andrieux lists this variety in 1885 as 'King Humbert Tomato' and says that the plum-shaped fruits are borne in clusters of 5–10. Plants are indeterminate, vigorous, and spreading. Vilmorin describes the skin color as bright scarlet, but existing modern forms are definitely pink. Fruits are sweet, juicy, and delicious; a historic variety; 75–90 days.

'Oxheart' (ca. 1925) p. 115
An old favorite whose shape resulted from a single gene mutation; its name is now synonymous with a separate tomato type. Indeterminate plants are large and open; grow in cages to help shade fruits from the sun. Fruits are deep rose-pink

and shallowly furrowed, 7 oz., and borne in clusters of 2–7. Flesh is meaty and firm, with few seeds and a mild flavor; good for slicing or sauce. Well adapted to regions with hot, humid summers; 80–95 days. 'Giant Oxheart' is a variety with larger, 1–2 lb. fruits.

'Pruden's Purple'

A great heirloom that has gained considerable favor in recent years among home gardeners. Indeterminate plants have potato-leaved foliage. Fruits are deep pink, smooth, flattened globes marked with shallow vertical ribs; average size 1 lb. or more. Tomatoes resist cracking. Flesh is crimson red, firm, meaty, and delicious, with few seeds. Similar to 'Brandywine', but earlier; 65–72 days.

'Zapotec Ribbed' ('Zapotec Pleated') p. 116

A beautiful tomato, originally from the Zapotec people of Oaxaca, Mexico. Ruffled pink fruits are hollow and perfect for stuffing and baking like a sweet pepper, or for cutting into rings for salads. Indeterminate plants; fruits are 4–8 oz. and resist cracking; sweet flavor. An unusual and very old type of tomato; 80–85 days.

Yellow-Orange Tomatoes

'Banana Legs' p. 116

It's rare to see a yellow paste tomato, but this variety is a good one. Plants are determinate with skinny, lacy leaves. Fruits are 3–4 in. long and 1–2 in. in diameter; skin color is yellow with longitudinal stripes that turn from light green to orange-yellow. Flesh is yellow, dry, sweet, and meaty, with few seeds. Use sliced in salads or cook down to make a novel, low-acid tomato sauce; 85–90 days.

While 'Banana Legs' is apparently a fairly recent introduction, another good variety named 'Banana' is a real heirloom hailing from the former Soviet Union. 'Banana' is the same as 'Banana Legs' in every respect save its skin color, which is orange, not yellow. David Cavagnaro of Seed Savers Exchange says this is the first truly orange paste tomato he's seen. 'Banana' is currently being preserved as part of SSE's Russian Seed Collection.

'Djena Lee's Golden Girl' (1920s)

Originally from Minnesota, this family heirloom won first prize at the Chicago Fair 10 years running. Vigorous, indeterminate vines. Fruits are obloid, 3–4 in. long, and golden-orange. Flesh is meaty and delicious, with a nicely balanced flavor; 80 days.

'Golden Queen' (1882) p. 117
An excellent and beautiful orange slicer. Medium-size indeterminate plants are bushy and prolific. Fruits are attractive,
4–6-oz. orange globes; flesh is sweet, mild, and subacid; some
tomatoes have hollow cavities; 75–80 days.

'Goldie' (1870s) p. 117
Vigorous, indeterminate plants. Fruits are large flattened
globes, mostly 1–2 lb., and an attractive golden-orange color.
Flavor is sweet, mild, and subacid; 85–95 days.

'Verna Orange' p. 118
An heirloom oxheart from Indiana. Vigorous, indeterminate
plants. Fruits are large, to 1½ lb., and ripen from yellow to
apricot-orange; shoulders are slightly ribbed. Flesh is very
meaty, with semihollow seed cavities and few seeds; flavor is
sweet, mild, and exceptional; 75–85 days.

'Yellow Pear' (before 1805) p. 118
This variety became the darling of restaurateurs and caterers
a few years ago as an attractive, shapely tomato for use in
both green and pasta salads. In fact, 'Yellow Pear' is a very
old type, probably dating back to at least the 1600s. Vines
are indeterminate and vigorous, with a rather open growing
habit; use cages to help contain them. Plants are disease-resistant and bear lots of 1-oz., pale yellow, pear-shaped fruits
that have a nice mild flavor; 70–80 days.

Other Tomatoes

'Big Rainbow'
A beautiful bicolored beefsteak; very large fruits are golden
with ruby red streaks radiating from the blossom end; red
color also runs through the flesh, making attractive slices. Indeterminate plants. Fruits are prone to some cracking and
catfacing (a malformation caused by imperfect pollination),
but their wonderful flavor makes them perfect for home gardeners; 80 days.

Several other good, similar bicolors are also available, including an heirloom variety called 'Striped German', which
got rave reviews at the 1994 Johnny's Selected Seeds tomato
tasting.

'Black Krim' p. 119
An odd-colored tomato that is named for the Crimean peninsula (Krim) on the Ukrainian Black Sea coast. Indeterminate,
medium-size plants, with either regular or potato leaves. The
skin color of the fruit is brownish purple, similar to 'Cher-

okee Purple' and other varieties, dark green shoulders. Medium-size fruits are prone to cracking and require a hot summer to attain their dark, ripe skin color. Flesh is deep reddish brown with a unique, full-bodied flavor that has been described as meaty, salty, and smoky. Well worth trying, especially in warm, long-season climates; 80–95 days.

'Evergreen'
This beefsteak tomato's skin is green with pale yellow highlights when it's fully ripe; slices make a nice contrast with other tomatoes on a platter. Indeterminate plants are tolerant of hot, humid weather. Fruits average 10–16 oz.; flesh is green with a good, mild flavor; 70–75 days.

'Tigerella' ('Mr. Stripey') p. 119
A very attractive English greenhouse variety with 2-in. fruits striped red and yellow-orange; immature fruits are light green striped with dark green. Indeterminate plants are very prolific and disease-resistant. Rich, tangy flavor is good in salads; 55–65 days.

'Tigerella' is the most famous striped variety, but I also recommend two lesser-known heirlooms. One is 'Schimmeig Creg' ("striped rock" in the Manx language), from the Isle of Man; the other is 'Tiger Tom', which apparently was developed in the former Czechoslovakia and found its way into the collection of the late Ben Quisenberry. Both of these varieties have about the same size, color, and earliness of 'Tigerella'.

'White Beauty' ('Snowball')
Fearing Burr mentions a white-skinned tomato in 1863, and 'White Beauty' may possibly derive from a variety called 'White Apple', which was grown before 1860. Large beefsteak fruits are slightly flattened and ribbed, medium-large (around 1 lb.), and creamy white inside and out when ripe. Indeterminate plants are bushy and produce abundant foliage; plants are not very disease-resistant. Flavor is mild and sweet; white tomatoes contain the same amount of acid as red tomatoes but have a higher sugar content. Unusual, but becoming rather popular among gourmets and home gardeners alike; 80–85 days.

Another good heirloom white tomato is 'Great White', which is similar to 'White Beauty' and a good slicer.

'Yellow Currant' (*Lycopersicon pimpinellifolium*) p. 120
This tiny-fruited variety belongs to a different species from the common garden tomato and has changed very little from its wild form. Plant breeders often use currant tomatoes in

making hybrid cherry tomatoes, since currants are sweet and bear fruit abundantly in grapelike clusters.

Plants are indeterminate, vigorous, and very disease-resistant. Tiny fruits are round and slightly over ½ in. across. The flavor is intense: crisp, sweet, and tart. The small fruits mature early and continue ripening until frost. Currants are terrific for using whole in salads, but the plants need to be picked frequently so fruits do not crack, split, or drop off the plant; 65 days.

'Red Currant' is also widely available, and the fruits of both varieties make a nice contrast when picked and used together in salads or other dishes.

Turnip

Brassica rapa, Rapifera group

Turnips belong to the large mustard or cabbage family and are probably native to both Europe and central or western Asia. They have been cultivated for thousands of years, and European settlers introduced them to North America as early as 1609.[69]

An easy-to-grow vegetable, turnips like cool weather and make a good crop in either spring or fall. In addition to the turnip's tender roots, its tasty and nutritious green leaves can be harvested for steaming, stir-frying, or salad use.

The Greek historian Plutarch tells the story of an ancient Roman general, Manius Curius, who after a long and successful career as a soldier retired to a modest home in the country. One day some ambassadors from the Samnites came to his cottage and found the old man boiling turnips in the chimney corner. When the ambassadors offered him gold, Manius Curius pointed to the turnips and asked them why a person who was satisfied with such a supper would have any need of gold. Even in Roman times, turnips were a source of simple pleasure.

How to Grow

Plant turnip seed in early to mid-spring for a spring crop, and from midsummer through early fall for a fall crop. Sow seeds thinly, about ¼–½ in. deep and ½ in. apart, in rows spaced 12–18 in. apart. Thin the young plants to 4–5 in. apart in the row.

Like other root crops, turnips prefer a loose or well-worked soil, but they grow well in nearly all soils. Fertilize the seedbed before planting by working in a little bone meal and a sprinkling of wood ashes.

Harvest

Begin harvesting turnip greens and small turnips about 30 days after seeding. Turnip roots are most tender and tasty when harvested small, about 2–3 in. in diameter. Roots that grow large or that mature during hot summer weather tend to become woody.

Most turnips do not store very well over an extended period in the root cellar. If your winter climate is relatively mild, you may be able to mulch turnip beds heavily in the late fall and continue harvesting roots from the garden.

Pests and Diseases

Control flea beetles by using a floating row cover over young plants; failing this, you can also dust leaves with rotenone. Floating row covers also help avoid damage from root maggots, as does sprinkling fine, dry wood ashes around the base of plants.

■ RECOMMENDED VARIETIES

'Gilfeather'™ p. 120
A tasty turnip from southern Vermont; developed by John Gilfeather of Wardsboro in the late 1800s. Roots are creamy white and egg-shaped, with green shoulders. Flesh is white and smooth-textured. Flavor is mild and sweet and remains good even when roots grow larger than 3 in.; 60–75 days.

'Golden Ball' ('Orange Jelly'; 1859)
Listed by Burr in 1863. Yellow roots are 3–4 in. across when mature; flesh is golden yellow with a fine, sweet flavor that resembles a rutabaga more than a turnip; medium-size cut-leaf tops. Flesh cooks down well for mashing; 45–65 days.

'Purple Top White Globe' (before 1880) p. 121
Still the standard market and home variety. Tops grow 14–22 in. tall. Roots are purplish red above ground, creamy white below; best harvested at 3–4 in., but remains tasty even when larger. White flesh is fine-grained, sweet, and mild-flavored; 45–65 days.

'Red Milan' ('De Milan Rouge'; before 1885) p. 121
Listed by Vilmorin-Andrieux in the 1880s, this turnip is fast-growing and good for spring planting. Roots are flattened globes, rose-colored above ground and pure white below. Thrives in very cool weather and should be picked when young and tender; 35 days.

'Seven Top' (1845)
This variety is specifically grown for its greens; roots are small, tough, and woody. Produces several crops of 16–22-in. tender green leaves that can be cut over a long season; leaves are most tender when harvested young. Very popular in the South, where it grows well in the winter and early spring; 45–50 days.

'Waldoboro Greenneck' (1780s)
Named for the town of Waldoboro, Maine, but perhaps French in origin. One story claims that the seed came from turnips that washed ashore when a ship, the *Cambridge,* ran aground. White roots and green shoulders; roots can grow very large without becoming woody. A rare heirloom variety; 50 days.

Watermelon

Citrullus lanatus
Watermelons have been cultivated for more than 4,000 years and come originally from the African tropics. Varieties range from small, round melons that grow successfully even in short-season areas, to oblong behemoths weighing 50 lb. or more. Some types have light green or striped rinds, while other fruits are almost black.

Northern gardeners who enjoy the sweet, cool taste of homegrown watermelon have always envied growers in the South, where the hot, humid summer weather ripens fruit beautifully. Mark Twain was a big fan of the watermelon, singing its praises in his book *Pudd'nhead Wilson* (1894):

> The true Southern watermelon is a boon apart, and not to be mentioned with commoner things. It is chief of this world's luxuries, king by the grace of God over all the fruits of the earth. When one has tasted it, he knows what the angels eat. It was not a Southern watermelon that Eve took; we know it because she repented.

How to Grow
In warm, long-season areas watermelons can be direct-seeded, planting 5–6 seeds in hills spaced 6–8 ft. apart; after plants emerge, thin to the best 2 plants in the hill. Or plant seeds 6–8 in. apart in rows spaced 5–6 ft. apart; thin young plants to 3 ft. apart.

In most regions, though, watermelons should be started indoors, sowing seeds 3–4 weeks before the last spring frost date in individual 2–3-in. pots or cells. Supply gentle bottom heating to keep soil temperatures warm (75–85°F) until germination occurs. Seedlings started too early in the season will start sprawling, which makes the job of transplanting them much more difficult.

Harden off plants and transplant to the garden after all threat of frost is past. Watermelons like rich, light, well-drained soil, so dig in plenty of compost or dried manure before transplanting. Set out plants 3 ft. apart in rows spaced 5–6 ft. apart.

Gardeners in cool regions can increase the soil temperature around plants by surrounding them with black paper or black plastic mulch and/or covering plants with a floating row fabric. The mulch will also help suppress weeds in the melon patch.

Fertilize watermelons by side-dressing with dried manure or other organic fertilizer when the plants are still upright and before the vines start to run on the ground. Remove the floating row cover once the plants produce female flowers (the ones with tiny fruits at the base of the blossom).

Late in the summer, pinch off the fuzzy tips at the ends of vines and remove any small fruits that won't have time to ripen. This helps concentrate the plant's energy on ripening the remaining fruits.

Harvest

To gauge the ripeness of a watermelon, look for the following three things: 1) the spot where the fruit rests on the ground should be yellow; 2) the tendril nearest the point on the stem where the fruit is attached should be dried-up and brown; and 3) the melon will make a hollow "punk" sound when you rap the rind with your finger (unripe fruits make a "pink" or "pank" sound).

Pests and Diseases

Control squash bugs and cucumber beetles by covering young plants with a floating row fabric; for serious infestations dust leaves with rotenone, pyrethrum, or sabadilla.

Watermelons are susceptible to various diseases, including anthracnose and stem-end rot. Examine fruits regularly and remove any shriveled or decayed ones that you see. Avoid working around the plants when they are wet, to prevent the spread of disease.

■ Recommended Varieties

'Cole's Early' ('Harris Early'; 1892)
An early watermelon with nearly round, medium-size fruits,

about 10 lb.; dark green with light stripes. Flesh is firm and dark red; medium rind. Recommended for short-season areas; rare; 75–80 days.

'Cream of Saskatchewan'

Another early "icebox-sized" melon for the North, one that comes highly recommended by Lawrence Hollander of CRESS. Available once again in the seed from Garden City Seeds and other sources; deserves to be more widely grown.

Round melons weigh 5–12 lb. and have a thin, brittle rind; pale green striped with dark green. Flesh is creamy white and very sweet; excellent flavor. One of the best heirloom home garden varieties for short-season areas; 80–85 days.

'Georgia Rattlesnake' ('Rattlesnake') p. 122

An old southern favorite, now becoming rare. Large, oblong fruits measure 22 in. long and 10 in. across; averages 25–30 lb.; rind is thin, hard, and pale green, with dark green, irregular "snakeskin" striping. Flesh is bright rose-red, firm and sweet; seeds are dull white with black tips; 90 days.

'Garrisonian' is the name of an improved variety of 'Georgia Rattlesnake', introduced in 1957 and grown for market in the South.

'Ice Cream' ('Peerless'; before 1885)

Large, oval fruits, 19 in. long and 9 in. across, to 25 lb. Pale green rinds are finely veined with dark green. Bright red flesh; white seeds; excellent quality; 75–90 days. A black-seeded strain is also available.

'Kleckley Sweet' ('Monte Christo', 'Wonder Melon'; before 1900)

Oblong fruits have square ends and a thin, glossy, dark green rind; 25–40 lb. Flesh is deep red and very sweet, with white seeds; a great home garden variety; 80–90 days.

'Moon & Stars' (before 1910) p. 122

Probably the most beautiful watermelon there is, this variety was once feared lost forever. In the early 1980s, Kent Whealy of Seed Savers Exchange rediscovered 'Moon & Stars' in Missouri, still being maintained by a man named Merle van Doren. Since that time this resurrected garden classic has enjoyed a tremendous surge in popularity, and many other strains have appeared. Some of them have yellow instead of pink or red flesh; others are family heirlooms or traditional strains preserved by the Amish or other groups. One "creation theory" suggests that 'Moon & Stars' may have come to the U.S. from the Volga River region of Russia.

The name 'Moon & Stars' comes from the bright yellow speckles and splotches that color the dark green leaves and melons; highly ornamental. Fruits are medium-large, 25–30 lb. or more, though the white-seeded Amish strain I have grown in the North is decidedly smaller. Rinds are thick and slightly ridged, though some types are entirely smooth. Flesh is pinkish red and very sweet; great flavor. Requires a rather long season so is best for warmer regions of the country. Highly recommended; 95–105 days.

'Nancy' (ca. 1885)
This variety was at one time a popular commercial variety but today is quite rare. Like 'Moon & Stars' it was recently "rediscovered," in this case growing wild in a Georgia cotton field. Excellent drought tolerance and disease resistance. Green-striped oval fruits average 25 lb. but can grow larger on good soil. Flesh is pinkish red, very sweet, and good-tasting all the way to the rind; white seeds. Produces good crops over an extended season; 90 days.

'Red-Seeded Citron' (*C. lanatus* var. *citroides*) p. 123
This is a real old-fashioned variety, also known as the "preserving melon." As that name suggests, it is not eaten fresh like other watermelons, but used to make pickles or preserves or candied in syrup and used in Christmas breads and fruitcakes. Despite the similar usage, though, this citron is not the same as the commonly candied type, which is actually a tree fruit *(Citrus medica)*.

Vines are hardy and prolific. Fruits are smooth and nearly round, 6–8 in. in diameter and 10–12 lb. The rind is pale green striped and spotted with darker green. Flesh is clear white and solid; seeds are bright red (a green-seeded variety also exists). Flavor is tasteless when fresh, but delicious when preserved, pickled, or candied. In 1863 Fearing Burr recommended "removing the rind or skin and seeds, cutting the flesh into convenient bits, and boiling in sirup [*sic*] which has been flavored with ginger, lemon, or some agreeable article." Still a good recipe today. Well worth trying; one plant will yield plenty of fruits for preserving; 80–100 days.

'Tom Watson' (before 1900)
A large-fruited variety for short-season areas. Fruits are 22–24 in. long and 10–12 in. across; rind is thin, hard, and green with darker green stripes; averages 25–40 lb. Flesh is dark red, coarse-textured, sweet, and firm; seeds are brown spotted with white. Productive; a popular home and market melon; 80–95 days.

Appendices

Hardiness Zone Map

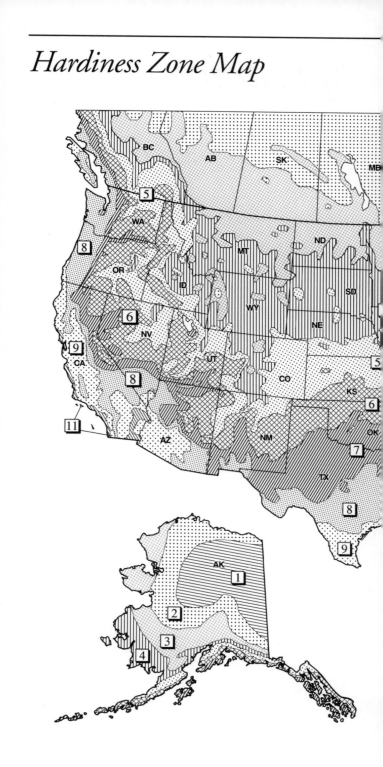

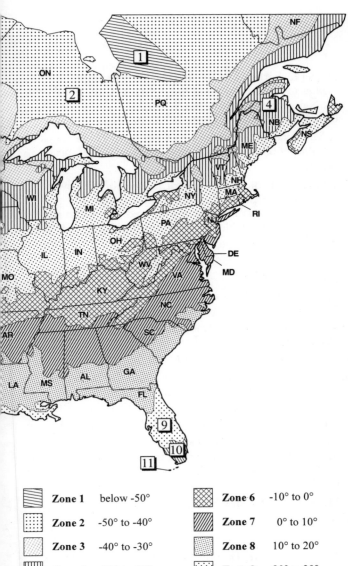

Zone 1 below -50°
Zone 2 -50° to -40°
Zone 3 -40° to -30°
Zone 4 -30° to -20°
Zone 5 -20° to -10°

Zone 6 -10° to 0°
Zone 7 0° to 10°
Zone 8 10° to 20°
Zone 9 20° to 30°
Zone 10 30° to 40°
Zone 11 above 40°

Notes

1. Daniel K. Early, "The Renaissance of Amaranth," in *Chilies to Chocolate: Food the Americas Gave the World,* ed. Nelson Foster and Linda S. Cordell (Tucson: University of Arizona Press, 1992), p. 26.

2. F. M. Hexamer, *Asparagus: Its Culture for Home Use and for Market* (New York: Orange Judd Cò., 1905), pp. 2–3.

3. Ibid., p. 17.

4. J. Smartt, "Evolution of American *Phaseolus* Beans under Domestication," in *The Domestication and Exploitation of Plants and Animals,* ed. P. J. Ucko and G. W. Dimbleby (Chicago: Aldine Publishing Co., 1969), pp. 455–57.

5. Ibid., p. 452.

6. Ibid., pp. 454, 458.

7. U. P. Hedrick (ed.), *Sturtevant's Edible Plants of the World* (New York: Dover, 1972), p. 593.

8. Smartt, "Evolution of American *Phaseolus* Beans," in *Domestication and Exploitation,* p. 452.

9. Hedrick, *Sturtevant's Edible Plants,* pp. 291–92.

10. Smartt, "Evolution of American *Phaseolus* Beans," in *Domestication and Exploitation,* p. 452.

11. Robert W. Schery, *Plants for Man,* 2nd edition (Englewood Cliffs, NJ: Prentice-Hall, 1972), p. 509.

12. Vilmorin-Andrieux, *The Vegetable Garden,* facsimile reprint of 1885 English edition, trans. William Miller, ed. W. Robinson (Berkeley, CA: Ten Speed Press, 1981), p. 132.

13. Hedrick, *Sturtevant's Edible Plants,* p. 115.

14. Ibid., p. 117.

15. Ibid., p. 234.

16. Lyman N. White, *Heirlooms and Genetics* (Cambridge, NY: Lyman N. White, 1988), pp. 24–25.

17. Schery, *Plants for Man,* p. 512.

18. Hedrick, *Sturtevant's Edible Plants,* p. 56.

19. Walton C. Galinat, "Maize: Gift from America's First Peoples," in *Chilies to Chocolate,* p. 47.

20. Ibid., pp. 49–50.

21. Edgar Anderson, *Plants, Man and Life* (Berkeley: University of California Press, 1967), pp. 211–12.

22. Ibid., p. 111.

23. Ibid., p. 117.

24. Hernando DeSoto, *The Discovery and Conquest of Terra Florida*, trans. Luis Hernandez de Beidma (London: Hakluyt Society, 1851), in *Sturtevant's Edible Plants*, p. 208.

25. Hedrick, *Sturtevant's Edible Plants*, p. 38.

26. Charles B. Heiser, *The Sunflower* (Norman: University of Oklahoma Press, 1976), p. 174.

27. Hedrick, *Sturtevant's Edible Plants*, p. 118.

28. Ibid., p. 37.

29. Ibid., p. 322.

30. E. Annie Proulx, *The Fine Art of Salad Gardening* (Emmaus, PA: Rodale Press, 1985), pp. 2–3.

31. Ibid., p. 18.

32. Hedrick, *Sturtevant's Edible Plants*, pp. 204–05.

33. Ibid., p. 302.

34. Ibid., p. 33.

35. Ibid., p. 32.

36. Ibid., p. 36.

37. Schery, *Plants for Man*, p. 504.

38. U. P. Hedrick et al., *The Peas of New York*, vol. 1, pt. 1, of *The Vegetables of New York* (Albany, NY: J. B. Lyon, 1928), p. 4.

39. Ibid., p. 7.

40. Ibid., p. 7.

41. Barbara Pickersgill, "The Domestication of Chili Peppers," in *Domestication and Exploitation*, p. 446.

42. Richard Schweid, *Hot Peppers: Cajuns and Capsicum in New Iberia, Louisiana* (Berkeley, CA: Ten Speed Press, 1989), p. 27.

43. Pickersgill, "Domestication of Chili Peppers," in *Domestication and Exploitation*, p. 448.

44. Jean Andrews, "The Peripatetic Chili Pepper: Diffusion of the Domesticated Capsicums since Columbus," in *Chilies to Chocolate*, p. 81.

45. Alfred W. Crosby, "The Potato Connection," *Civilization*, 2:1 (Jan./Feb. 1995), p. 56.

46. Alan Davidson, "Europeans' Wary Encounter with Tomatoes, Potatoes, and Other New World Foods," in *Chilies to Chocolate,* p. 12.

47. Crosby, "The Potato Connection," p. 56.

48. Davidson, "Europeans' Wary Encounter," in *Chilies to Chocolate,* p. 13.

49. Hedrick, *Sturtevant's Edible Plants,* p. 547.

50. Ibid., p. 484.

51. Clifford M. Faust, *Rhubarb: The Wondrous Drug* (Princeton, NJ: Princeton University Press, 1992), p. 38

52. Ibid., p. 213

53. White, *Heirlooms and Genetics,* p. 69.

54. Schery, *Plants for Man,* p. 529.

55. U. P. Hedrick et al., *The Cucurbits of New York,* vol. 1, pt. 4, of *The Vegetables of New York* (Albany, NY: J. B. Lyon, 1937), p. 3.

56. Anderson, *Plants, Man and Life,* pp. 129–30.

57. Heiser, *The Sunflower,* p. 43.

58. Ibid., pp. 56–57.

59. Schery, *Plants for Man,* p. 492.

60. Crosby, "The Potato Connection," p. 54.

61. Ibid., p. 55.

62. Jim Wilson, "All About Sweet Potatoes," *National Gardening,* 17:3 (May/June 1994), p. 59.

63. Schery, *Plants for Man,* p. 513.

64. Hedrick, *Sturtevant's Edible Plants,* p. 91.

65. Anderson, *Plants, Man and Life,* p. 131.

66. Schery, *Plants for Man,* p. 530.

67. Ibid., p. 531.

68. White, *Heirlooms and Genetics,* p. 80.

69. Schery, *Plants for Man,* p. 505.

Mail-Order Seed Sources

SEED COMPANIES SPECIALIZING IN HEIRLOOM VARIETIES

Abundant Life Seed Foundation, P.O. Box 772,
1029 Lawrence St., Port Townsend, WA 98368;
(206) 385-7192; catalog $2.
A nonprofit concern offering a good selection of heritage seeds, all untreated.

Ken Allan, 536 MacDonnell St., Kingston,
ON Canada K7K 4W7; SASE for price list.
Sells a range of sweet potato varieties as well as other vegetables.

Becker's Seed Potatoes, R.R. #1, Trout Creek,
ON Canada P0H 2L0; catalog SASE to Canadian customers.
Canadian supplier of seed potatoes; no orders to U.S.

Bentley Seeds, Inc., 16 Railroad Ave.,
Cambridge, NY 12816; (518) 677-2603.
Heirloom vegetable and flower seeds.

Elizabeth Berry, Galina Canyon Ranch, P.O. Box 706,
Abiquiu, NM 87510; seed list $1 plus long SASE.
Offers heirloom beans and other seeds.

Bountiful Gardens, 18001 Shafer Ranch Rd.,
Willits, CA 95490; (707) 459-6410.
Also publishes a separate Rare Seeds Catalog *($3), which helps preserve rare seed varieties by making them available to home gardeners and seed savers.*

D. V. Burrell Seed Growers Co., P.O. Box 150,
Rocky Ford, CO 81067; (719) 254-3318.
Founded in 1900, this family-owned business lists more than 300 varieties of herbs, vegetables, and flowers, but is most famous for its excellent melons and watermelons.

Le Champion Heritage Seeds, Box 1602,
Freedom, CA 95019; catalog $1.

Comstock, Ferre & Co., 263 Main St.,
Wethersfield, CT 06109; (203) 529-6255; catalog $3.
Established 1820.

The Cook's Garden, P.O. Box 535, Londonderry, VT 05148;
(802) 824-3400; catalog $1.
*Particularly strong selection of salad greens, flowers, and
European heirloom varieties.*

William Dam Seeds Ltd., P.O. Box 8400,
Dundas, ON Canada L9H 6M1; (905) 628-6641; catalog
free in Canada, $1 to U.S.

Deep Diversity, P.O. Box 15189, Santa Fe, NM 87506-5189;
catalog $4.
*Formerly Peace Seeds; catalog is organized botanically and
includes much good information for serious gardeners and
seed savers; features many heirloom and rare varieties.*

Degiorgi Seed Company, 6011 N Street,
Omaha, NE 68117-1634; (402) 731-3901; catalog $2.
*Family-owned company offering a mix of heirloom and
hybrid varieties.*

Down on the Farm Seed, P.O. Box 184, Hiram, OH 44234.
*Untreated seeds, with emphasis on old-time, open-pollinated
varieties.*

Evergreen Y. H. Enterprises, P.O. Box 17538,
Anaheim, CA 92817; catalog $2.
Seed for Oriental vegetables, fruits, and herbs.

Filaree Farm, Rt. 2, Box 162, Okanogan, WA 98840;
(509) 422-6940; catalog $2.
*The largest selection of garlics in the U.S., with more than
100 varieties for sale, all certified organic.*

Floating Mountain Seeds, P.O. Box 1275,
Port Angeles, WA 98362; catalog $2.

Fox Hollow Herb & Heirloom Seed Co., P.O. Box 148,
McGrann, PA 16236; catalog $1.

Garden City Seeds, 1324 Red Crow Road, Victor, MT 59875-9713; (406) 961-4837; catalog $1. *Specializes in open-pollinated seed varieties that are well adapted to the northern Rocky Mountain region and the northern Great Plains; all seeds untreated and many organically grown.*

Gleckler's Seedsmen, Metamora, OH 43540. *Specializes in unusual vegetable varieties.*

The Good Earth Seed Company, P.O. Box 5644, Redwood City, CA 94063. *Formerly Tsang & Ma; vegetables from the Far East.*

Good Seed Co., Star Route Box 73A, Oroville (Chesaw), WA 98844. *Committed to the preservation of old seed and tree varieties.*

The Gourmet Gardener, 8650 College Blvd., Dept. 205HA, Overland Park, KS 66210; (913) 345-0490; catalog $2. *Features many European varieties.*

Heirloom Seeds, Box 245, West Elizabeth, PA 15088-0245; catalog $1.

High Altitude Gardens, P.O. Box 1048, Hailey, ID 83333-1048; (208) 788-4363; catalog $3. *Through its affiliate, Seeds Trust, Inc., High Altitude has introduced a fine selection of short-season tomatoes from eastern Europe and the former Soviet Union.*

Howe Sound Seeds, Box 109, Bowen Island, BC Canada V0N 1G0; catalog SASE to Canada, $1 to U.S. *Specializes in late Victorian-era vegetable varieties.*

J. L. Hudson, Seedsman, P.O. Box 1058, Redwood City, CA 94064; catalog $1. *Hudson's Ethnobotanical Catalog of Seeds has some of the best and most complete information available on many plants.*

Le Jardin de Gourmet, P.O. Box 75, St. Johnsbury Ctr., VT 05863-0075; (800) 748-1446; catalog $1. *Excellent shallots, herb plants and seeds, and vegetable seeds from France.*

Johnny's Selected Seeds, Foss Hill Rd., Albion, ME 04910; (207) 437-4301.
Extensive in-house trials and breeding program; many introductions for cool-climate gardeners; good selection of heirlooms and traditional varieties.

Kalmia Farm, P.O. Box 3881, Charlottesville, VA 22903-0881.
Specializes in multiplier onions, both topsetting types and shallots.

Kitazawa Seed Co., 1111 Chapman St., San Jose, CA 95126; (408) 243-1330.
Oriental vegetable seeds since 1917.

D. L. Landreth Seed Co., P.O. Box 6426, Baltimore, MD 21230; (301) 727-3922; catalog $2.
America's oldest seed house; established 1784.

Long Island Seed Company, 1368 Flanders Rd., Flanders, NY 11901.
Specializes in genetically diverse seed blends for home gardeners; also carries separate single varieties, including more than 400 open-pollinated tomatoes.

Manhattan Farms, 3088 Salmon River Rd., Salmon Arm, BC Canada V1E 4M1.
Heirloom and unusual seeds, organically grown.

Milk Ranch Seed Potatoes, 20094 Hwy. 149, Powderhorn, CO 81243; catalog $1.
Carries 50 varieties of certified seed potatoes, some heirloom, some organically grown.

Nichols Garden Nursery, 1190 North Pacific Hwy., Albany, OR 97321; (503) 928-9280.
Offers some interesting and little-known varieties; many adapted to short-season growing areas.

Ornamental Edibles, 3622 Weedin Court, San Jose, CA 95132; (408) 946-7333.
Vegetables for edible landscaping and specialty market growers.

The Pepper Gal, P.O. Box 23006, Ft. Lauderdale, FL 33307; (305) 537-5540; SASE for price list.
More than 200 varieties of hot, sweet, and ornamental peppers.

Peters Seed & Research, 407 Maranatha Lane, Myrtle Creek, OR 97457; catalog $2.
Open-pollinated vegetables for short-season gardeners, many developed by Tim Peters. For a $5 fee gardeners can become PSR members and order seed from PSR's experimental breeding program.

Pinetree Garden Seeds, Box 300, New Gloucester, ME 04260; (207) 926-3400.
Offers small seed samples at lower prices for home gardeners with limited space.

Plants of the Southwest, Agua Fria, Rt. 6, Box 11A, Santa Fe, NM 87501; catalog $3.50.
Specializes in native plants and ancient vegetable varieties adapted to the Southwest.

Redwood City Seed Company, P.O. Box 361, Redwood City, CA 94064; (415) 325-7333; catalog $1.
Good selection of heirloom varieties.

Richters, 357 Hwy. 47, Goodwood, ON Canada L0C 1A0; catalog $2.
Specializes in herbs but also lists some unusual gourmet vegetables.

Ronniger's Seed Potatoes, Star Route 59, Moyie Springs, ID 83845; catalog $2.
Large selection of organically grown seed potatoes; many rare varieties.

Salt Spring Seeds, Box 33, Ganges, BC Canada V0S 1E0; catalog $3.
More than 100 varieties of beans, as well as tomatoes, heirloom grains, and a wide selection of garlics.

Seeds Blüm, HC 33, Idaho City Stage, Boise, ID 83706; catalog $3.
Jan Blüm's friendly, readable catalog features a large selection of heirlooms, including grains and many uncommon vegetables.

Seeds of Change, P.O. Box 15700, Santa Fe, NM 87506; (505) 438-6500.
One of the best selections of heirloom and traditional varieties; all seeds certified organic.

Shepherd's Garden Seeds, 30 Irene St., Torrington, CT 06790; (203) 482-3638.
Especially good selection of heirlooms and open-pollinated varieties from Europe.

R. H. Shumway, Seedsman, P.O. Box 1, Graniteville, SC 29829; (803) 663-9771.
Established 1870; good selection.

Southern Exposure Seed Exchange, P.O. Box 170, Earlysville, VA 22936; (804) 973-4703; catalog $2.
Informative catalog; good selection of untreated seed; varieties especially well adapted to the mid-Atlantic states.

Southern Seeds, P.O. Box 2091, Melbourne, FL 32902; (407) 727-3662; catalog $1.
Features varieties adapted to hot climates.

Terra Edibles, Box 63, Thomasburg, ON Canada K0K 3H0.
Varieties include heirlooms as well as space-saving and edible landscape plants.

Tomato Growers Supply Company, P.O. Box 2237, Fort Myers, FL 33902; (813) 768-1119.
Huge selection of tomatoes; also lists many varieties of peppers.

Tregunno Seeds Ltd., 126 St. Catharine St. North, Hamilton, ON Canada L8R 1J4.
Untreated seeds; catalog and sales to Canadian customers only.

Vermont Bean Seed Company, Garden Lane, Fair Haven, VT 05743; (802) 273-3400.
Lists around 100 varieties of beans, as well as other vegetables.

Wood Prairie Farm Certified Seed Potatoes, RR 5, Box 164F, Bridgewater, ME 04735; (800) 829-9765.
Many specialty varieties offered; all certified and organically grown.

OTHER SEED COMPANIES THAT LIST HEIRLOOM VARIETIES

W. Atlee Burpee Co., 300 Park Ave., Warminster, PA 18991;
(800) 888-1447.
Established in 1876. The largest U. S. mail-order seed com-
pany. Has introduced many classic varieties, including 'Ice-
berg' lettuce and 'Black Beauty' eggplant.

Gurney's Seed & Nursery Co., 110 Capital St., Yankton,
SD 57079; (605) 665-1671.
Established 1866.

J. W. Jung Seed Co., Box HS, Randolph, WI 53957;
(800) 297-3123.

Orol Ledden & Sons, P.O. Box 7, Sewall, NJ 08080;
(609) 468-1000.

Mellinger's, 2310 W. South Range Rd., North Lima,
OH 44452-9731; (216) 549-9861.

Prairie Grown Garden Seeds, Box 118, Cochin, SK Canada
S0M 0L0; catalog SASE to Canada, $1 to U.S.
Organically grown seed adapted to the Canadian prairies;
not all heirloom varieties are identified as such.

Seeds West Garden Seeds, P.O. Box 27057, Albuquerque,
NM 87125-7057; (505) 242-7474; catalog $2.50.
Specializes in flowers, herbs, and vegetables that grow well in
short-season growing regions.

Territorial Seed Company, P.O. Box 157, Cottage Grove,
OR 97424; (503) 942-9547.
Specializes in varieties adapted to the Maritime Northwest;
organically grown seed.

Thompson & Morgan Inc., P.O. Box 1308, Jackson,
NJ 08527; (908) 363-2225.
The American address for this famous English seed house;
catalog features predominantly flowers but also many
vegetables.

The Tomato Seed Company, P.O. Box 1400, Tryon,
NC 28782.

Seed Trusts and Historic Seed Programs

Abundant Life Seed Foundation
P.O. Box 772
Port Townsend, WA 98368

A nonprofit seed company and preservation project that operates the World Seed Fund, which sends seeds all over the world to community groups working to reduce hunger. In addition to selling untreated, nonhybrid vegetable seeds, Abundant Life also carries seed for herbs, flowers, trees, and shrubs. Send $2 for catalog. Suggested annual membership donation is $30; members receive the seed catalog and periodic newsletters.

CORNS
c/o Carl L. & Karen D. Barnes
Rt. 1, Box 32
Turpin, OK 73950

CORNS preserves and sells old open-pollinated varieties of dent corns, flint corns, and popcorns. Send a SASE for more information and a price list.

Eastern Native Seed Conservancy
CRESS Heirloom Seed Conservation Project
P.O. Box 451
Great Barrington, MA 01230

CRESS (Conservation and Regional Exchange by Seed Savers) is a regional seed exchange specializing in heirloom varieties that are endemic or acclimated to the Berkshire bioregion (western New England and eastern New York state). This sounds quite specific, but in fact many of the varieties offered are adaptable to other growing areas, particularly in the Northeast. Members receive an annual seed list and can order samples to grow out at home, returning a portion of the saved seed to CRESS. The basic yearly membership for individuals is $18.

Heritage Seed Program
RR 3
Uxbridge, ON L9P 1R3 Canada

Heritage Seed Program is a grassroots seed exchange founded by the Canadian Organic Growers in 1984 and dedicated to preserving heirloom and endangered varieties of vegetables, fruits, grains, herbs, and flowers. Members receive the HSP magazine three times a year and a yearly seed listing. Annual membership fees are $18 regular, $15 fixed income, and $25 supporting.

KUSA Research Foundation
P.O. Box 761
Ojai, CA 93023

KUSA is a nonprofit organization devoted to saving rare and endangered cereal crops. Grains are not only edible but can serve double duty as ornamentals or rotation crops for the gardener or small farmer. For a catalog send $2 plus a business-sized SASE.

Landis Valley Museum Heirloom Seed Project
2451 Kissel Hill Road
Lancaster, PA 17601

One of the many historical sites that now incorporates its own heirloom seed project. A seed list that includes more than 100 heirloom varieties with relevant background information is available for $2.50.

Native Seeds/SEARCH
2509 North Campbell Avenue, #325
Tucson, AZ 85719

Native Seeds/SEARCH is a nonprofit organization working to conserve traditional crops of the U.S. Southwest and northern Mexico, as well as their wild relatives. Their annual catalog features a broad and excellent assortment of native beans, corns, melons, chilies, and many other vegetables. Send $1 for catalog. Members receive a quarterly newsletter, the *Seedhead News*, as well as a 10 percent discount on all purchases. Basic annual membership is $18.

Old Sturbridge Village Museum Gift Shop
One Old Sturbridge Village Road
Sturbridge, MA 01566

The Old Sturbridge Village restoration is one of the more famous "living museums" and features kitchen and dooryard
gardens that are filled with varieties grown in the mid-19th
century. A seed list from the museum is available for $1, re-
fundable with order.

Seed Savers Exchange
3076 North Winn Road
Decorah, IA 52101

With more than 8,000 members, Seed Savers Exchange is
probably the largest nongovernmental organization in the
world working to save heirloom varieties of vegetables and
fruits from extinction. SSE members grow out these varieties
and offer them to other members through the exchange's annual Yearbook. SSE is also developing a network of plant col-
lectors in the former Soviet Union and Eastern Europe and
each year grows out and renews part of its in-house seed collection at Heritage Farm, with its five-acre gardens, its Heritage Orchard of old-time apples and grapes, and its herd of
rare White Park cattle.

Since its founding in 1975, Seed Savers Exchange has
grown to become an international clearinghouse for information on rare and heirloom vegetables. It publishes the *Garden Seed Inventory,* a "catalog of catalogs" that lists all of
the open-pollinated varieties carried by U.S. and Canadian
seed companies.

Although it is not a commercial seed company, SSE does
sell a limited number of heirloom seed packets to help support its work. Members receive an excellent journal three
times a year, as well as the annual Yearbook. Membership is
$20 a year in the U.S., $25 in Canada, and $35 overseas.

A separate but affiliated organization is the Flower and
Herb Exchange, which publishes its own yearbook. Membership in FHE is $7 a year in the U.S., $10 in Canada, and
$12 overseas.

Seed Shares
P.O. Box 226
Earlysville, VA 22936

A seed program affiliated with Southern Exposure Seed Exchange, Seed Shares is a "gardener's seed bank" that helps
preserve rare, heirloom, and unusual seed varieties. Seeds are

painstakingly stored and tested to ensure long viability and good germination. Send $1 for a current list of varieties.

The Thomas Jefferson Center for Historic Plants
P.O. Box 316
Charlottesville, VA 22902-0316

Thomas Jefferson was not only our third president and the author of the "Declaration of Independence," but an avid gardener and amateur meteorologist as well. Now some of the varieties familiar to this remarkable man are once again gracing his home gardens at Monticello. The Center for Historic Plants offers a seed listing of heirloom flowers and a few vegetables, which includes the Jefferson Sampler, 10 varieties that TJ grew himself. The seed list is available for $1; for $2 you also receive a copy of the Center's newsletter.

Further Reading

General and Historical Works

Chilies to Chocolate: Food the Americas Gave the World, ed. by Nelson Foster and Linda S. Cordell. Tucson: University of Arizona Press, 1992.

The Columbian Exchange: Biological and Cultural Consequences of 1492 by Alfred W. Crosby Jr., Westport, CT: Greenwood Publishing Co., 1972.

Garden Seed Inventory, ed. by Kent Whealy. 4th edition. Decorah, IA: Seed Saver Publications, 1995.

"Our Vegetable Travelers" by Victor R. Boswell, *National Geographic,* vol. 96, no. 2 (August 1949), pp. 145–217.

Cooking from the Garden

Cooking from the Garden: Creative Gardening and Contemporary Cuisine by Rosalind Creasy. San Francisco: Sierra Club Books, 1988.

The Cook's Garden: Growing and Using the Best-Tasting Vegetable Varieties by Shepherd Ogden and Ellen Ecker Ogden. Emmaus, PA: Rodale Press, 1989.

The Fine Art of Salad Gardening by E. Annie Proulx. Emmaus, PA: Rodale Press, 1985.

The Harrowsmith Salad Garden: A Complete Guide to Growing and Dressing Fresh Vegetables and Greens by Turid Forsyth and Merilyn Simonds Mohr. Camden East, ON: Camden House Publishing, 1992.

The Kitchen Garden Cookbook by Sylvia Thompson. New York: Bantam, 1995.

The Moosewood Restaurant Kitchen Garden: Creative Gardening for the Adventurous Cook by David Hirsch. New York: Simon & Schuster, 1992.

More Recipes from a Kitchen Garden by Renee Shepherd and Fran Raboff. Berkeley, CA: Ten Speed Press, 1995.

Potager: Fresh Garden Cooking in the French Style by Georgeanne Brennan. San Francisco: Chronicle Books, 1992.

Recipes from a Kitchen Garden by Renee Shepherd and Fran Raboff. Berkeley, CA: Ten Speed Press, 1993.

Ethnic and Ornamental Gardens

The Beautiful Food Garden by Kate Rogers Gessert. Pownal, VT: Garden Way Publishing, 1987.

Grow Your Own Chinese Vegetables by Geri Harrington. Pownal, VT: Garden Way Publishing, 1984.

Oriental Herbs and Vegetables. Plants & Gardens, Brooklyn Botanic Garden Record, vol. 39, no. 2 (Summer 1983). Handbook No. 101. Brooklyn, NY: Brooklyn Botanic Garden, 1985.

Growing Vegetables

Down-to-Earth Gardening Know-How for the '90s: Vegetables and Herbs by Dick Raymond. Pownal, VT: Storey Publishing, 1991.

The Harrowsmith Northern Gardener by Jennifer Bennett. Camden East, ON: Camden House Publishing, 1982.

The Kitchen Garden: A Passionate Gardener's Guide to Growing Good Things to Eat by Sylvia Thompson. New York: Bantam, 1995.

A New Look at Vegetables. Plants & Gardens, Brooklyn Botanic Garden Record, vol. 49, no. 1 (Spring 1993). Handbook No. 134. Brooklyn, NY: Brooklyn Botanic Garden, 1993.

The New Organic Grower's Four-Season Harvest by Eliot Coleman. Post Mills, VT: Chelsea Green Publishing, 1992.

The Random House Book of Vegetables by Roger Phillips and Martyn Rix. New York: Random House, 1993.

Rodale's Successful Organic Gardening: Vegetables by Patricia S. Michalak and Cass Peterson. Emmaus, PA: Rodale Press, 1993.

Solar Gardening by Leandre Poisson and Gretchen Vogel Poisson. White River Jct., VT: Chelsea Green Publishing, 1994.

Step by Step Organic Vegetable Gardening by Shepherd Ogden. New York: HarperCollins, 1992.

Vegetable Gardening by David Chambers and Lucinda Mays, with Laura C. Martin. New York: Pantheon Books, 1994.

Warm-Climate Gardening by Barbara Pleasant. Pownal, VT: Garden Way Publishing, 1993.

Organic Pest and Disease Control

The Gardener's Bug Book: Earth-Safe Insect Control by Barbara Pleasant. Pownal, VT: Storey Publishing, 1994.

The Gardener's Guide to Plant Diseases: Earth-Safe Remedies by Barbara Pleasant. Pownal, VT: Storey Publishing, 1995.

Rodale's Garden Insect, Disease & Weed Identification Guide by Miranda Smith and Anna Carr. Emmaus, PA: Rodale Press, 1988.

Preservation Issues

The Heirloom Gardener by Carolyn Jabs. San Francisco: Sierra Club Books, 1984.

Saving the Seed: Genetic Diversity and European Agriculture by Renée Vellvé. London: Earthscan Publications, Ltd., 1992.

Seeds of Change: The Living Treasure by Kenny Ausubel. San Francisco: Harper San Francisco, 1994.

Shattering: Food, Politics, and the Loss of Genetic Diversity by Cary Fowler and Pat Mooney. Tucson: University of Arizona Press, 1990.

Seed Saving and Plant Breeding

Breed Your Own Vegetable Varieties by Carol Deppe. Boston: Little, Brown, 1993.

The New Seed-Starters Handbook by Nancy Bubel. Emmaus, PA: Rodale Press, 1988.

Saving Seeds: The Gardener's Guide to Growing and Storing Vegetable and Flower Seeds by Marc Rogers. Pownal, VT: Storey Publishing, 1990.

Seed to Seed by Suzanne Ashworth. Decorah, IA: Seed Saver Publications, 1991.

Specific Vegetables

Growing Great Garlic by Ron Engeland. Okanogan, WA: Filaree Productions, 1991.

Hot Peppers: Cajuns and Capsicum in New Iberia, Louisiana by Richard Schweid. Berkeley, CA: Ten Speed Press, 1989.

The Pepper Garden by Dave DeWitt and Paul W. Bosland. Berkeley, CA: Ten Speed Press, 1993.

The Potato Garden: A Grower's Guide by Maggie Oster. New York: Harmony Books, 1993.

The Story of Corn by Betty Fussell. New York: Knopf, 1992.

The Sunflower by Charles B. Heiser Jr., Norman, OK: University of Oklahoma Press, 1976.

Bibliography

Anderson, Edgar. *Plants, Man and Life*. Berkeley: University of California Press, 1967.

Baron, Robert C., ed. *The Garden and Farm Books of Thomas Jefferson*. Golden, CO: Fulcrum, 1987.

Burr, Fearing, Jr. *The Field and Garden Vegetables of America*. Chillicothe, IL: The American Botanist, 1990. Originally published in 1863; this is a facsimile reprint of the 2nd edition (1865).

Crosby, Alfred W., Jr. *The Columbian Exchange: Biological and Cultural Consequences of 1492*. Westport, CT: Greenwood Publishing Co., 1972.

Dremann, Craig C. *Ground Cherries, Husk Tomatoes, and Tomatillos*. Redwood City, CA: Redwood City Seed Co., 1985.

Foster, Nelson, and Linda S. Cordell, eds. *Chilies to Chocolate: Food the Americas Gave the World*. Tucson: University of Arizona Press, 1992.

Foust, Clifford M. *Rhubarb: The Wondrous Drug*. Princeton, NJ: Princeton University Press, 1992.

Hedrick, U. P., ed. *Sturtevant's Edible Plants of the World*. New York: Dover, 1972. Originally published in 1919 as *Sturtevant's Notes on Edible Plants* by J. B. Lyon, Albany, NY.

Hedrick, U. P., et al. *The Vegetables of New York*. Albany, NY: J. B. Lyon.

    vol. 1, part 1. "The Peas of New York," 1928

    vol. 1, part 2. "The Beans of New York," 1931

    vol. 1, part 3. "The Sweet Corn of New York," 1934

    vol. 1, part 4. "The Cucurbits of New York," 1937

Heiser, Charles B., Jr. *Seed to Civilization: The Story of Man's Food*. San Francisco: W. H. Freeman & Co., 1973.

_____. *The Sunflower*. Norman: University of Oklahoma Press, 1976.

Henderson, Peter. *Garden and Farm Topics*. New York: Henderson & Co., 1884.

_____. *Gardening for Pleasure*. New York: Orange Judd, 1891.

_____. *Gardening for Profit*, ed. George DeVault. Chillicothe, IL: The American Botanist, 1991. Facsimile of 1886 edition (New York: Orange Judd Co.) and other works.

Hexamer, F. M. *Asparagus: Its Culture for Home Use and for Market*. New York: Orange Judd Co., 1905.

Johnson, Charles. *The Seed Grower's List of Vegetable Varieties Grown in the United States in 1906*. Redwood City, CA: Redwood City Seed Co., n.d. Facsimile reprint of last chapter of *The Seed Grower* (Marietta, PA, 1906).

Mangelsdorf, Paul C. *Corn: Its Origin, Evolution, and Improvement*. Cambridge: Harvard University Press, 1974.

Schery, Robert W. *Plants for Man*. 2nd edition. Englewood Cliffs, NJ: Prentice-Hall, 1972.

Stephens, James M. *Manual of Minor Vegetables*. Gainesville, FL: University of Florida Cooperative Extension Service, 1988. Bulletin SP-40.

Ucko, P. J., and G. W. Dimbleby, eds. *The Domestication and Exploitation of Plants and Animals*. Chicago: Aldine Publishing Co., 1969.

Vavilov, Nikolai Ivanovich. "The Origin, Variation, Immunity and Breeding of Cultivated Plants," trans. K. Starr Chester. *Chronica Botanica* vol. 13, nos. 1–6 (Spring 1951): 1–366.

Vilmorin-Andrieux. *The Vegetable Garden*. Trans. W. Miller. Berkeley, CA: Ten Speed Press, 1981. Facsimile reprint of 1885 English edition.

Whealy, Kent, and Arllys Adelmann, eds. *Seed Savers Exchange: The First Ten Years, 1975–1985*. Decorah, IA: Seed Saver Publications, 1986.

White, Lyman. *Heirlooms and Genetics: 100 Years of Seeds*. Cambridge, NY: Lyman White, 1988.

Photo Credits

Lucy Beckstead: 65A

David Cavagnaro: 24B, 25A, 26A, 27B, 28A, B, 29A, B, 31A, 32A, B, 33A, B, 34A, B, 35A, B, 36B, 37A, B, 38A, 39A, B, 40A, B, 41A, B, 42A, 45A, 52A, B, 55B, 58A, 59A, B, 61B, 62B, 63A, B, 64A, 65B, 66A, 68A, B, 69B, 71A, 72A, B, 73A, 74B, 75B, 76A, B, 79B, 80A, B, 81A, 84A, 86B, 87B, 88A, B, 89A, B, 90A, B, 91A, 92B, 93B, 94A, B, 95A, 100B, 102B, 105B, 108A, B, 109B, 110A, B, 111A, 112A, B, 113B, 114A, 115A, B, 116A, B, 117A, B, 118A, B, 119A, B, 122A, B, 123A

Priscilla Connell/PhotoNats: 103A

Rosalind Creasy: ii, viii, 7, 20

Wally Eberhart/PhotoNats: 56B

Derek Fell: 22A, B, 25B, 30B, 36A, 38B, 43A, 47B, 48A, B, 49A, B, 50A, B, 51A, 54A, 57A, B, 60A, 67A, 69A, 70A, B, 73B, 74A, 75A, 77A, 81B, 82B, 83A, B, 85A, B, 87A, 91B, 93A, 95B, 96A, 97A, B, 98A, B, 99A, 100A, 101A, B, 102A, 104B, 105A, 106A, B, 107A, B, 113A, 120A, B, 121A, 124

Jerry Howard/Positive Images: 64B

Johnny's Selected Seeds: 26B, 27A, 30A, 44A, 53A, B, 54B, 78B, 96B, 99B, 104A, 111B, 114B

Dency Kane: 14, 67B, 78A, 84B, 86A

John A. Lynch/PhotoNats: 109A

Robert E. Lyons/PhotoNats: 79A

A. Peter Margosian/PhotoNats: 23B

Shepherd Ogden: 44B, 51B, 55A

Jerry Pavia: 24A, 46A

Joanne Pavia: 43B

Ann Reilly/PhotoNats: 46B, 47A, 82A

Shepherd's Garden Seeds: 23A, 31B, 42B, 56A, 61A, 62A, 66B, 92A, 103B, 121B

Virginia Twinam-Smith/PhotoNats: 45B, 58B, 77B

Cathy Wilkinson-Barash/PhotoNats: 71B

Index

Numbers in **boldface** *type refer to pages on which color plates appear.*

Aaron Low Seed Co., 141
Abelmoschus esculentus, **79–81**, 218–20
Abundant Life Seed Foundation, 307, 314
Admire, George, 209
Aerial radishes, 251, 252, 254
Alegrias ("joy bars"), 128
All-American Selections
    Carrot 'Imperator,' **49**, 163
    Cucumber 'Straight 8,' 186
    Endive 'Broad-Leaved Batavian,' 191
    Melon 'Honey Rock' ('Sugar Rock'), 214
Allergies, to fava beans, 142
Allicin, 193
Allium
    ampeloprasum var. *porrum,* **68**, 204–6
    cepa, Aggregatum group, **84**, 221, 227–28
    cepa, Cepa group, **81–82**, 220–24
    cepa, Proliferum group, **83**, 221, 226–27
    fistulosum, **82–83**, 220–21, 225–26
    longicuspis, 193
    sativum, 193–97
    sativum var. *orphioscorodon,* **61–62**, 193, 194, 195–96
    sativum var. *sativum,* **63–64**, 193, 194, 196–97
    scorodoprasum, 194
Alternaria (early) blight, 18
Amaranth, 126–28
    'Coleus Leaf Salad', 127
    'Dreadicus', 127
    'Elephant Head', 127
    'Hopi Red Dye', 127
    'Joseph's Coat', **22**, 127
    'Komo', 127
    'Love-Lies-Bleeding', **22**, 126, 127
    'Merah', **23**, 127

'Mercado', 127
'Molten Fire', **23**, 128
'Summer Poinsettia', 128
Amaranthus
    caudatus, **22**, 126, 127
    cruentus, 127
    gangeticus 'Elephant Head', 127
    gangeticus 'Joseph's Coat', **22**, 127
    gangeticus 'Merah', **23**, 127
    gangeticus 'Molten Fire', **23**, 128
    hypochondriacus, 127
    tricolor, **22**, 127
Anasazi Indians, 179
Anderson, Edgar, 172, 265, 281
Angular leaf spot, 184
Annual plants, 8–9
Anthracnose, 133, 184, 297
Aphids
    on beet plants, 151
    on broccoli plants, 154
    on cabbage plants, 158
    on celery plants, 167
    on chicory plants, 170
    on fava bean plants, 143
    on lettuce plants, 208
    on pea plants, 235
    on pepper plants, 242
    on squash plants, 267
    use of rhubarb-leaf spray against, 257
Apium
    graveolens var. *dulce,* **51**, 166–68
    graveolens var. *rapaceum,* **50**, 166–68
Arancauo bean, 138
Arikara Indians, 275
Aristotle, 279
Arledge family, 242
Armyworm caterpillars, 278
Artichoke, globe, 2, 128–29
    'Green Globe', **24**, 129
    'Purple Sicilian', 129

Artichoke (Cont.)
　'Violetto', 129
Artichoke, Jerusalem, 2, **64–65,**
　197–99
Artichoke (common) garlic, **63,**
　194, 196–97
Ashworth, Suzanne, 189
Asparagus, 2, 9, **24,** 129–31
　'Argenteuil Early', 131
　'Conover's Colossal', 131
　'Giant Dutch Purple', 131
　'Martha Washington', 130
　'Mary Washington', 130
　Washington strains of, 130
Asparagus beans, 238
Asparagus beetles, spotted, 131
Asparagus broccoli, 153
Asparagus officinalis, **24,** 129–31
Augustus (Roman emperor), 129
Aztecs, 147, 240

Babur (emperor of India), 211
Bacterial wilt, 184, 267
Barbe de capuchin, 169
Bean mosaic virus, 133
Beans, 131–50
　dry (field) beans, **31–35,** 138–42
　fava (broad) beans, **36,** 132,
　　142–44
　horticultural (shell) beans,
　　29–31, 137–38
　lima (butter) beans, **36–39,**
　　144–46
　runner beans, **39–40,** 146–48
　snap beans, **25–28,** 132–36
　soybeans, **41,** 148–49
　tepary beans, **41,** 149–50
Bean weevils, 139
Becker's Seed Potatoes (company),
　307
Beet, 150–53
　'Albina Vereduna', 151
　'Bull's Blood', 151
　'Chiogga', **42,** 152
　'Crosby's Egyptian', 152
　'Cylindra', **42,** 152
　'Detroit Dark Red', **43,** 152
　'Dracena Beet', **44,** 153
　'Early Wonder', 152
　'Formanova', 152
　'Golden Beet', **43,** 152
　'Lutz Green Leaf', **44,** 152
　'MacGregor's Favorite', **44,** 153
　'Winter Keeper', 152

'Yellow Intermediate Mangel', 153
'Yellow Mangel', 153
Beetles, 151. *See also* Colorado
　potato beetles; Cucumber
　beetles; Flea beetles; Mexican
　bean beetles; Spotted
　asparagus beetles
Belgian endive, 169, 170, 171
Bell peppers. *See* Sweet peppers
Bentley Seeds, Inc., 307
Beta
　vulgaris, Cicla group, **110–11,**
　　279–80
　vulgaris, Crassa group, **42–44,**
　　150–52
Bibb lettuce, 207
Biennial plants, 8–9, 10
Biodiversity, 4, 5–6
Bird peppers, 242
Black-eyed peas, 238
Black heart, 151, 167
Black mustard, 216
Black rot, 278
Black salsify (scorzonera), 260
Blight. *See also* Corn blight; Early
　blight; Late blight; Leaf blight
　on asparagus plants, 131
　on bean plants, 133
　on corn plants, 5
　on spinach plants, 263
　on tomato plants, 18, 286
Blossom-end rot
　on pepper plants, 241
　on tomato plants, 286
Blum, Jan, 226
Bok choy, 216
Boothby family, 185
Boston lettuce, 207
Bountiful Gardens (seed company),
　307
Braganza cabbage, 159
Brassica
　hirta, 216
　juncea, **78–79,** 215–18
　napus, Napobrassica group, **99,**
　　258–59
　nigra, 216
　oleracea, 258
　oleracea, Acephala group,
　　65–66, 199–203
　oleracea, Botrytis group, **45,**
　　49–50, 153–55, 164–66
　oleracea, Capitata group, **46–47,**
　　157–60
　oleracea, Gemmifera group, **45,**
　　155–57

oleracea, Gongylodes group, **67,** 203–4
oleracea, Italica group, 153, 154
oleracea, var. *longata,* 202
rapa, 258
rapa, Chinensis group, 218
rapa, Japonica group, **78,** 215–18
rapa, Pekinensis group, **77,** 215–18
rapa, Rapifera group, **120–21,** 294–96
Briars, Dave, 199
Brill, Francis, 159
Broad (fava) beans, **36,** 132, 142–44
Broccoli, 153–55
  'Calabrese', 154
  'De Cicco', 154
  'Early Purple Sprouting', 155
  'Romanesco', **45,** 155
Brown mustard, 216
Brown scab, 151
Brown-skinned onions, 223–24
Brussel sprouts, 155–57
  'Bedford Fillbasket', 156
  'Catskill', 156
  'Long Island Improved', 156
  'Rubine Red', **45,** 156–57
Bt *(Bacillus thuringiensis),* 18
Bunching (Welsh) onions, **82,** 220–21, 225–26
  'Evergreen White Bunching', **83,** 225
  'He-Shi-Ko', **83,** 225
  'Red Welsh Bunching', 226
Burbank, Luther
  Amaranth 'Molten Fire' developed by, 128
  Potato 'Russet Burbank' developed by, 246, 250
  runner beans noted by, 147
  Tomato 'Burbank' developed by, 287
Burlingame, D.G., 134
Burpee Seed Co., 177, 215
Burr, Fearing, Jr.
  artichokes listed by, 129
  beans listed by, 143, 144
  beets listed by, 153
  broccoli listed by, 155
  cabbages listed by, 159
  carrots noted by, 162
  celery listed by, 168
  chicory listed by, 171
  citron listed by, 299

  corn listed by, 175, 179–80
  corn salad (mâche) listed by, 181
  endive (escarole) listed by, 191
  Jerusalem artichoke listed by, 198
  kale listed by, 201, 202
  kohlrabi listed by, 204
  melons listed by, 215
  onions listed by, 223, 226
  parsley listed by, 230
  parsnips listed by, 232
  peppers listed by, 243
  radishes listed by, 254
  rutabagas listed by, 259
  squash and pumpkins listed by, 268, 273
  tomatoes listed by, 284, 288, 293
  turnips listed by, 295
Bush beans, 132, 133
  dry (field) beans, **31–34,** 139–41
  horticultural (shell) beans, **29–30,** 137–38
  lima (butter) beans, **36–37,** 145
  runner beans ('Barteldes Bush Lima'), 147
  snap beans, 133–34
  tepary beans ('Sonoran Gold Bush'), 150
  wax beans, **27,** 135–36
Butter (lima) beans, **36–39,** 131, 144–46
Butterhead lettuce, 207

Cabbage, 157–60
  green cabbage, **46,** 159–60
  red cabbage, **47,** 160
  Savoy cabbage, **47,** 157, 160
Cabbage root maggots
  on broccoli plants, 154
  on radish plants, 252–53
  on rutabaga plants, 259
  on turnip plants, 295
Cabbage worms and loopers
  on broccoli plants, 154
  on Brussel sprout plants, 156
  on cabbage plants, 158
  on cauliflower plants, 165
  on kale and collard plants, 201
  on kohlrabi plants, 204
Calaloo, 126
Callahan, Miss (of Los Angeles), 136
Canadian Organic Growers, 315
Cantaloupes, true (French), 213, 215

Capsicum
  annuum, **90–95**, 239–45
  annuum var. *aviculare*, **89**, 242
  baccatum, 240
  chinense, 240
  frutescens, 240, 242
  pubescens, 240
Carolina beans, 144
Carrot rust flies, 162
Carrots, 160–64
  'Belgium White', 4, 162
  'Carotte Violette', 162
  'Chantenay', 1, 161
  'Chantenay Red Cored', **48**, 162
  'Danvers Half Long', **48**, 162
  'Dragon', 162–63
  'Early Scarlet Horn', 163
  'Guerande', 161, 163
  'Imperator', **49**, 163
  'Long Orange', 163
  'Long Orange Improved', 163
  'Nantes', 161
  'Oxheart', 161, 163
  'Paris Market', 163
  'Rondo', 163
  'St. Valery', 163
  'Topweight', 163
  'Touchon', 164
Carrot weevils, 162
Cartier, Jacques, 182
Casaba (honeydew) melons, **75**, 212, 213
Cauliflower, 164–66
  'Early Snowball', **49**, 165
  'Purple Cape', **50**, 165
  'Veitch's Autumn Giant', 165–66
Cavagnaro, David
  beans described by, 141, 148
  peas described by, 239
  squash described by, 268, 269
  tomatoes described by, 291
Celeriac (celery root), 166–68
  'Giant Prague', **50**, 167–68
Celery, 166–68
  'Golden Self-Blanching', **51**, 168
  'Golden Yellow', 168
  'Red Stalk', 168
  'Solid Pink', 168
  'Solid Red', 168
  'Zwolsche Krul', 168
Celery mosaic virus, 167
Chadwick, Alan, 287

Champlain, Samuel de, 197
Cherokee Indians, 135, 290
Chicons, 169, 170, 171
Chicorée frisée, 190
Chicorium
  endivia, **60**, 190–91
  intybus, **51**, 168–71
Chicory, 168–71
  radicchio and heading chicory, **51**, 171
  spring (cutting) chicory, 170–71
  witloof and root chicory, 171
Chili peppers. *See* Hot peppers
Chinese cabbage, 216–17
Chinese lantern, 281
Chinese spinach, 126
Ciboule onions, 221
Citron
  Citrullus lanatus var. *citroides*, **123**, 299
  Citrus medica, 299
Citrullus
  lanatus, **122–23**, 296–99
  lanatus var. *citroides*, **123**, 299
Citrus medica, 299
Clubroot, 165
Coleman, Eliot, 17, 128
Collards, 199–201, 202–3. *See also* Kale
  'Georgia', 202
  'Greasy Collards', 202
  'Green Glaze', 202
  'Morris Heading', 202–3
Colorado potato beetles
  on eggplant plants, 188
  on potato plants, 248–49
  on tomatillo plants, 282
  on tomato plants, 286
Columbus, Christopher, 240
Common beans, 131–32
Common (artichoke) garlic, **63**, 194, 196–97
Common (globe) onions, 220–24
  'Ailsa Craig Exhibition', **82**, 223
  'Australian Brown', 224
  'Italian Red Bottle', **81**, 223
  'Ox Horn', 223
  'Red Torpedo', **81**, 223
  'Red Wethersfield', 223
  'Silver Ball', 224
  'Silverskin', 224
  'Southport Red Globe', 223
  'Southport White Globe', 224
  'Spindle-Shaped', 223
  'White Portugal', 224

'White Rocca', 224
'Yellow Ebenezer', 224
'Yellow Globe Danvers', 224
Companion plantings, 18
Comstock, Ferre & Co. (seed
      company), 308
Conover, Michael, 175
Conover, S.B., 131
Conservation and Regional
      Exchange by Seed Savers
      (CRESS), 314–15
Cook's Garden (seed company),
      308
Corn, 172–80
   dent corn, **52–53**, 172–73, 174,
      178
   flint corn, 172, 174, 178–79
   flour corn, **53**, 173, 174,
      179–80
   pod corn, 173
   popcorn, **54**, 173, 174, 180
   sweet corn, **52**, 173, 174,
      175–78
Corn blight, 5
Corn borers, 175
Cornichons, 184
Corn salad (mâche), 180–82
   'A Grosse Graine', 181
   'Big-Seeded', 181
   'Candia', 182
   'Coquille', 181–82
   'Coquille de Louviers', **55**,
      181–82
   'D'Etampes', 182
   'Green de Cambria', 182
   'Mâche Ronde a Grosse
      Graine', 181
   'Verte de Cambrai', 182
   'Verte d'Etampes', 182
CORNS historic seed program,
      314
Corn smut, 175
Cos (romaine) lettuce, **74**, 207,
      211
Cowpeas, 238–39
   'Calico Crowder', 239
   'Hereford Pea', 239
   'Papago', **87**, 239
   'Polecat Pea', 239
   'Susanne', **88**, 239
   'Susanne Cream', 239
   'Whipporwill', **88**, 239
   'Zipper', **89**, 239
   'Zipper Cream Crowder', 239
Coy, E.L., 177
Cranberry beans, 137

Creasy, Rosalind
   beans described by, 145, 147
   beets recommended by, 151
   cucumbers recommended by,
      186
   eggplant recommended by, 189
   tomatoes described by, 289–90
CRESS (Conservation and
      Regional Exchange by Seed
      Savers), 314–15
Crookneck squashes, summer and
      winter, **107**, 265, 272
Crop rotation, 16
Cross-pollinating annuals, 9
Crowder peas, 238
Cucumber beetles, 183, 267, 297
Cucumber mosaic virus, 184
Cucumbers, 182–86
   'Boothby's Blonde', **55**, 185
   'Boston Pickling', 184
   'Chicago Pickling', 184
   'China Long', 185
   'Chinese Three Feet', 185
   'Crystal Apple', 185
   'Early Cluster', 184
   'Early Russian', 184
   'Emerald', 186
   'Japanese Climbing', 185
   'Lemon', **56**, 185
   'Longfellow', 186
   'Long Green Improved', 185–86
   'Long Green Turkey', 185
   'Straight 8', 186
   'Suyo Long', **56**, 186
   'Vert de Massy', 184
   'West Indian Gherkin', 186
   'White Wonder', **57**, 186
Cucumis
   anguria, 186
   melo, Flexuosus group, 185
   melo, Inodorus and Reticulatus
      groups, 75–77, 211–15
   sativus, 55–57, 182–86
Cucurbita, 264–73
   maxima, 65, **100–104**, 267–69
   mixta, **104**, 265, 267, 269–70
   moschata, **105**, 265, 267,
      270–71
   pepo, **106–8**, 265, 271–73
Curius, Manius, 294
Currant tomatoes, **120**, 283,
      293–94
Cushaw squashes, **104**, 265,
      269–70
Cutting celery, 166, 168
Cutting (spring) chicory, 169, 170

Cutworms, 154, 158, 165, 241
Cymling squash, 273
Cynara scolymus, **24,** 128–29

Daikon radishes, 251, 252, 254
Daucus
    carota, 160
    carota var. *sativus,* **48–49,**
        160–64
Deep Diversity (seed company),
    308
Deer, 181
Degiorgio Seed Company, 308
Dent corn, 172–73, 174
    'Bloody Butcher', 178
    'Hickory King', **52,** 178
    'Nothstine Dent', **53,** 178
DeSoto, Hernando, 182
Dioscorea spp., 277
Dipel, 18
Diseases
    on asparagus plants, 131
    on bean plants, 133, 139
    on beet plants, 151
    on broccoli plants, 154
    on Brussel sprout plants, 156
    on cabbage plants, 158
    on carrot plants, 162
    on cauliflower plants, 165
    on celery plants, 167
    on chicory plants, 170
    on corn plants, 175
    on cucumber plants, 183
    on eggplant plants, 188
    on kale and collard plants, 201
    on lettuce plants, 208
    on lima bean plants, 144
    on mustard and Oriental greens,
        216, 217
    on okra plants, 219
    on onion plants, 222–23
    on pea plants, 234–35
    on pepper plants, 241
    on potato plants, 246, 247, 248,
        249
    on rutabaga plants, 259
    on spinach plants, 263
    on squash plants, 267
    on sunflower plants, 275
    on sweet potato plants, 278
    on tomatillo plants, 282
    on tomato plants, 18, 286
    on watermelon plants, 297
    use of organic controls, 14–19
D.L. Landreth Seed Co., 310

Dow gauk, 238
Down on the Farm Seed (seed
    company), 308
Downy mildew
    on bean plants, 133
    on cucumber plants, 184
    on okra plants, 219
    on spinach plants, 263
    on squash plants, 267
Drip irrigation, 17
Dry (field) beans, 138–42
    bush beans, **31–34,** 139–41
    pole beans, **35,** 141–42
—bush
    'Anasazi', 140
    'Arikara Yellow', 139–40
    'Black Coco', 140
    'Black Turtle', **31,** 140
    'Cannellini', 140
    'Cannelone', 140
    'China Yellow', 141
    'Dwarf Red Cranberry', 140–41
    'Eureka', 141
    'Great Northern', 140
    'Hutterite', **32,** 140
    'Jacob's Cattle', **32,** 140
    'Johnson Bean', 141
    'Low's Champion', **33,** 140–41
    'Molasses Face', 141
    'Montana White', 140
    'Santa Maria Pinquito', 141
    'Soldier', **33,** 141
    'Sulphur', **34,** 141
    'Swedish Brown', 6, **34,** 141
    'Trout', **32,** 140
    'Turtle Soup', 140
    'Yellow Eye', 141
—pole
    'Mostoller Wild Goose', **35,**
        141–42
    'Ruth Bible', **35,** 142
D.V. Burrell Seed Growers
    Company, 307
Dye plants, 127

Early blight, 18
Earworms, 175
Eastern Native Seed Conservancy,
    314–15
Eastwood, J.W., 215
Edible-podded (sugar or snow)
    peas, 233, 234, 237
    'Dwarf Gray Sugar', 237
    'Golden Sweet', **86,** 237

'Mammoth Melting Sugar', **87**, 237
Eggplant, 187–90
  'Black Beauty', 1, **57**, 188
  'Listada de Gandia', **58**, 188–89
  'Pintong Long', **58**, 189
  'Rosa Bianca', **59**, 189
  'Thai Green', 189
  'Turkish Italian', 189
  'Turkish Orange', **59**, 189
  'Violette di Firenze', 190
Egyptian (topset) onions, **83**, 221, 226–27
  'Catawissa Onion', 227
  'McCullar's White Topset', 227
Elephant garlic, 194
Elizabeth Berry (seed company), 307
Endive (escarole), 190–91
  'Batavian', 191
  'Broad-Leaved Batavian', 191
  'Frisée', **60**, 191
  'Green Curled Ruffec', **60**, 191
  'Grosse Bouclee', 191
  'Tres Fine Marachiere', **60**, 191
Endive, Belgian, 169, 170, 171
Engeland, Ron, 193–94
Escarole (endive), **60**, 190–91
European wild cabbage, 258
Evergreen Y.H. Enterprises (seed company), 308

Farr, Charles N., 271
Fava (broad) beans, 132, 142–44
  'Agua-Dulce Long-Podded', 143
  'Aquadulce Claudia', 143
  'Broad Windsor', **36**, 143
  'Castillo Franco', 143
  'Crimson-Flowered', 144
  'Red or Scarlet Blossomed', 144
  'Seville Long-Pod', 143
  'Windsor', 143
Fedco Seeds (seed company), 313
Fencing, 16–17
Fennel, Florence, 192
Fertilizers, 17–18
Fetticus, 180
Field (dry) beans, **31–35**, 138–42
Field peas
  Pisum sativum var. *arvense*, **86**, 233, 235
  Vigna unguiculata, **87–89**, 238–39
Filaree Farm (seed company), 308
Filet beans, 132, 133, 134

Finocchio, 192
Flageolet beans, 137
Flea beetles
  on broccoli plants, 154
  on cabbage plants, 158
  on cauliflower plants, 165
  on eggplant plants, 188
  on mustard and Oriental greens, 216, 217
  on pepper plants, 241–42
  on radish plants, 252
  on tomato plants, 286
  on turnip plants, 295
Flint corn, 172, 174
  'Garland Flint', 178
  'Longfellow Flint', 178
  'Narragansett', 179
  'Rhode Island White Cap', 178–79
Floating Mountain Seeds (seed company), 308
Florence fennel, 192
  'Romy', **61**, 192
Flour corn, 173, 174
  'Anasazi', 179
  'Hopi Blue', 179
  'Mandan Bride', **53**, 179
  'Taos Pueblo Blue Corn', 179
  'Tuscarora', 179–80
Flowering cabbage, 200
Flowering kale, 200
Foeniculum vulgare var. *azoricum*, **61**, 192
Ford Seed Co., 141
Fox Hollow Herb & Heirloom Seed Co., 308
French beans, 132, 133, 134
French (true) cantaloupes, 213, 215
French (true) pumpkins, **103**, 265, 269
Frisée, 190
Fusarium root rot, 158
Fusarium wilt, 131, 219, 234, 286

Garden beans, 132
Garden City Seeds (seed company), 309
Gardner, Jo Ann, 280
Garland, George, 178
Garlic, 2, 193–97
  'Carpathian', **61**, 195
  'Chesnok Red', 196
  'German Red', **62**, 195–96
  'Greek', 196

Garlic (Cont.)
  'Greek Blue', 196
  'Inchelium Red', **63**, 196
  'Lorz Italian', **63**, 196–97
  'Nootka Rose', **64**, 197
  'Romanian Red', 196
  'Silverskin', 197
  'Spanish Roja', **62**, 196
Georgia Agricultural Experiment
  Station, 278
Germplasm, 6
Gherkins, 186
Gilfeather, John, 295
Girasole articiocco, 197
Gleckler's Seedsmen (seed
  company), 309
Globe artichoke, **24**, 128–29
Globe (common) onions, **81–82**,
  220–24
Glycine max, **41**, 132, 148–49
Good Earth Seed Company, 309
Good Seed Co., 309
Gourmet Gardener (seed
  company), 309
Gray mold, 131
Green cabbage
  'Brunswick', 159
  'Christmas Drumhead', 159
  'Couve de Tronchuda', 159
  'Danish Ballhead', **46**, 159
  'Early Jersey Wakefield', **46**, 159
  'Glory of Enkhuizen', 159
  'Late Flat Dutch', 159–60
  'Premium Late Flat Dutch',
    159–60
Green onions, 220
Green peas. *See* Peas
Greens
  beet greens, 150, 151
  chicory, **51**, 168–71
  endive (escarole), **60**, 190–91
  kale and collards, **65–66**,
    199–203
  lettuce, **69–74**, 206–11
  mustard and Oriental greens,
    77–79, 215–18
  Swiss chard, **110–11**, 279–80
  turnip greens, 295, 296
Gregory, J.H., 268
Ground cherry, 5, 281
Gurney's Seed & Nursery Co., 313

Hale, I.D., 214
Hand pollination, 9

Hardiness zones, USDA (map),
  302–3
Hardneck (ophio) garlic, **61–62**,
  193, 194, 195–96
Havasupai Indians, 275
Head lettuce, **70–73**, 207, 209–11
Hedrick, U.P.
  beans listed by, 135, 136, 138,
    141, 145, 146, 147
  corn listed by, 175–76, 177,
    179
  cucumbers listed by, 185
  melons listed by, 213, 214, 215
  peas listed by, 236, 237
  squash and pumpkins noted by,
    264, 268, 269, 270, 271
Heirloom Seeds (seed company),
  309
Heirloom vegetables
  adaptation of, 7
  definition of, 2–3
  mail-order seed sources for,
    307–13
  preservation of, 7–8
  reasons for growing, 3–5
Helianthus
  annuus, **108–9**, 273–76
  debilis var. *cucumerifolius*, **109**,
    275–76
  maximiliani, 276
  tuberosus, **64–65**, 197–99
Henderson, Peter, 130, 159, 165,
  236, 273
Heritage Seed Program (Canada),
  315
Herodotus, 207
Hibiscus esculentus. *See*
  Abelmoschus esculentus
High Altitude Gardens (seed
  company), 309
Hill, Luther, 176
Hinn choy, 126
Historic seed programs and trusts,
  6, 314–17
Hollander, Lawrence
  beans noted by, 135, 142
  corn noted by, 175, 180
  onions noted by, 224
  peppers noted by, 243
  sunflowers noted by, 275
  tomatoes noted by, 289
  watermelons noted by, 298
Honeydew (casaba) melons, **75**,
  212, 213
Hooker, Ira, 176

Hopi Indians, 127
Horse beans, 142
Horticultural (shell) beans, 137–38
  bush beans, 29–30, 137–38
  pole beans, 30–31, 138
—bush
  'Chevrier Vert', 137
  'Dwarf Horticultural', 29, 137
  'Horto', 137–38
  'Tongue of Fire', 29, 137–38
  'Vermont Cranberry Bush', 30,
    138
—pole
  'Lazy Wife', 30, 138
  'London Horticultural', 31, 138
  'Vermont Cranberry Pole', 138
  'White Cranberry', 138
  'Wren's Egg', 31, 138
Hot peppers, 240–41, 242–44
  'Arbol', 242–43
  'Arledge Hot', 242
  'Chiltepine', 89, 242
  'Chimayo', 90, 242
  'Czechoslovakian Black', 242
  'De Arbol', 242–43
  'De Comida', 243
  'Grandpa's Home Pepper', 90,
    243
  'Karlo', 91, 243
  'Long Cayenne', 243
  'Long Red Cayenne', 91, 243
  'Louisiana Hot', 242
  'Mushroom Pepper', 92, 243–44
  'Pico de Gallo', 243
  'Red Squash', 92, 243–44
  'Squash Pepper', 243
  'Texas', 242
  'Tree Chili', 242–43
  'Yellow Squash', 244
  'Zapotec di Comida', 243
Howe Sound Seeds (seed
    company), 309
Hubbard, Elizabeth, 268
Hummingbirds, 146
Huron Indians, 197
Husk tomato, 5, 281

Iceberg lettuce, 207
Incas, 240
Insecticidal soap, 19
Inulin, 198
Ipomoea batatas, 110, 276–78
Iroquois Nation, 180
Italian corn salad, 181
Italian dandelions, 169

Jackson, Thomas, 145
Jefferson, Thomas, 182, 210, 317
Jerusalem artichoke, 2, 64, 197–
    99
  'Dave's Shrine', 199
  'Garnet', 199
  'Judy's Red', 199
  'Maine Giant', 199
  'Smooth Garnet', 65, 199
  'Wolcottonian Red', 199
J.L. Hudson, Seedsman (seed
    company), 309
Johnny's Selected Seeds (seed
    company), 310
Johnson, Charles, 211, 224, 232
Johnston, Rob, Jr., 136, 138, 175
"Joy bars," 128
J.W. Jung Seed Co., 313

Kale, 199–203. *See also* Collards
  'Buda Kale', 202
  'Cavalo Nero', 201
  'Dwarf Blue Curled
    Scotch', 65, 201
  'Dwarf Green Curled Scotch',
    201
  'Jersey Kale', 202
  'Lacinato', 66, 201
  'Pentland Brig', 201
  'Ragged Jack', 66, 201–2
  'Red Russian', 66, 200, 201–2
  'Thousand-Headed', 201, 202
  'Tree Cabbage', 202
  'Tuscan Black Palm', 201
  'Walking Stick', 202
Kalmia Farm (seed company),
    310
Kapuler, Alan, 140
Keeney, Calvin, 134, 136
Keller, C.D., 176
Ken Allen (seed company), 307
Kershaw, Charles, 257
Kidney beans, 131, 132
Kim chee, 157
Kitazawa Seed Co., 310
Knight, Thomas A., 233
Kohlrabi, 203–4
  'Early Purple Vienna', 67, 204
  'Early White Vienna', 67, 204
  'Gigante', 204
  'Gigant Winter', 204
Komatsuna, 216, 218
Krupnick, Wendy, 279–80, 287
KUSA Research Foundation,
    315

Lactuca
  sativa, **69–74,** 206–11
  sativa var. *capitata,* **70–73,** 207,
      209–11
  sativa var. *crispa,* **69–70,** 207,
      208–9
  sativa var. *longifolia,* **74,** 207,
      211
  serriola, 207
Lamb's lettuce, 180
Landis Valley Museum Heirloom
      Seed Project, 315
Landreth Seed Co., 134
Larsen Agricultural Experiment
      Station, Penn State University,
      187
Late blight, 246
Laxton, Thomas, 233, 235
Leaf blight, 175
Leaf miner flies, 263
Leaf mustard, **78–79,** 215–18
Le Champion Heritage Seeds
      (company), 308
Leeks, 204–6
  'American Flag', **68,** 206
  'Bleu de Solaise', 206
  'Blue Solaise', **68,** 206
  'Giant Caretan', 206
  'Giant Musselburgh', **68,** 206
  'Giant Rouen', 206
  'Lyon', 206
  'Prizetaker', 206
  'Scotch Flag', 206
Le Jardin de Gourmet (seed
      company), 309
Lettuce, 206–11
  'Balloon', 211
  'Balon', 211
  'Bibb', 210
  'Black-Seeded Simpson', **69,**
      208–9
  'Bronze Arrow', 209
  'Brune d'Hiver', 208, 209
  'Deer Tongue', **69,** 209
  'Four Seasons', **71,** 210
  'Grandpa Admire's', 209
  'Grandpa's', 209
  'Hanson', 209
  'Iceberg', **70,** 207, 210
  'Limestone Bibb', **71,** 210
  'Matchless', **69,** 209
  'Merveille des Quatre Saisons',
      71, 210
  'Mescher', **72,** 210
  'Oak Leaf', **70,** 209
  'Paris White Cos', **74,** 211

  'Pirat', **72,** 210
  'Red Deer Tongue', 209
  'Red Oak Leaf', 209
  'Red Winter', **74,** 211
  'Romaine Blonde Marachiere',
      211
  'Rouge d'Hiver', **74,** 211
  'Royal Oak Leaf', 209
  'Schweitzer's Mescher Bibb', 210
  'Speckled', **73,** 210
  'Spreckled', 210
  'Tennis Ball', 210
  'Tom Thumb', **73,** 210–11
Lettuce mosaic virus, 208
Lima (butter) beans, 131, 144–46
  bush limas, **36–37,** 145
  pole limas, **37–39,** 145–46
—bush
  'Henderson', 145
  'Hopi Orange', **36,** 145
  'Jackson Wonder', **37,** 145
—pole
  'Black', **37, 39,** 145
  'Christmas', **38,** 145
  'Civil War', 145
  'Dr. Martin', 146
  'Florida Butter', 145
  'King of the Garden', **38,** 146
  'Red Calico', **39,** 146
  'Willow Leaf White', **39,** 146
Lind, Jenny, 214
Long Island Seed Company, 310
Looseleaf (cutting) lettuce, **69–70,**
      207, 208–9
Louis XIV, court of, 232
Lucullus, Lucius Licinius, 280
Lycopersicon
  lycopersicum, **112–19,** 283–94
  pimpinellifolium, **120,** 283,
      293–94

Mâche (corn salad), **55,** 180–82
Maggots, 223. *See also* Cabbage
      root maggots; Sunflower
      maggots
Mail-order seed sources, 307–13
Maintenon, Madame de, 232
Maize, 172–80
Mandan Indians, 140, 177, 179
Mangels (mangel-wurzels), 150
Manhattan Farms (seed company),
      310
Map, of USDA hardiness zones,
      302–3
Marie Antoinette, 246

Maximilian of Wied (Prussian prince), 276
McMahon, Bernard, 192
Meader, Elwyn, 157, 180, 204
Medicinal plants
    Asparagus officinalis, 129–30
    Brassica oleracea, Botrytis group, 153
    Rheum rhabarbarum, 255
Mellinger's (seed company), 313
Melons, 211–15. *See also* Watermelons
    'Admiral Togo', 213
    'Banana', 213
    'Casaba, Golden Beauty', **75**, 213, 215
    'Charentais', 215
    'Collective Farmwoman', **75**, 213
    'Eden Gem', **77**, 215
    'Golden Champlain', 213–14
    'Hale's Best', **76**, 214
    'Hearts of Gold', 214
    'Honey Dew', 214, 215
    'Honey Rock', 214
    'Jenny Lind', **76**, 214–15
    'Lake Champlain', 213
    'Netted Gem', 215
    'Nutmeg', 215
    'Perfection', 215
    'Rocky Ford', **77**, 215
    'Sugar Rock', 214
    'Vedrantais', 215
    'White Antibes', 214
Mesclun mixtures, 170, 180, 191, 217. *See also* Greens
Mexican bean beetles, 133
Mice, 248
Mildew. *See* Downy mildew; Powdery mildew
Milk Ranch Seed Potatoes (company), 310
Milky spore disease, 18
Mizuna, **78**, 216, 217
Monk's beard, 169
Morrill, Roland, 214
Mosaic virus
    on bean plants, 133
    on celery plants, 167
    on cucumber plants, 184
    on lettuce plants, 208
    on spinach plants, 263
    on squash plants, 267
Mulching, 17, 18
Multiplier onions, 221, 227–28
    'Hill Onion', 228

'Mother Onion', 228
'Odetta's White Shallot', 228
'Pregnant Onion', 228
'Yellow Potato Onion', **84**, 228
Muskmelons, **76**, 212, 213
Mustard and Oriental greens, 215–18
    'Giant Red', 218
    'Kyona', **78**, 217
    'Michihili', **77**, 217
    'Mizuna', **78**, 216, 217
    'Osaka Purple', **78**, 217
    'Red Giant', **79**, 218
    'Southern Giant Curled', 216, 218
    'Tendergreen', 218
Mustard spinach, 216, 218
Myatt, Joseph, 255, 257
Myatt, William, 255

Napa cabbage, 216
Narragansett Indians, 179
National Seed Storage Laboratory, 6
Native Seeds/SEARCH, 315
Nearing, Helen and Scott, 16
Nematodes, beneficial, 18
Nero (Roman emperor), 205
New World crops
    beans *(Phaseolus vulgaris),* **25–35**, 131–50
    corn *(Zea mays),* **52–54**, 172–80
    Jerusalem artichoke *(Helianthus tuberosus),* **64–65**, 197–99
    potatoes *(Solanum tuberosum),* **96**, 245–51
    squash and pumpkins *(Cucurbita* spp.), **100–108**, 264–73
    sunflowers *(Helianthus annuus),* **108–9**, 273–76
    tomatillo *(Physalis ixocarpa),* **111**, 281–83
    tomatoes *(Lycopersicon lycopersicum),* **112–19**, 283–94
New Zealand spinach, 263
Nichols Garden Nursery (supplier), 310
North Dakota Agricultural Experiment Station, 268
NORTHPLAN/Mountain Seed (seed company), 313
Nutrients, for plants, 17

Ogden, Shepherd, 170, 182
Okra, 218–20
    'Cow Horn', **79**, 219
    'Louisiana Green Velvet', **80**,
        220
    'Purple Okra', **80**, 220
    'Red Okra', **80**, 220
    'Star of David', **81**, 220
Old Sturbridge Village Museum,
    316
Onions
    bunching (Welsh), **82–83**,
        220–21, 225–26
    common (globe), **81–82**, 220–24
    Egyptian (topset), **83**, 221,
        226–27
    multiplier, **84**, 221, 227–28
Open-pollinated (OP) varieties, 2,
    4, 5, 7
Organic gardening, 14–19
Oriental greens. *See* Mustard and
    Oriental greens
Ornamental Edibles (seed
    company), 310
Ornamental kales, 200
Orol Ledden & Sons (seed
    company), 313
Orzolek, Michael, 187
Oscar H. Will & Co., 139, 140,
    177
Oyster plant, 260

Parsley, 228–30
    'Dwarf Curled', 230
    'Giant Italian', 230
    'Gigante d'Italia', **84**, 230
    'Hamburg Root Parsley', **85**,
        230
    'Moss Curled', 230
Parsnips, 230–32
    'Hollow Crown', **85**, 231, 232
    'Offenham', 231–32
    'Student, The', 232
    'Sutton's Student', 232
Pastinaca sativa, **85**, 230–32
Pattypan (scallop) squash, 265,
    266, 271–72, 273
Peas, 232–37. *See also* Cowpeas
    edible-podded (sugar or snow),
        86–87, 233, 234, 237
    shelling, **86**, 233, 235–37
    snap, 233, 234
    soup, 233, 234
Peery, Susan, 257
Pepper Gal (seed company), 310

Peppers, 239–45
    hot, **89–92**, 240–41, 242–44
    sweet, **92–95**, 240–41, 244–45
Perennial plants, 8–9
Perry, Comm. Matthew, 148
Pests
    on asparagus plants, 131
    on bean plants, 133, 139
    on beet plants, 151
    on broccoli plants, 154
    on Brussel sprout plants, 156
    on cabbage plants, 158
    on carrot plants, 162
    on cauliflower plants, 165
    on celery plants, 167
    on chicory plants, 170
    on corn plants, 175
    on corn salad plants, 181
    on cowpea seeds, 238–39
    on cucumber plants, 183–84
    on eggplant plants, 188
    on fava bean plants, 143
    on kale and collard plants, 201
    on kohlrabi plants, 204
    on lettuce plants, 208
    on lima bean plants, 144
    on mustard and Oriental greens,
        216, 217
    on onion plants, 222–23
    on pea plants, 234–35
    on pepper plants, 241–42
    on potato plants, 248–49
    on radish plants, 252–53
    on rutabaga plants, 259
    on spinach plants, 263
    on squash plants, 267
    on sunflower plants, 275
    on sweet potato plants, 278
    on tomatillo plants, 282
    on tomato plants, 286–87
    on turnip plants, 295
    on watermelon plants, 297
    use of organic controls, 14–19
Peter Henderson & Co. *See*
    Henderson, Peter
Peters Seed & Research (seed
    company), 311
Petroselinum
    crispum, 228–30
    crispum var. *neapolitanum,* **84**,
        230
    crispum var. *tuberosum,* **85**,
        229, 230
Phaseolus
    acutifolius, **41**, 149–50
    coccineus, **39–40**, 146–48

lunatus, **36–39**, 144–46
vulgaris, 6, **25–35**, 131–42
Physalis
  alkekengi, 281
  ixocarpa, **111**, 281–83
  philadelphica, 283
Phytophthora infestans, 246
Pickett, J.G., 177
Pickling cucumbers, 182, 184
Pie plant, 255
Pimienta, 240
Pimiento, 240
Pinetree Garden Seeds (seed
    company), 311
Pisum
  sativum, 232–37
  sativum var. *arvense,* **86**, 235
  sativum var. *macrocarpon,*
    86–87, 233, 237
  sativum var. *sativum,* 233,
    235–37
Plants of the Southwest (seed
    company), 311
Pliny, 193, 207
Plutarch, 294
Pod corn, 173
Poisson, Gretchen, 174
Poisson, Lea, 263
Pole beans, 132, 133
  dry (field) beans, **35**, 141–42
  horticultural (shell) beans,
    30–31, 138
  lima (butter) beans, **37–39**,
    145–46
  snap pole beans, **25–26**, 134–35
  wax pole beans, **28**, 136
Popcorn, 173, 174
  'Dwarf Strawberry', 180
  'Pennsylvania Butter-Flavored',
    180
  'Strawberry', **54**, 180
  'Tom Thumb Yellow', **54**, 180
Porcelain garlic, 194, 196
Portuguese cabbage, 159
Potatoes, 2, 245–51
  'All Blue', **96**, 249
  'Anna Cheeka's Ozette', 249
  'Beauty of Hebron', 249
  'Bintje', 249–50
  'Blue Marker', 249
  'Cow Horn', 250
  'Early Ohio', 250
  'Early Rose', 250
  'Garnet Chile', 250
  'Green Mountain', 250
  'Lady Finger', 250

  'Lumper, The', 246
  'Netted Gem', 250
  'Ozette', 249
  'Purple Peruvian', 249
  'Russet Burbank', 246, 250
  'Russian Banana', **96**, 251
  'Seneca Horn', 250
Potatoes, sweet. *See* Sweet potatoes
Potato onions, **84**, 221, 227–28
Powdery mildew
  on cucumber plants, 184
  on pea plants, 234
  on squash plants, 267
  on sunflower plants, 275
Prairie Grown Garden Seeds (seed
    company), 313
Preserving melon, 299
Pumpkins
  'Cheese Pumpkin', **105**, 270
  'Connecticut Field', **106**, 272
  French (true), **103**, 265, 269
  'Luxury Pie Pumpkin', 273
  'New England Pie', 273
  'Seminole Pumpkin', 271
  'Small Sugar', 273
  'Winter Luxury', 273
  for jack-o'-lanterns, 265
  for pies, 265, 271, 273
Purple-skinned onions, 223
Purple stripe garlic, 194, 196

Queen-Anne's-lace, 160
Quisenberry, Ben, 288, 289, 293

Rabbits, 181, 208
Raccoons, 175
Radicchio, 169, 170
  'Castelfranco', 171
  'Pain de Sucre', 171
  'Pan di Zucchero', 171
  'Rossa di Treviso', 171
  'Rossa di Verona', 171
  'Sugar Loaf', **51**, 171
Radishes, 251–55
  'All Seasons', 254
  'Beer Garden', 253
  'Birra di Monaco', 253
  'China Rose', 253
  'D'Avignon', 253
  'French Breakfast', **97**, 253
  'French Golden', 253
  'Gournay Violet', 254
  'Lady Finger', 254
  'Long Black Spanish', **97**, 253,
    254

Radishes (Cont.)
'Madras Radish', 254
'Mongri', 254
'Munchener Bier', 253
'Munich Bier', 253
'Rat's Tail', 254
'Round Black Spanish', 254
'Snake Radish', 254
'Tokinashi', 254
'Violet de Gournay', 254
'White Icicle', **98**, 254
'Wood's Frame', 254–55
Raleigh, Sir Walter, 245
Raphanus
bipinnatus, 254
caudatus, 254
sativus, 97–98, 251–55
Red cabbage, 157, 160
'Mammoth Red Rock', **47**, 160
'Red Danish', 160
Red-skinned onions, 223
Redwood City Seed Company, 311
R.H. Shumway, Seedsman (seed
company), 312
Rheum rhabarbarum, **98**, 255–57
Rhubarb, 2, 9, 255–57
'German Wine', 257
'Glaskin's Perpetual', 257
'Myatt's Victoria', 257
'Paragon', 257
'Victoria', **98**, 257
Richardson, F.W., 214
Richters (seed company), 311
Rocambole garlic, **61–62**, 194,
195–96
Romaine (cos) lettuce, **74**, 207,
211
Ronniger's Seed Potatoes (seed
company), 311
Root parsley, **85**, 229, 230
Root rot, 234
Rot. *See* Black rot; Blossom-end-
rot; Fusarium root rot; Root
rot; Stem-end rot; Stem rot
Rotenone, 19
Royal Agricultural Society
(Cirencester, England), 232
Runner beans, 131, 146–48
'Aztec Dwarf White', **39**, 147
'Barteldes Bush Lima', 147
'Blackcoat', 147
'Black Runner', 147
'Czar', 147
'Painted Lady', **40**, 147
'Scarlet Runner', **39**, **40**, 148
'Seneca Indian Bear Paw', 148

'White Dutch Runner', 148
Russell, J.B., 269
Rust
on asparagus plants, 131
on bean plants, 133
on sunflower plants, 275
Rutabaga, 258–59
'American Purple Top', 259
'American Purple Top
Improved', 259
'Bristol White', 259
'Laurentian', **99**, 259
'Macomber', 259
'Pike', 259
'Sweet German', 259

Salad greens. *See* Greens; Mesclun
mixtures
Salsify, 260–61
'Mammoth Sandwich Island',
99, 261
Salt Spring Seeds (seed company),
311
Savoy cabbage, 157, 160
'Drumhead Savoy', 160
'January King', **47**, 160
Scab
on beet plants, 151
on cucumber plants, 184
on potato plants, 247, 248, 249
Scallions, **82–83**, 220, 225–26
Scallop (pattypan) squash, 265,
266, 271–72, 273
Scorzonera (black salsify), 260–61
'Geante Noire de Russie', 261
Scorzonera hispanica, 260–61
Scotch beans, 142
Sea Kale cabbage, 159
Seed banks, 6
Seeds
mail-order sources of, 307–13
saving of, 7–13
sharing of, 8
viability and germination of,
12–13
Seed Savers Exchange, 6, 7, 316
Seeds Blum (seed company), 311
Seed Shares, 316–17
Seeds of Change (seed company),
311
Seeds West Garden Seeds (seed
company), 313
Self-pollinating annuals, 9
Seminole Indians, 271
Seneca Indians, 142

Shakespeare, William, 205, 255
Shallots, **84**, 221, 227–28
Shell (horticultural) beans, **29–31**, 137–38
Shelling peas, 233, 235–37
  'Alaska', 235
  'Alderman', 234, 235
  'American Wonder', 235
  'Blue Bantam', 236
  'Blue Pod Capicijners', **86**, 235–36
  'Champion of England', 235, 236
  'Daisy', 236
  'Duke of Albany', 235
  'Dutch Grey', 235–36
  'Dwarf Telephone', 236
  'Earliest of All', 237
  'Freezonian', 237
  'Gradus', 237
  'Holland Capucijners', 235–36
  'Homesteader', 236
  'Hundredfold', 236
  'Improved American Wonder', 236
  'Laxtonian', 236
  'Lincoln', 236
  'Little Gem', 235
  'Little Marvel', 234, 236
  'Pilot, The', 236–37
  'Stratagem', 236, 237
  'Tall Telephone', 235
  'Telegraph', 235
  'Telephone', 235, 236
  'Thomas Laxton', 237
  'William Hurst', 236
Shen nung, 148
Shepher's Garden Seeds (seed company), 312
Sieva beans, 144
Silica gel, 12
Silver-leaf beet, 279
Silverskin garlic, **64**, 194, 197
Slicing cucumbers, **55–57**, 182, 185–86
Slugs, 170, 208
Smallage, 166
Snake melons, 185
Snap beans, 132–36
  snap bush beans, 133–34
  snap pole beans, **25–26**, 134–35
  wax bush beans, **27**, 135–36
  wax pole beans, **28**, 136
Snap bush beans, 133–34
  'Black Valentine', 133
  'Bountiful', 134

  'Burpee's Stringless Green Pod', 134
  'Canadian Wonder', 134
  'Fin des Bagnols', 134
  'Masterpiece', 134
  'Red Valentine', 134
  'Shoestring Bean', 134
  'Stringless Black Valentine', 133
  'Tendergreen', 134
  'Triomphe de Farcy', 134
Snap peas, 233, 234
  'Butter Pea', 233
Snap pole beans
  'Blue Coco', 134
  'Cherokee Trail of Tears', 135
  'Hickman', **25**, 135
  'Hickman's Soup', 135
  'Kentucky Wonder', **25**, 135
  'Old Homestead', 135
  'Oregon Giant', 135
  'Paul Bunyan', 135
  'Romano Pole', **26**, 135
  'Trionfo Violetto', **26**, 135
Snow peas, **86–87**, 233, 234, 237
Softneck garlic, **63–64**, 193, 194, 196–97
Soil testing, 17
Solanum
  integrifolium, **59**, 189
  melongena, **57–59**, 187–90
  tuberosum, **96**, 245–51
Soup peas, 233, 234
Southern Exposure Seed Exchange, 228, 312, 316
Southern peas, 238
Southern Seeds (seed company), 312
Soybeans, 132, 148–49
  'Agate', **41**, 149
  'Lammer's Black', **41**, 149
Spagetti squash, 273
Spanish-type onions, 223
Spinach, 262–64
  'Bloomsdale', 263
  'Bloomsdale Long Standing', **100**, 263
  'Giant Nobel', 264
  'King of Denmark', 264
  'Long-Standing Gaudry', 264
  'Monstrueux de Viroflay', 264
  'Norfolk', 1, 264
  'Old Dominion', 264
  'Virginia Savoy', 264
  'Viroflay', 264
Spinach beet, 279

Spinacia
  oleracea, **100**, 262–64
  oleracea var. *inermis*, 262
Spotted asparagus beetles, 131
Spring (cutting) chicory, 169, 170
  'Asparagus Chicory', 170–71
  'Catalogna', 170–71
  'Italian Dandelion', 170–71
Sprouting broccoli, 153
Squash and pumpkins, 264–73
  summer squash, **106–8**, 265, 266, 271–73
  winter squash and pumpkins, **100–105**, 265, 266–71
Squash bugs, 267, 297
Squash vine borers, 267
Stem-end rot, 297
Stem rot, 278
Stem turnip, 203
Stowell, Nathan, 177
Sturtevant, E. Lewis, 142, 166, 209
Sugarloaf chicory, 169
Sugar peas, **86–87**, 233, 234, 237
Suggested readings, 318–21
Sulforaphane, in broccoli, 153
Summer crookneck squash, 265, 266
Summer squash, 265, 266, 271–73
  'Benning's Green Tint Scallop', 271–72
  'Black Zucchini', 272
  'Cocozelle', **106**, 272
  'Early Yellow Summer Crookneck', **107**, 272
  'Farr's Benning White Bush', 271–72
  'Golden Custard', 273
  'Rampicante Zucchetta', 271
  'Ronde de Nice', **108**, 272–73
  'Summer Crookneck', 272
  'Tromboncino', 271
  'White Bush Scallop', 273
  'Yellow Bush Scallop', 273
Sunchoke (Jerusalem artichoke), **64–65**, 197–99
Sunflower artichoke, 197
Sunflower maggots, 275
Sunflowers, 273–76
  'Arikara', **108**, 275
  'Havasupai Striped', 275
  'Italian White', **109**, 275–76
  'Mammoth Russian', **109**, 276
  'Maximilian', 276
  'Tarahumara White', 276
Swede turnip, 258

Sweet corn, 173, 174
—hybrid
  'Silver Queen', 176
—white
  'Black Aztec', 175–76
  'Black Mexican', 4, 175–76
  'Black Sweet', 175
  'Catawba', 176
  'Country Gentleman', 176
  'Early White Market', 177
  'Hooker's Sweet Indian', 176
  'Howling Mob', 176
  'Luther Hill', 176
  'Shoe Peg', 176
  'Stowell's Evergreen', 177
—yellow
  'Golden Bantam', 1, **52**, 177
  'Golden Early Market', 177
  'Golden Sweet', 177
  'Mandan Red Sweet', 177–78
  'Nuetta', 177–78
Sweet peppers, 240–41, 244–45
  'Aconcagua', **92**, 244
  'Bull Nose', 244
  'Cherry Sweet', **93**, 244
  'Chinese Giant', 245
  'Corno di Toro, Giallo', 244
  'Corno di Toro, Rosso', **93**, 244
  'Giant Aconcagua', 244
  'Golden Summit', **94**, 244
  'Hungarian Wax Sweet', **95**, 245
  'Jimmy Nardello's Sweet Frying Pepper', 245
  'Large Bell', 244
  'Merrimack Wonder', **94**, 244
  'Nardello', 245
  'Quadrato d'Asti Giallo Rosa', **95**, 245
  'Red Cherry', 244
  'Ruby Giant', 245
  'Ruby King', 245
  'Sweet Banana', **95**, 245
  'Sweet Mountain', 244
  'World Beater', 245
  'Yellow Banana', 245
Sweet potatoes, 2, **110**, 276–78
  'Choker', 278
  'Nancy Hall', 278
  'Poplar Root', 278
  'Porto Rico Bush', 278
  'Red Wine Velvet', 278
  'Southern Queen', 278
  'White Yam', 278
Swiss chard, 279–80
  'Argentata', 279–80

'Five Color Silver Beet', **110,** 280

'Fordhook Giant', 280

'Lucullus', 280

'Perpetual Spinach', 280

'Rainbow Chard', **110,** 280

'Rhubarb Chard', **111,** 280

'Ruby Chard', 280

'Spinach Beet', 280

Symnel squash, 273

Taino Indians, 276

Tampala, 126

T'ch'ang Te, 211

Teosinte, 172

Tepary beans, **41,** 131, 149–50

  'Mitla Black', 150

  'Sonoran Gold Bush', 150

Terra Edibles (seed company), 312

Territorial Seed Company, 313

Testa, 139

Tetragonia expansa, 263

Thomas Jefferson Center for Historic Plants, 317

Thompson & Morgan Inc., 280, 313

Thorburn, 272

Thweat family, 146

Timberleaf Soil testing, 17

Tinker, Rev. J.E., 176

Titus, 147

Tomatillo, 281–83

  'Purple de Milpa', 5, **111,** 282

  'Tomatillo Verde', 283

  'Toma Verde', 283

Tomatoes, 283–94

  'Abraham Lincoln', 287

  'Amish Paste', 287

  'Anna Russian', **114,** 289

  'Banana', 291

  'Banana Legs', **116,** 291

  'Big Rainbow', 292

  'Black Krim', **119,** 292–93

  'Brandywine', **114,** 289–90

  'Brimmer Pink', 290

  'Burbank', 287

  'Camp Joy Cherry', 287

  'Chadwick's Cherry', **112,** 287

  'Cherokee Purple', 4, **115,** 290, 292–93

  'Costoluto Genovese', **112,** 287–88

  'Cuostralee', 288

  'Dad's Mug', 288

  'Djena Lee's Golden Girl', 291

'Eva Purple Ball', 290

'Evergreen', 293

'Gardener's Delight', **113,** 288

'Giant Oxheart', 291

'Golden Queen', **117,** 292

'Goldie', **117,** 292

'Great White', 293

'Indische Fleisch', 290

'King Humbert Tomato', 290

'King Umberto', 290

'Lincoln', 287

'Marmande', 288

'Mr. Stripey', **119,** 293

'Old Brooks', 288

'Oxheart', **115,** 290–91

'Pruden's Purple', 291

'Red Brandywine', 289

'Red Currant', 294

'Red Pear', 283, 288

'Riesentraube', 289

'Schimmeig Creg', 293

'Snowball', 293

'Striped German', 292

'Sugar Lump', 288

'Super Italian Paste', **113,** 289

'Sweet 100' cherry, 2

'Tigerella', **119,** 293

'Tiger Tom', 293

'Umberto Pear', 290

'Verna Orange', **118,** 292

'White Apple', 293

'White Beauty', 293

'Yellow Brandywine', 290

'Yellow Currant', **120,** 293–94

'Yellow Pear', **118,** 283, 288, 292

'Zapotec Pleated', 291

'Zapotec Ribbed', **116,** 283, 291

Tomato Growers Supply Company, 312

Tomato hornworms, 282, 286–87

Tomato Seed Company, 313

Topset (Egyptian) onions, **83,** 221, 226–27

Totally Tomatoes (seed company), 313

Tragopogon porrifolius, **99,** 260–61

Trap plants, 18

Tree onions, 221, 226

Tregunno Seeds Ltd. (seed company), 312

True (French) cantaloupes, 213, 215

True (French) pumpkins, **103,** 265, 269

Trusts and historic seed programs, 6, 314–17
Turnips, 258, 294–96
  'De Milan Rouge', **121**, 295
  'Gilfeather'™, **120**, 295
  'Golden Ball', 295
  'Orange Jelly', 295
  'Purple Top White Globe', **121**, 295
  'Red Milan', **121**, 295
  'Seven Top', 296
  'Waldoboro Greenneck', 296
Tuscarora Indians, 179
Twain, Mark, 164, 296

USDA Hardiness Zone Map, 302–3

Valerianella
  eriocarpa, 181
  locusta var. *olitoria*, **55**, 180–82
van Doren, Merle, 298
Van Siclen, Abraham, 131
Vermont Bean Seed Company, 312
Verticillium wilt, 188, 286
Vicia faba, **36**, 132, 142–44
Vigna
  unguiculata, **87–89**, 238–39
  unguiculata var. *sesquipedalis*, 238
Vilmorin-Andrieux
  asparagus listed by, 131
  beans listed by, 143
  beets listed by, 153
  Brussel sprouts listed by, 155
  cabbages listed by, 160
  carrots developed by, 161
  carrots listed by, 162
  celery listed by, 168
  chicory listed by, 171
  corn salad (mâche) listed by, 181, 182
  kale listed by, 201, 202
  leeks listed by, 206
  melons listed by, 214
  onions listed by, 223, 224, 227
  parsnips listed by, 232
  peas listed by, 233
  radishes listed by, 254
  spinach listed by, 264
  tomatoes listed by, 290
  turnips listed by, 295
Virginia Agricultural Experiment Station, 264

Walking onions, **83**, 221, 226
Walrath, H.J., 213
Watering, 17
Watermelons, 296–99
  'Cole's Early', 297–98
  'Cream of Saskatchewan', 298
  'Garrisonian', 298
  'Georgia Rattlesnake', **122**, 298
  'Harris Early', 297–98
  'Ice Cream', 298
  'Kleckley Sweet', 298
  'Monte Christo', 298
  'Moon & Stars', 4, **122**, 298–99
  'Nancy', 299
  'Peerless', 298
  'Rattlesnake', 298
  'Red-Seeded Citron', **123**, 299
  'Tom Watson', 299
  'Wonder Melon', 298
Wax bush beans
  'Brittle Wax', 135
  'Buerre de Rocquencourt', **27**, 135
  'Dragon Langerie', **27**, 136
  'Dragon's Tongue', **27**, 136
  'Golden Wax', 136
  'Mont D'Or', 136
  'Pencil Pod Black Wax', 136
  'Round Pod Kidney Wax', 135
Wax pole beans
  'Goldmarie', 136
  'Kentucky Wonder Wax', **28**, 136
  'Meraviglia di Venezia', 136
  'Wonder of Venice', 136
  'Yellow Annelino', **28**, 136
Wax snow pea 'Golden Sweet', **86**, 237
Weevils. *See also* Bean weevils; Carrot weevils
  on beet plants, 151
  on cowpea seeds, 238–39
  on onion plants, 223
Wegscheider, Anneke, 274
Welsh (bunching) onions, **82–83**, 220–21, 225–26
Whealy, Kent, 5, 298
White, Arthur, 156
White mustard, 216
White-skinned onions, 224
Wild cabbage, 157
Wild tomatillo, 283
Will, Oscar H., 139, 140, 177
William Dam Seeds Ltd. (seed company), 308

Wilt. *See* Bacterial wilt; Fusarium wilt; Verticillium wilt
Windsor beans, 142
Winter kohlrabi, 203–4
Winter squash and pumpkins, 265, 266–71
  'Acorn', 265, 269
  'Acorn, Table Queen', 271
  'Autumnal Marrow', 268
  'Baby Blue Hubbard', 268
  'Banana', 268
  'Blue Banana', **100**, 267
  'Blue Hubbard', 265, 268
  'Boston Marrow', 1, **101**, 267–68
  'Buttercup', **101**, 265, 268
  'Butternut', **105**, 270
  'Cheese Pumpkin', **105**, 270
  'Chicago Warted Hubbard', 268
  'Connecticut Field', **106**, 272
  'Delicata', **107**, 272
  'Essex Hybrid', **101**, 268
  'Etampes', 269
  'French Turban', 269
  'Golden Hubbard', 268
  'Green Hubbard', 268
  'Green-Striped Cushaw', **104**, 269–70
  'Hubbard', **102**, 268
  'Kikuza Early White', 270
  'Kitchenette', 268
  'Luxury Pie Pumpkin', 273
  'Neck Pumpkin', 270
  'New England Pie', 273
  'North Georgia Candy Roaster', **102**; 268
  'Orange Hokkaido', 269
  'Quality', **101**, 268
  'Queensland Blue', 268–69
  'Rampicante Zucchetta', 271
  'Red Kuri', **103**, 269
  'Rouge Vif d'Etampes', **103**, 269
  'Seminole Pumpkin', 271
  'Small Sugar', 273
  'Spagetti Squash', 273
  'Tromboncino', 271
  'True Hubbard', 268
  'Turk's Turban', **104**, 265, 269
  'Upper Ground Sweet Potato', 271
  'Vegetable Spagetti', 273
  'Waltham Butternut', 270
  'White Jonathan Cushaw', 270
  'Winter Luxury', 273
Wireworms, 162

Withee, John, 146
Witloof chicory, 169, 170
  'Belgian Endive', 171
  'Coffee Chicory', 171
  'Large-Rooted Magdeburg', 171
  'Witloof', 171
Woodchucks, 181, 208
Wood Prairie Farm Certified Seed Potatoes (seed company), 312
World Seed Fund, 314

Yams, 277
Yard-long beans, 238
Yellow mustard, 216
Yellow-skinned onions, 223–24

Zapotec Indians, 243
Zea mays, 52–54, 172–80
Zucchini, **106**, **108**, 265, 266, 272–73
Zuni tomatillo, 283